JOHN NELSON,
MERCHANT ADVENTURER

JOHN NELSON

MERCHANT ADVENTURER

A Life Between Empires

RICHARD R. JOHNSON

New York   Oxford
OXFORD UNIVERSITY PRESS
1991

Oxford University Press

Oxford   New York   Toronto
Delhi   Bombay   Calcutta   Madras   Karachi
Petaling Jaya   Singapore   Hong Kong   Tokyo
Nairobi   Dar es Salaam   Cape Town
Melbourne   Auckland

and associated companies in
Berlin   Ibadan

Published by Oxford University Press, Inc.,
200 Madison Avenue, New York, New York 10016

Oxford is a registered trademark of Oxford University Press

Library of Congress Cataloging-in-Publication Data
Johnson, Richard R., 1942–
John Nelson, merchant adventurer : a life between empires /
Richard R. Johnson.
p. cm.   Includes bibliographical references.
ISBN 0-19-506505-0
1. Nelson, John, d. 1734.   2. Boston (Mass.)—Biography.
3. Adventure and adventurers—Massachusetts—Boston—Biography.
4. Merchants—Massachusetts—Boston—Biography.
5. Boston (Mass.)—History—Colonial period, ca. 1600–1775.
I. Title.   F73.4.J67   1991
974.4′6102′092—dc20
[B]   90-33286

1 3 5 7 9 8 6 4 2
Printed in the United States of America
on acid-free paper

PREFACE

This book seeks to recover the life of a man—John Nelson, who died in 1734 in his eighty-first year—more honored by his contemporaries than by posterity. True, many of those closest to him remained attentive to his memory: relatives both distant and direct preserved his portrait (the artist John Singleton Copley was called upon to repair one treasured copy), and a string of sons christened John Nelson have borne their ancestor's name even down to the present day.[1] Scattered echoes of his life reverberate elsewhere—a glowing footnote in Thomas Hutchinson's *History of Massachusetts-Bay*, a page in one of Francis Parkman's volumes, an historical romance from the pen of a nineteenth-century Boston antiquarian, even a public park bearing Nelson's name on the south shore of Boston Harbor, hard by what was once his island home.[2] All testify to a life of unusual enterprise and daring that ranged across the face of the late seventeenth-century North Atlantic community, from London, Boston, and the Bay of Fundy, to Quebec, the Bastille in Paris, the corridors of England's Whitehall, and back once more to Boston.

The very character of this life suggests, however, why Nelson's contemporary fame proved fleeting: restless, adventurous, and careless of political power or office, he built no monuments to himself. Neither did his ways and beliefs match up to any pattern of emerging American

nationalism appealing to a later, republican age. Yet different genera-
tions find new windows into the past, and from my own perspective—
and in apologia for recovering another's life—it was precisely this restless
ubiquity that drew me to retracing Nelson's career. In the course of
writing a more general account of the New England colonies during
these years, I found myself continually intrigued by how often his name
surfaced amid familiar events, linking farflung personalities and powers
in ways I had not previously suspected. In some of these events, as in
New England's relations with Acadia and Boston's overthrow of Governor Andros in 1689, Nelson played a formative role; in others, as
during his long imprisonment by the French and his years in London,
his part was more passive but still exceptionally revealing of larger forces
at work.

The study that follows, therefore, aspires to be both biography and
something more than biography. It certainly seeks to relate (in both
senses of the word) Nelson's lives as spy, speculator, multinational merchant, memorialist, politician, prisoner, parent, friend, and gentleman.
This is a story worth telling for its own sake. Yet—and with apologies
to an individual who clearly disdained being used by anybody—it also
endeavors to employ his protean career as a symbol of, and guide
through, the abrupt changes and fierce conflicts overtaking the North
Atlantic world during the span of Nelson's life. For even as New England
and New France moved into closer political conjunction with their parent
countries, so they also plunged into conflict with each other—a double
pas de deux joined to form a deadly quadrille, with America's first
settlers, the Indians, entangled in the dance. The complexities of this
interplay, and its significance for the history of each participant as well
as for that of the whole, are often neglected by studies centered on
particular colonies, peoples, or nation-states. Nelson supplies a thread
through this labyrinth, one that in marking his own particular path is
nonetheless sufficiently intricate and wide-ranging to illuminate the
whole.

In addition, I believe, Nelson's career suggests the importance during
these years of a handful of individuals who were neither typical of their
time nor set in the highest seats of authority. Recent scholarship has
taught us much about both the broad socioeconomic forces that confi-
gured colonial society and the goals and mechanisms of London's policy-
making. Yet there remains a missing ingredient. On the one hand, social
history tells us little about the forces and personalities shaping the day-
to-day events of this intensely political age. On the other, to chart the
unfolding of transatlantic ties during these years too exclusively in terms

of London's actions slights the extent to which royal officialdom did not so much initiate events as respond to situations set in motion by others. We have been too ready to read a purposeful, Victorian-style imperialism into what was more accurately the working out of the ambitions of adventurers, traders, land-hungry settlers, and religious visionaries; and we must give more credit to the shaping of events and policy by private solicitation and personal enterprise. A variety of such individuals appear in the pages of this book, some pursuing their ambitions within the service of the Crown, and others shifting their loyalties to match their circumstances. Still others, a more shadowy and forgotten group, preferred to remain more on the margins of their respective worlds. Entrepreneurs operating ahead of the governments and settled societies they came from, they interwove conventions and conditions derived from a variety of different and often competing cultures, precipitating both conflict and accommodation. John Nelson, these pages argue, was such a man.

* * *

Both the cosmopolitanism of Nelson's life and its distance from the present day raise certain problems of presentation that require explanation to the modern reader. With the exception of a few phrases, I have translated into English all direct quotations from French materials. French names and titles have been rendered according to the guidelines provided by the invaluable *Dictionary of Canadian Biography*. Overall, when quoting from seventeenth-century materials, I have reproduced spelling and punctuation as it appears in the printed and manuscript materials of the time, save for expanding abbreviations and replacing the old usages of "v", "j", and "þ" (thorn) with "u", "i", and "th". A more complex and potentially more confusing problem arises from Protestant England's stubborn refusal, until 1751, to adopt the Gregorian or New Style calendar used by Catholic countries since 1582. The loyalty of seventeenth-century Englishmen to the Julian or Old Style calendar meant that they continued to begin each year on March 25 instead of January 1 and that they had come to lag ten (and, after 1700, eleven) days behind those using the New Style calendar. Hence it was possible for John Nelson—in imitation of the young man named Bright whose speed was much faster than light—to leave English Boston, sail for a week, and still arrive in French Port Royal several days before his departure, according to the calendars in use in each country. This should be kept in mind, for rather than redating all French documents to accord with English Old Style reckoning I have cited them according to the

French New Style employed by their authors. In keeping with the usual scholarly practice, however, I have modernized all Old Style dates to conform with both modern American usage and a calendar year beginning January 1, so that a date recorded by Nelson and other Englishmen as 15 February, 1685 (or 1685/6), is given as February 15, 1686.

In the making of this book, I have come to realize, my greatest debt is owed to its subject, for living such a life and for requiring my acquaintance with so many fascinating people and places. To a believer in original sin, there is nothing quite so gratifying as a working holiday with scholarly pretensions, and I have much enjoyed my duty of pursuing John Nelson's trail through New England, Nova Scotia, Ottawa, France, England, southern California, and the Caribbean. Nelson did not visit quite all these places, but all contain some record of his life, and I gratefully acknowledge the courtesies and hospitality extended by the staffs of the Massachusetts Historical Society, the Massachusetts State Archives, Harvard University's Houghton Library, the Boston Public Library, the American Antiquarian Society, the Library of Congress, the Public Archives of Canada, England's Public Record Office, the Bodleian and University Libraries of Oxford and Cambridge Universities, the municipal archives of Angoulême, and the Henry E. Huntington Library in San Marino, California. I acknowledge, too, the permission granted to me by these institutions to quote from the manuscript materials in their care. The Huntington Library not only opened up its incomparable collections to me but also provided a six-month period to study there in the form of a fellowship funded by the National Endowment for the Humanities, for which I am deeply grateful to the Library and its officers, especially Robert Middlekauff and Martin Ridge. Closer to my professional home, the staff of the University of Washington's superb Suzzallo Library never failed in their advice and assistance. I am also conscious of a considerable debt owed to scholars who have mapped out many of my paths before me by editing source materials or by writing their own analyses of the period. I hope that my footnotes acknowledge a part of this indebtedness, but I would pay particular tribute, for inspiration and guidance, to the work of Francis Parkman, W. J. Eccles, George A. Rawlyk, Jean Daigle, and John G. Reid.

Scholarly projects provide wonderful opportunities to renew old friendships and weave new ones, and this book is no exception. At several points along the way, Jonathan Chu and John McCusker provided advice and warm hospitality; in Virginia, Mr. and Mrs. Orme Wilson not only introduced me to a clan of distinguished descendants of John Nelson but allowed me access to the portrait of Elizabeth Nelson reproduced in this book. Richard Saunders of Middlebury College, Thomas Gardiner, and John Tyler of the Colonial Society of Massachusetts also furnished valuable help in tracking down portraits and illustrations. I am grateful to Gail Cooper and Karen Wolny of Oxford University Press for their editorial skills, and to John Murrin of Princeton University for advice and support over many years. Back in Seattle, my colleagues in the Department of History are also, to my great good fortune, my close friends, and I am especially grateful to Carol Thomas and Bill Rorabaugh for reading the manuscript and offering encouragement and correction. Peter Hansen, now of Brandeis University, helped in many ways. And without the interest shown by the members of the Department's History Research Group, I should not have realized that Nelson's life had its parallels as far away as Hapsburg Hungary and seventeenth-century Formosa. Finally—and most deeply and satisfyingly—I am indebted to Carol and Mary Susan, dearest friends, for their love, concern, and support.

CONTENTS

ILLUSTRATIONS

JOHN NELSON,
MERCHANT ADVENTURER

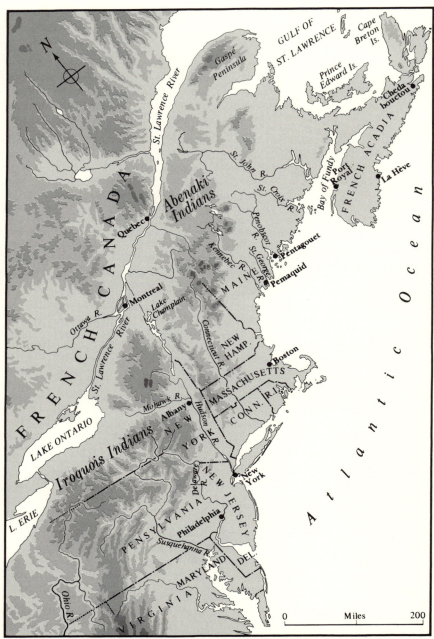

ENGLISH NORTH AMERICA AND FRENCH CANADA IN 1692

the main French and English settlements made it a battleground between rival camps, a pawn in the maneuvering of larger forces. As one scholar has observed, the region became one of marginal colonies dependent on forces outside their control: their European mother countries, the stronger and more self-sufficient colonies to their north and south, and the region's native Indian population.[1]

Yet Acadia's role had not always been so peripheral. Though English and French explorers came late on the New World scene—so late they had to make do with founding the United States and Canada—they were quick to take advantage of one of the continent's greatest resources, the fish that swam in fabulous profusion off its northern shores. From Newfoundland south to the aptly named Cape Cod, the shallow waters over the projecting continental shelf provided a natural breeding ground; and by the mid-sixteenth century, fleets from numerous western European ports gathered to fish and trade together. So abundant were the fish, it was said, that they would bite every hook of a line immediately it was proffered, or throng to fill a basket simply lowered into the sea. John Winthrop and his fellow Puritan migrants found fiction close to truth even before they landed in New England—on sighting America in the shape of Cape Sable at the southern tip of Acadia, they put down "a few hooks" and took up sixty-seven codfish in less than two hours, "some a yard and a half long, and a yard in compass."[2] Acadia's geography thrust it like a massive hammerhead into the center of this magnificent bounty, and fishermen who opted to land and dry their catch ("dry fishing" as opposed to the "wet fishing" of salting down the "green" cod aboard ship for transport directly to market) soon made use of its rocky shores and numerous inlets for this purpose.

More permanent settlement began in the first years of the seventeenth century, and Acadia was again its focal point. Indeed, if a three-year gap in occupation after 1607 is overlooked, the lands around Port Royal (close to the modern town of Annapolis Royal) can boast of having the longest history of sustained European settlement in the Americas north of Florida, since its first French colonists came in 1605, two years before the English landed at Jamestown. The planting of Port Royal within a spacious harbor opening into the Bay of Fundy, facing west and away from the Atlantic coast, served a variety of plans for settlement: while still adjacent to the fisheries, its colonists could also establish the ties with the local Indians—Micmac, and on the mainland, Malecite and Abenaki—that would permit trading for the furs in high demand in Europe. The St. John River, forty miles across the bay, gave access to the peoples and peltry of the mainland's interior as well as to an arduous route communicating overland with the French settlements later established on the St. Lawrence. With Port Royal's first colonists came missionaries whose preachings among the tribes, coupled with the exchange of furs and trade goods, formed bonds between French and Indians that would prove of vital significance to each during their long contest with the English.

Of almost equal importance in establishing Port Royal—and decisive in ensuring its permanence as a settlement—was its capacity for agricultural self-sufficiency. In contrast to the craggy and indented face of the region's Atlantic coastline, the shoreline bordering the Bay of Fundy is one of low hills and ridges separated by broad river valleys, of which the longest, where Port Royal was planted, runs some sixty miles parallel to the shore. This valley, with others later settled by the French at the head of the Bay around Chignecto and Minas Basin, contains deep beds of grassy marshland, washed and in storms flooded by the exceptional tidal variations in the Bay of Fundy. The Port Royal settlers learned how to dike and drain these marshes with sluiceboxes—"aboiteaux"—designed to draw off the fresh water and repel the salt.[3] As salt marshes, like those further south at the mouth of the Piscataqua in New England, they provided excellent grazing for cattle; drained and desalinized, they were fertile land for wheat, fruit, and vegetables. The name "Acadia" has been assigned two origins, one stemming from the classical Arcadia, famed for its rural simplicity and contentment, and the other from a Micmac Indian word, "quoddy," or in French "cadie," signifying a good piece of land. Whichever is correct, both convey the satisfaction the settlers took in their new land, a contentment illustrated in the names they gave to some of the grasslands at Chignecto and upriver from Port Royal—Champs Elysées and Paradis Terrestre, the "Elysian fields" and the "terrestrial paradise."[4]

Yet Paradise begat temptation and a supporting cast of serpents, and the very bounty that drew colonists to Acadia also exposed them to jealousy and danger. The very variety and wealth of the region's resources, coupled with its natural geography, made it more exploited than exploiting, more vulnerable to having its bounty harvested by outsiders than itself becoming a center able to dominate its neighbors. As Samuel de Champlain, one of Port Royal's founding fathers, quickly perceived, Acadia was easy to settle but difficult to hold. As with the islands of the Caribbean, its infinite number of harbors required large forces for their defense.[5] Nor, as events proved, could it depend upon the Caribbean islands' greatest natural defense—tropical disease—to deter attackers. At a time when most Europeans coming to the New

World were thinking more of instant riches than of migration and settlement, it was of little use to gather fish or furs if some freebooter could step in and reap the harvest.

Under Champlain's guidance, therefore, the main thrust of French colonization shifted north and west into the valley of the St. Lawrence, a point closer to the resources of the interior, farther from rival European settlements, and where a single fortress, Quebec, could defend against intruders. Even Quebec succumbed to an English blockade in 1629; but with its return to French hands soon afterwards, its walls, cliffs, and winter ice would repel all assaults—and secure New France—for the next one hundred and thirty years. Port Royal, by contrast, would fall to external attack no fewer than six times during the seventeenth century alone, episodes in an almost continuous series of plunderings of the settlements strung out along the Acadian coast.

The source of most of these attacks, and the development that completed Acadia's transition to being a region sandwiched between two stronger and rival camps, was the burgeoning English settlement down the coast in New England. First at Plymouth, and then in the 1630s with the spectacular growth of Massachusetts and Connecticut, the English established a depth and density of settlement along the northeastern seaboard that the French could never match: by mid-century, Massachusetts' settlers alone numbered five times those in all New France, forty times those in Acadia. English traders began to probe up the coastline of Maine, cutting into the Acadians' dealings with the Indians. More threatening still, successive colonizing groups laid claim to an ever-increasing extent of northeastern coastline by virtue of charters solicited from the Stuart Crown, claims that reached as far north as the St. Lawrence River by a grant of 1621 to Sir William Alexander for a lordship to be known as New Scotland or Nova Scotia—the origin of the English name for Acadia. For a few years in the late 1620s, Alexander maintained several groups of Scots colonists in Acadia, including one group that occupied Port Royal. The French colonizing "Compagnie de la Nouvelle-France," for its part, claimed not only Acadia but a coastline of "Canada," defined as stretching from Florida to the Arctic Circle. The groundwork was laid for a crazy quilt of overlapping French and English claims, shot through with such questions as which Maine river formed the proper boundary and whether "Acadia" and "Nova Scotia" were distinct from each other or one and the same, questions that would keep clerks and diplomats in Europe employed for more than a century to come.[6]

With the return of Acadia to French hands by treaty in 1632, Louis

XIIIe and his ministers sought to make it a key component of a reorganized New France. Colonists and supplies were sent to Port Royal and the region's government brought under direct royal control. Other settlements and trading posts were founded or enlarged, along the Atlantic coast at La Hève and Cape Sable, and across the Bay of Fundy at the mouths of the St. John and Penobscot rivers. Unhappily for the new settlers, however, the death of royal governor Isaac de Razilly in 1635 set off a prolonged succession struggle between two able and determined claimants, Charles de Menou d'Aulnay and Charles de Saint-Étienne de La Tour. Paris compounded the confusion by allowing each in turn to claim he had royal sanction for his actions. Ships were battered into surrender, forts taken by storm, and garrisons slaughtered without quarter. La Tour's gallant wife, Françoise, left in command of his principal trading post at the mouth of the St. John River during his absence, was forced to watch her comrades fall around her and the survivors hanged by d'Aulnay's besieging forces. She herself died soon afterwards in captivity. With the fortunes of civil war turned against him, La Tour sought aid from New England. The Massachusetts government refused any official assistance. Under pressure by merchants eager to break into the Acadian fur trade, however, and persuaded that La Tour's sympathies were slightly more attuned to English Protestantism than those of his rival, the government twice allowed him to hire men and ships to prosecute his cause. But La Tour not only lost the war, he then reneged on his debts to Boston, hijacking a ship lent to him by his backers and taking refuge in Quebec—the first but not the last time Massachusetts merchants would find the profits of dabbling in Acadian waters abruptly offset by war or double dealing.[7]

By the late 1640s, d'Aulnay was undisputed master of Acadia. Massachusetts grudgingly apologized for its aid to his rival, sending as token of peace an ornate sedan chair, a gift from the Viceroy of Mexico to his sister in Spain that had been intercepted by New England freebooters. No one in Boston could find a use for it, so the magistrates thriftily converted it into a present appropriate for a popish governor, even one in the depths of rural Acadia.[8] At the moment of his triumph, however, in the spring of 1650, d'Aulnay drowned in the icy waters of Port Royal harbor. The resourceful La Tour immediately crossed to France and persuaded Paris to restore him to power in Acadia. He then hastened back to Port Royal and enticed his rival's widow to unite with him in marriage and joint indebtedness to their numerous creditors. But the long arm of European intervention, hitherto felt mainly by the multiplication of contradictory orders and titles, now reached out in direct and forceful fashion. The late d'Aulnay's principal creditor, Emmanuel Le Borgne, a merchant of La Rochelle in France, dispatched a succession of expeditions to recoup his investment by plundering the Acadian settlements. Having taken Port Royal and La Hève, Le Borgne moved against the La Tours in Fort St. John in July 1654, only to be forestalled by a second and more powerful European force, a expedition sent out from England by way of Boston. By September, English garrisons held all the principal French posts around the Bay of Fundy, from Port Royal west to Pentagouet on the Penobscot.

Ironically, although in keeping with the often haphazard character of European intervention during these years, the English force had set out to attack a different objective, Dutch New Netherland (present-day New York) rather than French Acadia. Its mere arrival in American waters, however, marked a new and significant turn in English colonial policy. In the wake of Parliament's victory in the English Civil War and the execution of King Charles I, power had passed into the hands of Oliver Cromwell and his fellow Puritans. Flushed with patriotic and Protestant pride, they initiated an aggressive foreign policy that set England at odds with every major western European power in turn—the Netherlands, France, and finally Spain. In place of costly Continental interventions, however, Cromwell and his merchant allies sought revenue and profit through the building up of English sea power, both naval and commercial, and its deployment in ways that would weaken the nation's rivals and enlarge its trade. In this scheme of things, English America and its staple products of sugar, tobacco, and fish were recognized as invaluable resources worth protecting and exploiting, a fact brought home to officials in London by the many Puritans who had returned from the colonies during the struggle with Charles I and who now held high office in Cromwell's Commonwealth. Indicative of this new interest in matters American were the Navigation Acts passed by Parliament in 1650 and 1651 that stressed the colonies' subordination to their mother country and required that the bulk of their commerce (and England's overseas trade) be conducted in English or English colonial shipping. Simultaneously, a powerful squadron was sent to range through Caribbean and Chesapeake waters, where it reduced colonies still loyal to the monarchy to obedience to Parliament. In 1654 came the expedition that attacked Acadia, and then the main thrust of Cromwell's "Western Design," a fleet that aimed at Spanish Hispaniola and finally, after huge expenditure of blood and treasure, brought Jamaica into England's overseas empire.

Behind this unprecedented assertion of English state power in America lay two main purposes linked by a third—to show the flag to wavering colonists, to exclude foreigners (and especially the Dutch) from England's Atlantic trade, and, finally, in the great tradition of Drake and his fellow freebooters, to provide a quick infusion to the national exchequer by what amounted to state-authorized piracy. A little of all three goals was evident in the expedition that seized Acadia. It originated in a call by the New Haven and Connecticut colonies in New England for English aid in forestalling what was rumored to be an imminent Dutch attack on them from neighboring New Netherland. Cromwell responded by giving the message bearers, Robert Sedgwick and John Leverett of Massachusetts, a small force of ships and English soldiers to attack the Dutch, along with a commission to enlist more men in New England. But just as an army was mustering in Boston, the unwelcome news came that peace with the Dutch had broken out, causing Massachusetts to withdraw its aid. Undaunted, Sedgwick determined to pass the time before returning to England with a cargo of timber by, as he told Cromwell, "rangeing the coast against the French."[9] Sedgwick's earlier career as a merchant and investor in the northern fisheries and fur trade doubtless inclined him to look towards Acadia. In addition, the Massachusetts government was visibly anxious to get "Cromwells boyes" (as the boisterous English veterans termed themselves) out of town, particularly in light of a rumor that they were part of a plan by London to impose a governor-general on New England.[10] True, France was still at peace with England, but gold, glory, and the gospel (the last to be served by expelling "that deluding Crew" of Catholics who had "crept in among the blind Indians" in Acadia) could all be won in a manner much closer to Massachusetts' political and commercial interests than by an attack on the Dutch.[11]

Whether the English had mounted a raid or a conquest, however, remained to be seen. Sedgwick took away much plunder; to the value, it was later said, of ten thousand pounds. But he left garrisons behind him, and Massachusetts expressed its readiness to annex the region providing it would not be obliged to assume past debts or claims. Significantly, it floated this proposal in England, through the colony's agent there, instead taking matters into its own hands as it might have done before Cromwell's ascendancy. This proved to be a realistic, if unavailing, assessment of the situation, for Acadia's fate was now decided in London and Paris rather than in America. The English government, in its new expansionist mood, wished to hold on to the captured forts; French officials were unwilling to let the matter jeopardize their hopes for an alliance against Spain. By a treaty signed at Westminster in the fall of 1655, England was permitted to retain its conquest until such time as special commissioners could decide on its legality—a formula amounting to a diplomatic sanctification of the status quo.[12]

With the forts retained, London began to plan for their disposition under English control. Instead of simply assuming title by right of conquest, care was taken to draw a delicate veneer of legality over the proceedings by means of the versatile Charles de La Tour, who had been carried captive to England by Sedgwick. La Tour now unveiled himself to Cromwell's Council of State as the legitimate English as well as French ruler of Acadia by virtue of a grant he had received back in 1629 (but had then refused to take up) from Sir William Alexander, the former proprietor of Nova Scotia. Through the spring and summer of 1656, an agreement took shape whereby La Tour would hold title to the land and government of "Lacadie and that parte of the Country called Nova Scotia"—"Acadia" here defined as extending west from halfway down the peninsula's Atlantic coast to the borders of New England—providing he assumed the cost of paying the garrisons of the forts, reimbursed Boston merchants for the more than three thousand pounds he owed them from his previous adventures, and took into partnership two Englishmen, William Crowne and Thomas Temple. Soon afterward, his function as intermediary and legitimizer fulfilled, he relinquished his share to Crowne and Temple in return for their assumption of his debts and a five percent cut in their future profits. Since La Tour had sold what was no longer his to sell, had escaped his debts, and later received regular dividends from his former partners, he surely deserves to be remembered as one of early America's most creative entrepreneurs.[13]

Through Crowne and Temple, finally, we approach the start of John Nelson's career, for it was through Temple, his uncle, that Nelson first came to America. Yet this still lay ten years in the future. For the moment, the two partners were left to develop their encumbered heritage. Neither man had hitherto made any perceptible mark on English society, and both now came to the fore more by the backing of patrons and relatives than by their own prominence or initiative. Crowne, despite his later claims that he had provided the bulk of the money spent, always accepted the role of junior partner. Upon a division of their title, he received the smaller and less valuable western segment, around Pentagouet. He later leased it to others, retiring to Massachusetts and poverty by the 1670s.[14]

Temple, by contrast, possessed the political influence and family ties that were even more essential than hard cash for a seventeenth-century colonial venture. Born in 1614 into a prominent, exceptionally prolific, and financially hard-pressed Buckinghamshire family, he joined with his relatives in taking up arms against the king in the Civil War—two of his brothers and an uncle were colonels in the parliamentary armies and Temple himself had risen to that rank, though no details survive of his military career. Politically, he had friends at the Cromwellian court through his great-aunt's marriage to "Old Subtlety," the noted Puritan politician (and prominent investor in colonial enterprises), William Fiennes, Viscount Say and Sele.[15] Both Say and Sele's son, Nathaniel Fiennes, and son-in-law, Sir Charles Wolseley, were members of Cromwell's Council of State at the time of the grant to Temple and his partners, and both appear in Temple's letters as backers of his Acadian venture. Later, a younger member of the Wolseley clan served as Temple's lieutenant in America. Other investors in the "Company" formed to finance Temple included Crowne's wealthy relative, William Watts, and two London merchants who had fingers in almost every colonial venture during the 1650s, Martin Noell and Thomas Povey.[16]

The merchants' participation and the joint-subscription form of organization, coupled with the language of the grant, all reveal this as a venture planned for trade rather than settlement, importing the land's products rather than selling it off to settlers. Temple and Crowne were in effect glamorously titled "factors," agents fronting for others whose official positions made the grant of Acadia politically feasible and yet necessitated their names' being kept from public view. Temple in particular emerges as the seventeenth-century equivalent of a remittance man, furnished with a job and a one-way ticket providing he left England's shores. Several of his relatives who had fought for Parliament were sufficiently alienated from Cromwell's radical course by the 1650s to be suspected of royalist sympathies, and Temple himself later claimed, after the restoration of the monarchy, that he had schemed with his brother Edmund to free the king from his imprisonment. Among the martyred Charles I's last words, Temple recalled, was a request that his son take care of "Honest Tom Temple." This attempt to serve the Stuarts, Temple claimed, had brought down Cromwell's wrath upon his head, prompting Nathaniel Fiennes to advise Temple to absent himself until the storm had blown over.[17]

This romantic and, after the monarchy's return, politically convenient story passes over the more than eight-year hiatus between Temple's alleged plotting to free the king and the visiting of Cromwell's resentment. It may contain a grain of truth. In 1658, looking back "from the Deserts of America whither my unhappy fate had led me," Temple spoke of his hopes "to hyde my blushes in the shades of this wooden world free from the scorchings I had felt in the other." Another of his brothers, Purbeck Temple, later testified at the trial of Charles I's judges that he, too, had plotted to rescue the king, even to the point of eaves-dropping (from a hiding place in the Palace of Westminster) on a con-frontation between Charles and the Cromwellian leadership.[18] It is more likely, however, that Thomas Temple's embarrassments by the mid-1650s were more pecuniary than political. He was a needy younger son of a family in financial straits—for his well-placed Fiennes relatives to find him a post at once honorable and distant was a happy solution all round.[19]

Temple left England for America early in 1657. Like many another migrant, he planned to live the life in the New World that his upbringing had promised, but had failed to provide, in the old. Landing in Boston at the head of a small army of retainers, he soon established himself as an openhanded and congenial man about town—"as fine a Gentleman," it was said, "as ever sat foot on the American strand." Over the next fifteen years, he became a substantial landowner in and around Boston Bay, a benefactor of Harvard College, and a member of the Reverend Increase Mather's church in the town's North End. The Bostonians, for their part, liked his politics, deprecated his domestic arrangements (un-married, he was reputed to keep a mistress), and worked busily to relieve him of his financial assets.[20]

Almost immediately, Temple ran into difficulties on two fronts. Charged with upholding the boundaries and government of Nova Scotia, he found himself obliged to equip and maintain a succession of costly expeditions to construct trading posts along the coast and hold them in the face of French raids. In Boston, meanwhile, his genteel reluctance to sully his hands in trade allowed the local merchants he took into partnership or permitted to trade on their own account to skim the cream off the profits of the fish and fur trade with Acadia, leaving little over to satisfy his obligations to Crowne, La Tour, and the latter's creditors. "I fear," wrote one of Temple's friends soon after his arrival, "that his Noble Spiritt will nott suite with Acadie, or at least the profitts of Acadie will nott mayntayne his post."[21] Temple's letters to his English patrons soon took on a querulous tone; his brothers back in England loved only money and no longer sent out any worthwhile goods for trade; his Boston associates were exploiting him; Povey and Nathaniel Fiennes were besought to use their influence to patch up a truce with the French and furnish a further—and positively final—injection of cap-ital to stave off the quite exceptional string of misfortunes temporarily afflicting his affairs. Something was bound to turn up, however; perhaps a sudden bonanza from the pieces of supposedly ore-bearing Nova Scotian rock that Temple kept shipping back to London.[22]

Back in England, however, the only mining undertaken was directed against Temple's position as proprietor. The restoration of the Stuart monarchy in 1660 resurrected a variety of claimants to Nova Scotia eager to discredit titles awarded during the Cromwellian Interregnum. Temple's own agent in London, Boston merchant Thomas Breedon, struck an alliance with the politically most influential claimant, a courtier named Thomas Elliott, and had himself named governor of Nova Scotia in Temple's place. Temple was forced back to England in his own defense. There, after much soliciting at court, bolstered by freshly minted recollections of his deep-rooted royalism, he won both confirmation of his title to the land and government of Nova Scotia and the new title, as baronet, of Sir Thomas Temple, but at the cost of buying off Elliott with an annual payment of £600.[23]

Back in Boston by 1663, Temple seemed at last to have fought and wheedled his way into secure possession of his province. He had ridden out the storm of political change in England and made the transition from Cromwellian colonel to royal governor and baronet. His new patent—a true proprietorship—conferred much fuller powers of government than those allowed him by his earlier title. He had plans, he told Lord Chancellor Clarendon, the dominant minister in Charles II's government, to bring Acadia's fisheries and fur trade under his personal supervision in ways that would bring great prosperity to North America and new revenues to the Crown. The Massachusetts authorities, for their part, showed themselves willing to cooperate with Temple to uphold his authority and exclude interlopers from his dominions. A pattern of trade was taking shape—bartering woollen cloth and other items with the Indians for furs and skins, supplying the European settlers of the region with manufactured goods, and dispatching cargoes of fish to southern European ports in return for wines and other commodities marketable in Boston—that would be the basis of English dealings with Acadia for years to come.[24]

In reality, however, Temple's position remained as precariously balanced as that of Acadia/Nova Scotia itself, poised between divergent and intermittently contending forces. Most of the region's settlers around the Bay of Fundy accepted English commercial and political hegemony, provided that they were left undisturbed in possession of their lands. But they had not been settled there as Temple's adherents, and they felt no loyalty to his cause. They remained French in culture and sympathies, and hence receptive to the plans being laid in Quebec and Paris to recapture Acadia and reverse the momentary consequence of English aggression. French claimants were encouraged to contest control of the Atlantic coastline and the offshore fisheries with Temple's forces; and Louis XIVe's ambassadors in London now pressed his fellow monarch hard to return lands seized during the usurpation of the Interregnum. Charles and his ministers, despite their confirmation of Temple's title, felt no particular commitment to retaining territories that seemed to profit the merchants of the stiff-necked Puritan commonwealth of Massachusetts more than the royal purse. And even the Boston authorities, friendly to a political arrangement that served to insulate their eastern borders and enhance their trade, were not prepared to repeat their mistakes of mid-century by providing it or its ruler with any form of direct support.

Temple, in fact, was caught in what was already proving to be the classic dilemma of the seventeenth-century colonial proprietor, one shared by the would-be seigneurs of French Canada and by such grantees as the Masons of New Hampshire and the Calverts of Maryland. Assigned broad acreage and political powers, they could only protect their grandiose titles by trying to make them a reality. Their resources, however, were generally too scanty, their ambitions too purely personal, and their vulnerability to external constraint and intervention too great to permit them to build up the kind of sustained, subordinate, and revenue-producing polities that would have made their proprietorial powers effective and enduring. A few, like the Calverts in Maryland (and later in the century, the Penns in Pennsylvania), achieved a measure of success by forming alliances with broadly based interest groups and by lighting on exceptionally favored and protected locations for their enterprises. But Temple's venture was more typical, both in its dependence on the perseverance of a single individual and in the incessant challenges it incurred by reason of its exposed position on the shifting margins of European colonial expansion. In the years ahead, men ambitious for similar power would come to recognize that success depended on swimming alongside rather than ahead of the authority and protection of the mother country; on being a camp follower rather than a forward skirmisher in the battle for empire.

Temple, meanwhile, faced unrelenting difficulties with no reliable allies. He was beset by rival claimants; his emissaries to London had cheated and betrayed him; and the Boston merchants supported him only so long as he could provide protection for their ventures and cargoes for them to handle. His Fiennes relatives had fallen from power, and their representative in America, Temple's cousin and chief lieutenant, Ralph Wolseley, had perished in a shipwreck off Cape Sable. Searching for support, Sir Thomas turned to his disgruntled Temple relatives in England. Bound to him by ties of blood and debt, the Temples were now reaping the harvest of their political ambiguity in the years before Charles II's restoration in the form of their own return to wealth and office. Among those who now arrived in America to see what could be made of Sir Thomas' embattled heritage was his sister's son, a boy barely into his teens—John Nelson.

II

T R A D E R
TO THE EASTWARD

When John Nelson reached America in the late 1660s, little in his early life had prepared him for what lay before him. Nelson himself left no record of his childhood or upbringing, but enough fragments survive to be pieced together. To judge by the coat of arms he set upon documents in New England, his ancestors descended from a cluster of Nelson families long established in central Lancashire in northern England. How and when his branch of the family moved south to live in London remains uncertain, but they surely responded to the same magnetic attractions of opportunity and professional advancement that were drawing other ambitious provincials to the capital in the early seventeenth century: John Winthrop, for example, exchanged his native East Anglia for government office as a lawyer in London before leaving crown and country in 1630 to become the first governor of Massachusetts.

Robert Nelson, John's grandfather, left no comparable mark on history; but by 1641, the year of his death in London, he, too, had established himself as a lawyer, a member of Barnard's Inn, one of the city's Inns of Chancery. His son, a second Robert (and John Nelson's father), rose several rungs further up the legal ladder: leaving Barnard's Inn in 1631 for Gray's Inn, a more prestigious training ground, he won admission to the ranks of "utter barristers" fifteen years later and joined its elite of senior members—"the grand Company of Auncients"—in 1654, a few months after John's birth.[1] Through these years, Gray's Inn, the largest of the Inns of Court, was renowned for its members' loyalty to Parliament in the latter's struggle with the Crown, and the younger Robert Nelson was no exception. By 1653, following King Charles I's defeat and execution, he was serving the Commonwealth government set up by Parliament as a justice of the peace for the London suburb of Westminster. Several subsequent letters he addressed to John Thurloe, Protector Oliver Cromwell's secretary and spymaster, testify to his zeal to serve the new regime, whether by searching out fugitive Catholic priests or unmasking the plots of radical Protestant extremists.[2]

By then, too, Robert Nelson had signalled his entry into the lower ranks of Cromwell's ruling oligarchy by buying a house in St. Martin's Lane, half a mile west of his chambers in Gray's Inn and London's medieval walls. Running north from what is now Trafalgar Square, and linking the churches of St. Martin-in-the-Fields and St. Giles-in-the-Fields, the lane stood on the very edge of London's urban sprawl, with large, newly constructed houses looking out over the open countryside to the west, which would soon in turn succumb to the city's sprawl and become the new suburbs of Piccadilly and Pall Mall. Scarred with "great muckhills" earlier in the century, the area still bore marks of its past in its surrounding horse stables and streets with such fragrant names (not yet sanitized by property developers) as Dirty Lane and Dunghill Mews.[3] Where there had been muck, however, top military and political brass now came to live: by the mid-1650s, Robert Nelson's neighbors in St. Martin's Lane included Major Generals Fleetwood and Mytton of the parliamentary army, the Earl of Leicester, and Lady Mary Armine, widow of a member of Cromwell's Council of State.[4] Another neighbor who was also the widow of a parliamentary leader, Lady Catherine Perceval, became his client when he defended her from charges of royalism and Catholicism, one of several such cases that underwrote the comfortable affluence Robert Nelson had achieved by the early 1650s.[5] Such Puritan neighbors could hardly have imagined, as they journeyed soberly to church each Sabbath, that their staid street would become the heart of twentieth-century London's theater district.

But a different near neighbor had the most lasting effect upon the Nelson family's fortunes, and John's in particular. A few doors down the street in the early 1650s stood the house of Thomas Temple, the future proprietor of Acadia. This proximity surely cemented—and may well have initiated—the alliance of the two families formed by Robert Nelson's marriage to Temple's sister, Mary. The years that followed brought Robert and Mary a succession of children—a son, Temple, who followed his father into membership of Gray's Inn in 1662 but died childless and unmarried in 1671; two daughters, Margaret and Ursula; a second son, Robert, born in 1651, who seems to have died in childhood; John, the third son; and a last boy, described by his grieving father after his death at the age of eleven as "a most beautiful and forward Child" proficient in both Latin and French.[6] John, therefore, was neither the heir nor the Benjamin of the family; and though he was destined to become Robert Nelson's sole surviving son while still a young adolescent, the relationship between father and son seems to have been formal and increasingly distant. All might have been different had his mother lived; but, heartbroken by the death of her youngest child, she died and was buried with him, in 1669. In her last sickness, Robert Nelson told her brother in America, she "talked often of you and her sonne Jacke"— a son who still wrote letters to his parents. But this correspondence ebbed, and in later years it was to the Temple side of the family that John Nelson looked for help and news of affairs in England. True, the Temples were a far more numerous and politically well-placed clan than the Nelsons—indeed, John's earliest claim to fame derived from his Temple rather than his Nelson ancestry; from the contemporary estimate that he was the seven-hundredth (and last) direct descendant of his mother's grandmother, Lady Hester Temple, born during her lifetime.[7] Uncles and distant Temple cousins were baronets, diplomats, government officeholders, city merchants, and members of Parliament. Robert Nelson, by contrast, never matched his in-laws' adroit transition from service under Cromwell to loyalty to a restored Stuart monarchy. Retreating into social and political obscurity, he married again, and in his will (proved in 1698, after his death) bequeathed all his possessions to his "deare and kind" wife Susanna "to whom my love and affection is so great that I cannot reward her too much." Nothing of sentiment or substance was left to John. His only mention was as "my son" who owed the estate—his father estimated—twelve hundred pounds.[8]

John Nelson's migration to New England in his early teens, therefore, was in every sense a point of departure in his life—tying him henceforward to the ambitions and interests of his mother's family and transforming his horizons from the crowded, plague-stalked streets of London to the green depths of North America's bays and forests. In an England where the lion's share of a family's property was held for the eldest son, it was common practice for a younger to be sent out to make his own way in the world. Moreover, Robert Nelson was among the hapless investors in his brother-in-law's Acadian venture. Hence John's dispatch was both a way of keeping an eye on the investment and of placing a possible heir in the way of a childless relative.[9] Had any letter accompanying John survived, it must have read like that dispatched with another restless young Temple nephew rescued from an apprenticeship and sent out to make his way a few years later: the boy's genius, wrote his elder brother to their uncle Sir Thomas, "leads him to an Active stirring life rather than be confined to a Shop by a Trade. My uncle Sir Purbeck [Temple] and I have brought his master to a composition and thought it best to send him to you whom I humbly beg you to entertaine and get him some Imploiment."[10]

John Nelson's "genius" would likewise lie in the direction of "an Active stirring life." For the moment, however, his arrival in America passed unrecorded amid the stream of emigrants travelling to New England in the 1660s following the restoration of the Stuarts. Many were Puritans distressed by the reestablishment of the Anglican church and its bishops; they included a young minister, Increase Mather, returning to his native Boston where he and his son Cotton, born in 1663, would become the town's most prominent (and certainly most published) exponents of the New England way. Less welcome arrivals, presaging the looming conflict between the Mathers' Massachusetts and the forces of English royal government, were the four Crown-appointed commissioners who accompanied the expedition sent out against the Dutch colony of New Netherland in 1664. The conquest completed, and New Netherland become New York, the commissioners travelled on through the New England colonies, investigating conditions there and sending back a series of reports blistering the settlers' lack of respect for royal authority. Nelson probably arrived just too late to witness the Massachusetts government's humiliating repulse of the indignant visitors, expressed by a proclamation denying their authority, delivered to them at daybreak by sound of trumpet outside the windows of their Boston lodgings. But the clash of wills forecast the larger contest between London and Boston that would underlie much of his subsequent life in America, a contest born out of the closer political and economic ties being spun across the Atlantic and symbolized by Nelson's own migration. In its starkest form, the conflict pitted intransigent Puritans, determined to maintain their Bible Commonwealth free of external contamination, against royal officials bent on imposing English commercial regulation and political authority. Between these extremes, however, would emerge a spectrum of individual solutions and accommodations made by those who, like Nelson, sought to found their own careers—and preserve their own particular brand of Englishness—in a time of rapid political change.

Even as Nelson reached New England, moreover, another and almost equally important influence upon his life was taking fresh shape, as the French Crown began what amounted to a second founding of the colony of New France, bringing its administration under closer control and dispatching men and money to its aid. The arrival in Quebec of the one-thousand-strong regiment of Carignan-Salières in 1665—doubling the colony's adult male population—brought officers and administrators who would found most of French Canada's great military families and dominate its government for the next half century. Many would become Nelson's friends, customers, and political rivals in the years ahead. In these years, also, arrived two men, Father Jacques Marquette and René-Robert Cavelier de La Salle, whose explorations through the Great Lakes and down the Mississippi would point the way for a French empire circumscribing the English settlements in America. By chance, Nelson arrived as one of a generation whose lives would reshape the map of European North America.

Like almost every transatlantic traveller journeying to New England during these years, Nelson surely landed first in Boston. A bustling settlement of three thousand inhabitants and three churches crowding the shores of the bulbous Shawmut peninsula thrusting out into Boston Bay, it boasted a lively trade with Europe, the Caribbean, and lesser ports along the New England coast. Once landed, Nelson lodged with his uncle in the town's North End and doubtless accompanied him to hear Increase Mather's sermons in the nearby North Church, where Temple later accepted membership. Yet Nelson's stay there must have been brief, for, by the fall of 1667, he was already out at a point of contact with French power, employed in his uncle's service along the coast of Acadia. "I charge you as you expect my love," wrote Sir Thomas Temple from Boston to his nephew, "to vallue truth in all your words and actions about any thing. Carry yourself liberally and manly in all things and fear not but that God your Lord will provide for you in all conditions." More practically, he enjoined him to be obedient to "Mr. Rhoades"—John Rhoades, a veteran pilot assigned the task of tutoring the fourteen-year-old in the arts of navigating the dangerous waters and the even trickier trading conditions of his new home. "In the spring," Temple breezily concluded, "I hope to send you all things you want." For now, he enclosed three pairs of stockings and two cheeses. Nelson and his companions were left to spend the winter literally holding the fort: the string of stockaded trading posts that Temple maintained around the Bay of Fundy and up the eastern seacoast as far as La Hève.[11]

Nelson served his apprenticeship well enough so that in March 1670 his uncle, citing the proprietorial powers conferred upon him by Charles II, made his teenage nephew Deputy Governor of Nova Scotia. John was charged to keep the land against all invaders, to protect the trade with the Indians, and to sink or burn the boats of all interlopers who contested his authority.[12] Yet this authority was already hollow: for what the king had given Temple, the king had already taken away. By the Treaty of Breda signed in 1667, which ended the brief Anglo-French war, Charles II had surrendered English title to Acadia in exchange for the return of the half of the island St. Christopher recently captured by the French. The logic, if not the justice, of the decision was impeccable—control of a Caribbean island producing sugar and a revenue to the Crown was much more valuable to England than a string of trading posts whose profits, if any, were ending up in the pockets of the notoriously recalcitrant New Englanders. To English officials familiar with the reports of the commissioners recently returned from New England, the complaints received from Boston about how the terms of the treaty would harm the interests and authority of Massachusetts must have been more a source of satisfaction than of sorrow.[13]

To Sir Thomas Temple, however, the news came as a devastating blow and meant the sudden ruin of ten years of building up his proprietary with other people's money. He had, he claimed, invested sixteen thousand pounds and fallen deeply in debt to backers in England and rapacious merchants in Boston. Thirteen thousand pounds were still owed him by his trading partners in Nova Scotia. For a while he resisted, questioning the language of the treaty and arguing that to return to Acadia would still leave him in possession of part of Nova Scotia between Acadia and northern New England. But in the face of a direct order from the Crown, he gave way; and late in 1670, only a few months after becoming the New World's youngest deputy governor, John Nelson surrendered his command of Temple's fort at the mouth of the St. John River to the new French governor. Sir Thomas briefly contemplated accepting French sovereignty and citizenship if he could retain his commercial investments. At length, however, even his perennial optimism subsided. Liquidating his extensive landholdings in Boston to satisfy his creditors, he returned to London and died, despairing and impoverished—"his spirit broken, his inward estate darke"—at the home of his former mistress, in 1674. In his will, Sir Thomas left his nephew, in addition to "Wearing Cloaths and Linnen and some few Books," a principal share of the compensation he believed was due him from the Crown for the loss of his proprietorship—"if ever paid." Needless to say, it never was.[14]

For some part of the time before his uncle's death, John Nelson was once more at sea, but in Caribbean waters: in an earlier will drafted in 1671, Temple had bequeathed his nephew a ketch and its cargo, then in Nelson's charge at the island of Nevis. By 1674, however, he was in England by his uncle's bedside. He listened to the dying man dictate the terms of his last will and served as one of its executors.[15] His fortunes had fallen with his uncle's, and he might have been expected to have remained in England now that his brothers' deaths had left him his father's one remaining son. Yet by the fall of 1675 he had returned to Boston to act in the affairs of another recent English immigrant who would become a lifelong friend, James Lloyd. Two years later, Nelson was already well established in Boston's trade with what was now French Acadia.[16] Perhaps he found little to keep him in England after his mother's death. He may also have been commissioned by his uncle's two brothers, Colonel Edmund and Sir Purbeck Temple, who had invested heavily in the Nova Scotia venture, to go back and salvage what he could from its ruins. Ultimately, after a series of lawsuits between the administrators of Sir Thomas' estate and Nelson as its executor, the estate did reach the respectable sum, on paper, of nearly two thousand pounds.[17] But if Nelson's later life is any guide, it was above all the force of an incorrigibly adventurous temperament, unleashed by the opportunities revealed by his earlier venture, that led him back to New England and the far fringes of English expansion.

Once back in Boston, Nelson found the 1670s to be a decade of even greater confusion—and hence opportunity—than the days of his uncle's proprietorship. An energetic new governor, Louis de Buade, Count Frontenac, ruled in Quebec after 1672, but he proved more intent upon recouping his own and New France's fortunes by expanding the western fur trade around the Great Lakes than upon consolidating French power along the Atlantic coastline. Even the official instructions sent to Acadia's governor tacitly acknowledged his province's dependence on a continued English connection by urging Acadians to stay on good terms with the Boston authorities and to look to New England when necessary for supplies. French merchants who had expected to enjoy exclusive control of the region's trade and fisheries appealed in vain for some authority that might deter English interlopers: "if it were only an old contract in parchment with a large seal of yellow or red wax, it does not matter which," wrote one, "it will be sufficient to dazzle the scum of this country."[18] But French power was too distant, and the Acadian dependence on the New Englanders too pressing; and all that officials could contrive was a continuation of the system of selling licenses to foreign traders begun by Sir Thomas Temple. Indeed, for some years during the mid-1670s, French control over Acadia vanished altogether, after a small Dutch force took advantage of the outbreak of war in Europe to launch an attack on the colony. Guided by Nelson's old mentor, John Rhoades, the Dutch overran the French forts, pillaged the settlements, and carried off their plunder and prisoners to Boston. Ultimately, their evenhanded looting of vessels trading in Acadian waters won them Massachusetts's enmity as well. Setting one freebooter to catch another, the Boston authorities dispatched an expedition headed by ex-buccaneer Samuel Mosely that captured Rhoades and his men after a sea battle in the Bay of Fundy. Brought back to Boston in 1675 and condemned to death for piracy, Rhoades escaped the gallows only by accepting a sentence of banishment from New England.[19]

In the meantime, Massachusetts' own claims to authority in northeastern New England suffered an equally abrupt setback as the outbreak of war with the Indians in New England in 1675 was followed by a more prolonged conflict with the powerful Abenaki Indians of Maine that lasted until 1678. Scores of New England towns were damaged or destroyed, and English settlement along the northeast coast was driven back a hundred miles, to the outskirts of Wells and Saco. Finally, to compound the tangle of French, Dutch, and Massachusetts claims, one more English actor took the stage when Governor Edmund Andros of New York decided to make a reality of the title that his master, the Duke of York, possessed to the land between the Kennebec and St. Croix Rivers by virtue of New York's royally granted charter of 1664. In June of 1677, Andros sent a force of men and ships to build and garrison a fort at Pemaquid, a few miles east of the mouth of the Kennebec, on land the French claimed by their interpretation of the terms of the Treaty of Breda and within the area that Massachusetts, too, claimed to govern. The New Yorkers were intent on upholding their newly claimed authority and intolerant of the pragmatic arrangements for trade and coexistence set up before the violence of the 1670s, and their efforts to occupy and control the buffer zone between Massachusetts and Acadia remained a constant source of irritation for a dozen years to come.

While governments wrangled, however, trade made its way through whatever channels it found open at the moment needed; and by the early 1680s John Nelson had established himself as a dominant, and certainly the best known, figure in New England's trade with Acadia. He may have served in the war with the Indians: half a century later his name appeared on a list of surviving Boston veterans claiming land in southern Massachusetts as reward for their enlistment.[20] More certainly, he capitalized on his own background and the character of Acadia's government and commercial dependence to forge ties with French officials in the colony. On paper, the succession of French army officers who commanded in Acadia possessed only limited authority, shared with civil officials appointed by the Crown. They were expected to support themselves by supplementing their meager military pay with inherited wealth and the revenues of the seigneurial land grants most sought and received after their arrival in Canada. In practice, few of the younger sons and minor gentry who ended up in Canadian regiments possessed much inherited wealth, and fewer still profited from their seigneuries. The remedy was irresistibly simple: Acadia's remoteness and the officers' domination of what was in effect a garrison community allowed them broad authority, which they used (while Quebec looked the other way) to profit from every form of economic life within their grasp, through methods ranging from fees and personal ventures to self-proclaimed monopolies and the private use of men and monies entrusted to their command. The very fact that trade with New England flew in the face of a policy of economic self-sufficiency made official connivance essential to its success, entrenching it within the levels of government charged with its restriction.

In these circumstances, Nelson—urbane, openhanded, European-born, and well connected—was far better equipped to ease the social discomfort of officers and gentlemen driven to dabble in trade than the majority of his fellow New Englanders. One tie he soon forged was with Pierre de Joybert de Soulanges et de Marson, acting governor of Acadia during the mid-1670s until his death in 1678. Marson had visited Boston during the negotiations for Sir Thomas Temple's submission after the Treaty of Breda and again, involuntarily, following his capture during the Dutch conquest of Acadia in 1674. As acting governor, he administered Acadia from his seigneury at Fort Jemseg on the St. John River, upstream from where he had received Nelson's surrender of Temple's fort in 1670. Nelson's second, and more exotic, link was with the remarkable Jean-Vincent d'Abbadie de Saint-Castin. Like Marson and many other future leaders of New France, Saint-Castin had come to Canada from France in 1665 as an officer in the regiment of Carignan-Salières. In other respects, however, he had much in common with Nelson—both were motherless younger sons cast loose to make their way in the world; both reached the New World and their teens almost simultaneously; and both quickly headed for a life of adventure on America's margins. Soon after arriving in Acadia under Marson's command, Saint-Castin had left the immediate service of the Crown to settle at the mouth of the Penobscot River at Pentagouet, close to the ruins of the northernmost English settlements. There he had established an enduring friendship with the local Indians, one cemented by his marriage to the daughter of an Abenaki chieftain. Not even inheriting the family title could lure him back to France. Quebec officials sneered at the baron's unorthodox and, in their eyes, ungentlemanly way of life—his "libertinage" and "vye vagabonde." But they were quick to note his value as an essential link in the chain of friendship (and common fear of English expansion) that drew the eastern Indians into alliance with France.[21]

In the aftermath of the Dutch conquest, as French control returned, both Marson and Saint-Castin looked to Boston, and Nelson in particular, for supplies in return for Acadia's products. When, in early 1677, the Massachusetts government sought to cut off the shipment of arms and ammunition to hostile Indians by imposing an general embargo on trade to Maine and parts beyond, the reaction from affected merchants revealed a regular trade to eastern waters. William Tailer of Boston sought permission for a ship owned by Marson and Saint-Castin to return to Acadia with its cargo: Marson, he argued, was a valued (and heavily indebted) customer as a shipper of moose and beaver pelts and a buyer of goods from Boston. The embargo would only divert this trade elsewhere. In addition, it would hurt the the venture of John Nelson, who had just sailed up the coast with "a considerabell Cargo and hath great favour shown him Amongst the French." At first, the Massachusetts government refused Tailer's request: the Frenchmen's ship could only return if empty of cargo. Later, it permitted the dispatch of limited quantities of food and clothing to Marson—flour, pork, beef, rum, tobacco, salt, and some cotton goods and blankets—but not the six axes and ten dozen knives he and Saint-Castin had requested.[22] An inventory of a cargo captured in Acadian waters some months earlier suggests that Tailer's shipments to and from the region were typical of the larger pattern of trade: it listed many of the same goods, including details of the purple and scarlet shades of cloth favored by the Indians, and added fishing tackle, wine, and—another important Acadian product—bags of feathers to the items of exchange.[23]

Tailer and Nelson were not the only New Englanders trading to Acadia during the 1670s. The names of others—Daniel Dennison, John

Poole, William Waldron, Oliver Duncomb, John Freake, John Alden, and Christopher Smith—emerge from the records in the wake of complaints and legal wranglings surrounding their activities.[24] Some of the Acadian settlers, too, had begun to deal directly with New England on their own account. Plainly the trade demanded special skills, among them a capacity to cater to a clientele divided by a range of European and Indian tongues and seeking to barter an even greater diversity of goods—from fish, fur, and feathers, through rum and raisins, to pots and pans. The knowledgeable merchant had to be able to distinguish at a glance the best "winter beaver" pelt from its less valuable spring- or summer-trapped cousin, or "good merchantable cod" fit for European tastes from the "refuse" fish destined for the diet of slaves on West Indian plantations. All this amid a hostile environment where pirates or raiding Indians might burst suddenly out of dense fog, or tidal flurries smash a vessel on what was one of the world's most treacherous and unforgiving coasts.

Yet Tailer and Nelson emerged at the head of this select fraternity, and their alliance suggested the additional combination of skill and status likely to ensure success. Tailer had been a leading commercial property owner in Boston since the 1660s. A partner in the Atherton Proprietors, New England's most powerful and socially distinguished group of land speculators, and married to the sister of Massachusetts magistrate William Stoughton, he possessed the local standing and political connections that the younger man still lacked. Nelson remained the agent and man out front, bearing and relishing the risk of trading face to face with his French and Indian customers, while Tailer balanced the books at home.[25]

Yet Nelson also brought assets to the partnership over and above his youth and vigor. Through his uncle's paper legacy he could claim a legally tattered but still impressive right to trade beyond the boundaries of New England and along Acadia's shores. His family background offered access to English capital and political influence. Finally, as his whole life showed, Nelson himself was not the kind of man to let such assets go to waste. For all his seemingly sheltered childhood, he had quickly shed that shell of self-satisfied insularity that even then cut off most of his fellow Englishmen from communicating with those unfortunates fated to be born foreigners. Perhaps the very shock of emigration at a formative age had opened his eyes and mind to cultures beyond his own. Already a veteran of eastern waters, he was fast perfecting the skills of speech and diplomacy that would cause Frenchmen to speak of his complete command of their language, and himself to note his capacity to negotiate with Abenaki Indian leaders in their own tongue behind the backs of his fellow Europeans.[26] Born a child of London's streets, Nelson was already a full citizen of the North Atlantic sea-world.

During these years, in consequence, Nelson built up a web of trading relationships that prompted the French governor of Acadia in 1686 to describe him as one who "has always traded on this coast and who has brought much benefit to the inhabitants by the large loans he has made to them in their greatest necessity." In the same year, Intendant Jacques de Meulles, New France's highest official after the governor, visited Acadia and identified Nelson as one of the two Bostonians who dominated the trade in fish, furs, and provisions around the Bay of Fundy.[27] Nor was this the hand-to-mouth business it had been back in mid-century. By 1686, the number of French settlers in Acadia had almost doubled from fifteen years before, to some eight hundred souls, three quarters of them living on the rich marshlands around Port Royal. Along the Atlantic coast of Acadia, the crews of the numerous fishing boats from New England who landed to salt and dry their catch composed another profitable market for itinerant traders.[28] No record survives of Nelson's—or any other Englishman's—dealings with the region's Indians during these years, but the character of the trade, in conjunction with Nelson's determination to learn their language, suggests that this, too, was an important component of his commercial success: later in the century, a French visitor to Acadia reported, with disbelief, the contention of Saint-Castin and a local Jesuit priest that as much as eighty thousand livres (some £6,500) of furs could be harvested each year from the Penobscot River valley alone.[29]

As trade increased, however, so did the tensions and the stakes involved in this interplay of French political authority with English commercial penetration. Here, too, Nelson took on an important, mediating role, protecting his investments and his exposed position. Following Temple's surrender of his proprietorship, the French authorities had tried with limited success to continue his system of requiring fees from New England fishermen visiting Acadian waters. Early in the 1680s, the French tried again, coupling this offensive with complaints against English vessels trading with the Acadian Indians and mining coal on Cape Breton Island without permission.[30] In response, the Massachusetts government dispatched John Nelson to Canada on an exploratory mission to see what form of compromise was possible. Carrying a letter from Governor Simon Bradstreet, Nelson left Boston by ship early in June 1682 and reached Quebec after a voyage of about six weeks. He was agreeably impressed with the capital of New France, set upon frowning cliffs commanding the St. Lawrence River. The town, he later reported, was "advantagiously and pleasantly situated," its churches and other religious buildings a match in structure and design for those in Europe.[31] Once there, he held conversations with French officials that ranged beyond Acadian affairs to include the workings of English trade in furs from New York and Hudson Bay.[32] Two circumstances intervened to impede his mission. A disastrous fire broke out during his visit that destroyed much of Quebec's commercial district below the walls of the citadel. In addition, Governor Frontenac happened to be upriver in Montreal during Nelson's stay, so that Massachusetts got no official satisfaction for its protest against the tightening of French control.[33] What did emerge during the summer was an effective acceptance by the Bostonians of the reality of French authority, an acceptance that put Nelson in the position of middleman and broker. Shortly after his return to Boston, and perhaps as a result of stopping off in Acadia on the way home, he was empowered by Frontenac's lieutenant then stationed at Beaubassin, Governor Michel Leneuf de La Vallière, to sell licenses (five pounds seems to have been the usual fee) to his fellow New Englanders to fish in Acadian waters. The Massachusetts General Court, for its part, provided indirect endorsement of the arrangement by voting to condemn any "irregularityes" occurring in the trade with Acadia and expressing hopes for "a good correspondence" with "our neighbors" to the north. Any violators, the Court declared, must expect to suffer at the hands of the appropriate authorities.[34]

French officials proud of their territorial sovereignty still chafed at the economic dependence that made such an arrangement necessary. New England fishermen and traders, for their part, remained incorrigible individualists, reluctant to hold to any set way of trading and quick to take their profits whenever and wherever they could. The whole coast from Maine to the mouth of the St. Lawrence River, dotted with scattered settlements unable to withstand even a single ship or a determined Indian war party, lay as vulnerable as ever to any visitor who might decide to supplement diplomacy with force. But while officials in Boston and Quebec—or, at one more remove, London and Paris—were content to turn a blind eye to the informal arrangements emerging on the fringes of their authority, there was room for a balance of interests in which intermediary figures such as John Nelson could have a significant and profitable position. Nelson, in particular, seemed on the verge of reestablishing the commercial position his uncle had established twenty years before, but without its costly political burdens. Yet even as the complexity of intersecting economies, political systems, and cultures generated opportunity, so their variety also rendered such opportunity vulnerable to a much greater range of challenges and dislocations. Only time would tell if, as so often in Acadia's history, the arrangements that favored Nelson's enterprises would prove to be but a deceptive lull between storms.

III

SEEKING "TO LIVE INDIFFERENT"

Fifteen years after his migration from England, John Nelson had emerged from his uncle's eclipse to establish a position of his own in the commercial life of his adopted land. As if buoyed by the prospects before him, he began to put down social and domestic roots in Boston. In 1681, he joined the town's Ancient and Honorable Artillery Company, founded in 1638 and modelled on that of London. Ostensibly an association for military training, it served as the nearest thing in seventeenth-century Boston to a gentleman's club, where the town's social and political elite could come together on easy terms under the guise of civic purpose. Early in the following year, he bought land to build a house in the center of town on the "Long Back Street" (later Hanover Street) that led from the southeastern base of Beacon Hill to Boston's North End. From that site, it was an easy walk of some two hundred paces to the Town Dock, the center of commercial life. A few yards to the east, at the point where Hanover intersected with Hudson's (later Wings) Lane, stood the mansion of William Tailer and his family, Nelson's associate in the Acadia trade.[1]

Within the year, however, during Nelson's voyage to Quebec in the summer of 1682, came a tragedy that caught the attention of contemporary diarists and remained vivid in the memory of one, Samuel Sewall,

John Nelson in old age. Painted by John Smibert in 1732, two years before Nelson died at the age of eighty-one. (*Courtesy of The Fine Arts Museums of San Francisco. Gift of Mr. and Mrs. John D. Rockefeller III*)

more than forty years later. In a fit of depression compounded by business losses, Tailer, "one of the greatest merchants in Boston," walked to his warehouse, knelt, and "hang'd himself with a new Snaffle Bridle." As the sensation and the pulpit homilies on the sin of suicide subsided,

Nelson joined with Tailer's widow Rebecca to serve as administrator of his friend's estate.[2] Soon afterward, and at some point before the summer of 1684, Nelson wed the Tailers' eldest child, Elizabeth, a girl still in her teens and a dozen years his junior, launching a partnership that would encompass more than fifty years of married life, many separations, and six children surviving into maturity.[3] An heiress by her father's holdings of lands, wharves, and mills in Boston as well as by her expectations from her childless uncle William Stoughton, Elizabeth further buttressed her new husband's standing. By the late 1680s, Nelson's assessment for taxes on his real and personal estate in Boston put him among the wealthiest six percent of the town's fifteen hundred adult males.[4] As acting head of the Tailer family interests (the elder of Elizabeth's two brothers was still under guardianship and not yet ten years old), Nelson now assumed his late father-in-law's position, casting the accounts and serving as agent and banker in Boston while others voyaged on his behalf. Seldom mentioned in the records as present in Boston before 1682, he was frequently called upon to act in court during the next several years in matters relating to Frenchmen trading with Massachusetts—translating their depositions, collecting debts due, and serving as Saint-Castin's attorney in the latter's suit to recover eighty-three moose skins taken from him by pirates and brought to Boston. Meanwhile, with land received as part of his wife's marriage settlement, Nelson built a brick house, wharf, and warehouse down at Boston's town dock, on the northeast side of "Merchants' Row," close to the present-day site of Faneuil Hall.[5]

Yet, however much Nelson might seem to have blended into Massachusetts society, he still stood apart from it in several significant ways. Loyal to his native Church of England, a church as yet without any formal place of worship in Puritan Boston, he did not seek membership in any of the town's Congregational churches. He was never admitted a freeman of the colony (a privilege generally though not wholly restricted to male Congregational church members) and so remained ineligible to vote in elections for the magistrates and deputies of the colony's General Court. Nor did he serve in any of the numerous offices—more than one hundred chosen each year, ranging from selectman to the lowly tasks of scavenger and hogreeve—of Boston's town government. A prominent and even famous inhabitant of the town by the mid-1680s, he never took up the status of leading citizen that his prosperity seemed to warrant.

Some part of this detachment from civic life stemmed from Nelson's youth, his immigrant origins, and his frequent absences at sea. That it

Elizabeth Tailer Nelson. A portrait by an unknown artist that remains in the possession of the family's descendants. (*Courtesy of Mr. and Mrs. Orme Wilson*)

persisted after his marriage and settlement in Boston (and through the rest of his long life), however, suggests an alienation both self-fashioned and imposed, one linked to his chosen career as a merchant. As Bernard Bailyn has shown, John Nelson was not the only New Englander with trading interests who stood apart in this fashion. From the first years of settlement, some merchants arriving in the Bay Colony paid more heed to establishing their prosperity than to the work of building a Bible Commonwealth. Others found their personal religious beliefs at odds with the ruling canons of Puritan orthodoxy, or felt themselves deficient in the spiritual self-assurance they deemed essential to participation in public life. Yet these choices were also responses to the currents of public opinion, and at the root of many merchants' detachment lay a widely held perception—even among merchants themselves—that the interests of trade and its practitioners ran at odds with those of the community as a whole. Images of the moneychangers in the temple and the corruption wrought by wealth found practical expression in denunciation of the ways trade seemed to be luring the "city on a hill" into the international marketplace, provoking French hostility and English regulation. "I see no reason," wrote one of Massachusetts' emissaries to England in a widely circulated letter, "why the Countrey should be involved and made obnoxious by a few rich merchants." Let it not be forgotten, cried the Reverend John Higginson, in a sermon preached to the Massachusetts General Court just before Nelson's arrival in Boston, "that *New-England is originally a Plantation of Religion, not a Plantation of Trade*. Let Merchants and such as are increasing *Cent per Cent* remember this . . . that worldly gain was not the end and design of the people of *New-England*, but *Religion*."[6]

Higginson's rhetoric was slanted. It ignored the way trade and its returns had become an indispensable prop of Massachusetts' economic and, by extension, political and religious autonomy. It slighted the enduring and often ardent loyalty of the great majority of the colony's mercantile community to the established Puritan order. Skill in the service of Mammon did not preclude a dedication to the ways ordained by God. Yet it was true that a number of merchants, both loyalists and others less so, had taken the lead in demanding a more conciliatory attitude to the Crown in the wake of the restoration of the Stuart monarchy in England—William Tailer, for example, had signed a petition of 1666, one of several from coastal communities, that counselled a greater respect for royal authority.[7] The prompt rejection of this advice by a General Court dominated by a vocally Puritan and rurally based majority not only served to discourage merchants as a group from similar initiatives in the future, hardening their distaste for political involvement. It also gave added weight to a persistent sentiment against allowing such critics political power commensurate with their economic and social status. Not until 1681 was Boston, with its wealth and a population of some five thousand (an eighth of that of the whole colony), permitted to send any larger number of deputies to the Massachusetts General Court than the smallest rural community; and within the town itself, proposals to establish an English-style ruling oligarchy of mayor and aldermen in which the merchants would have had a greater voice were consistently rejected in favor of keeping the reins of government in the hands of the town meeting.[8] The young Samuel Sewall conveyed some of the flavor of contemporary feeling—at once jealous, distrustful, and admiring—when he recorded in his diary, soon after his marriage to the daughter of a leading trader, an invitation to "Acquaint myself with merchants" and take part in their "caballs." A later diarist tied popular resentment directly to Nelson himself. When Nelson was proposed as leader of an expedition against the French, "the Country Deputies said he was a Merchant and not to be trusted."[9]

Yet that Nelson was a merchant ultimately mattered less to his standing in the colony than what manner of merchant he was. Sir Thomas Temple had come close to accepting foreign sovereignty and nationality to preserve his holdings. Nelson, despite similar temptations, had remained an Englishman. Yet he too was drawn by his chosen pattern of trade towards a cooperation with outsiders that could all too easily be construed as collaboration with New England's enemies. In the wake of Governor John Winthrop's ill-judged intervention in the war between La Tour and d'Aulnay in the 1640s, many in Massachusetts had concluded that none but the directly self-interested stood to profit from further meddling with matters Acadian. Suspicion flared into active resentment amid rumors that the hand of France was behind the outburst of Indian resistance within New England and on the eastern frontier during the years following 1675. Not English land hunger, nor tribal resentments, but "a premeditated Jesuiticall device completed long before" explained the conflict.[10] Ultimately, French officials would indeed embrace such a policy; in the meantime, rumor found other scapegoats even closer to hand in the form of the English merchants trading up the eastern coast, charged with supplying their French and Indian customers with the very munitions employed to cut down English frontier families. Must we be involved in a bloody war, asked one Connecticut leader, "for the sake of a beaver trade, to be upheld by the point of the sword for the enriching of a few mercenary spirited men"?[11] Such feelings prompted the embargo of 1677 on eastern trade; and in the following year only the veto of the Massachusetts magistrates saved John Nelson from an investigation by the deputies of the lower house into charges that he had exported gunpowder from Boston without permission. Ten years later, it was an item of popular belief that Nelson had shipped sufficient cargoes to Saint-Castin for every Indian who engaged to attack New England to receive a pound of powder and two of lead.[12]

The evidence needed to sustain such charges was never forthcoming, and Nelson might have escaped a measure of the suspicion he incurred by a humbler or, when appropriate, more penitent stance. In church or court in Massachusetts, black sheep who professed guilt and a hope of reconciliation were offered a way back into the fold. Merchants who confessed ill-gotten gains could atone for their sins against the community. Others avoided censure by heeding popular feeling. Captain John Alden, for example, another trader to the eastward, stayed in better odor by enlisting in the public service and supplying English settlements on the frontier.

But Nelson's temperament was already set in a different mold. Secure in his right to trade by virtue of his inheritance and his own acquired skills, he saw no reason to pay blind obedience to the Bay Colony's traditions and beliefs. Proud of his network of friendships transcending the limits of race, religion, and nationality, he scorned to play down his ability to converse with Indians in their own tongue, loan money to Acadian settlers, conduct what amounted to his own foreign policy, and carouse with French seigneurs. Years later, the historian Thomas Hutchinson, a young man at the time of Nelson's death, recalled the latter's "gay free temper" that set him at odds with authority; equally revealing—and a central clue to Nelson's image of himself—was Hutchinson's classification of him as a gentleman.[13] To modern ears, the term lacks significance where it does not inspire derision: we no longer allocate church seating according to social status or ponder long and hard before dubbing John Smith "Mr." or assigning him the higher rank of "Esquire." To late seventeenth-century society, however, these were titles endowed with responsibility as well as privilege, earned no less than inherited, and kept untarnished only by a consistent pattern of personal relationships and behavior. Friendships must be honored at personal and even patriotic cost, excess abhorred, and the lure of mere accumulation subordinated to the living of a life that would be, in the words of a eulogist after Nelson's death, "Genteel, Enlarged, [and] Liberal." To take upon oneself, as Nelson was to do, the public character of "John Nelson Gentleman," and to assume the social and armorial bearings of that rank, was to pledge allegiance to standards of behavior that transcended the provincial boundaries of Puritan New England.[14]

Whatever Nelson's success in embodying such standards, they clearly provided him with a lifelong image of what he sought to be. To pursue such aspirations on the edge of empire did not diminish their force. To the contrary, such an arena provided a matchless opportunity for younger sons to resolve the disparity between what they were raised to be and the means allotted them to achieve it, a chance to put breeding to the test by exemplifying gentility in the wild. Nelson was neither the first nor last gentleman-adventurer to try his hand in the New World. But he found himself unusually constricted by the society in which he chose to live. Indeed, French Canada's world of scattered seigneuries and transplanted Languedoc gentry offered a better proving ground for such ideals than Puritan Boston, and it was one of the ironies of Nelson's life that he became and remained more akin in spirit to those cast as his enemies than to his adopted fellow New Englanders. Given a proprietorship or a seigneury, he too, might have become a Saint-Castin. In this light, to go against the grain of Boston society was a step toward self-identity: like the Tories of a later generation, Nelson seems to have taken a certain wilful pride in maintaining his singularity and standing out as a lightning rod for popular suspicion.

One path away from such isolation, had Nelson chosen to take it, lay through the political realignments now emerging within New England. Exasperated by the refusal of Massachusetts to accept any effective degree of royal regulation, officials in London had begun a prosecution of the colony's charter, the legal basis of its political autonomy. In the fall of 1684, word reached Boston that the charter had been annulled. For more than a year, Crown plans for a new government were delayed by the death of King Charles II, the succession of his brother James, and a brief spasm of rebellion in England. Yet a settlement was inevitable, one likely to involve not just Massachusetts but neighboring colonies as well. Throughout New England, men at odds with the existing order or simply convinced of the need for compromise pondered how to come to terms with the new political opportunities appearing over the horizon. In New Hampshire, the Crown had already established a royal government, but one administered for the most part by the colonists themselves. Might not it now consent to a regime in which moderate New Englanders, neither extreme Puritans nor royalist newcomers, held a preponderant voice? The news of the charter's fall, wrote one such moderate to a leading official in London, "makes all good subjects thoughtful how they may best express their obedience."[15]

By background and experience, Nelson seemed well fitted to assume a place in this emerging coalition. Indeed, it took shape almost literally on his own doorstep. One of its key figures was Edward Randolph. The Crown-appointed collector of Customs in New England, Randolph had worked tirelessly since his arrival in Boston in 1676 to gather information for the prosecution of the charter and draft plans for a royal government in New England. Another was William Tailer's longtime business associate, Richard Wharton, a restless entrepreneur at the center of a web of speculative schemes likely to benefit from a change of government. But the group's most important leaders, in terms of their public prestige and ability to provide fearful colonists with a sense of continuity from the old Puritan regime, were three former Massachusetts magistrates: Joseph Dudley, Peter Bulkeley, and Nelson's uncle by marriage, William Stoughton. During the months that the charter's fate hung in the balance, these leaders met regularly to plan strategy at the home of Stoughton's sister (who was also Nelson's mother-in-law), the widowed Mrs. Rebecca Tailer, a few yards down the street from Nelson's house.[16] When, in May 1686, word arrived of London's establishment of a Dominion of New England stretching from Maine to the borders of Rhode Island, to be governed by a Crown-appointed council headed by Dudley and Stoughton, these men stepped forward as the new rulers of Massachusetts.

In the event, however, Nelson himself moved only marginally closer to the center of power than before. Though named to a committee of merchants to suggest ways of improving trade, he took no political office under the new regime. One reason seems to have been immediate and personal—the recently bereaved Randolph, he came to believe, had designs on the person and estate of his widowed mother-in-law, prompting him to write what Randolph termed "a very indiscreet letter" that the royal official circulated among his Boston allies with instructions to read and then burn. "I am unwilling to expose him for Mrs. Taylor's sake."[17] Randolph had aroused violent hatreds in Massachusetts by his unbending zeal in prosecuting the charter, and to Nelson he must have seemed as obnoxious a potential father-in-law as any of the charter's equally zealous Puritan defenders. Yet alongside the clash of temperaments ran a conflict of interests of the kind that led other New England merchants to shy away from Randolph's embrace even as they strove to avoid his enmity: as a loyal Crown official, Randolph was determined to curb the very kind of commerce, ranging freely through the Atlantic community across political boundaries, that was crucial to the colony's prosperity.

By 1686, moreover, Nelson had become only too well aware of the special threat to his interests posed by a greater degree of royal intervention, whether directed from London or from Paris. Even as the English Crown was forcing through its reorganization of government in

New England, Louis XIVe and his ministers were committing new resources to the protection and expansion of New France on a scale not
seen since the 1660s. Frontenac was replaced as governor; several shipments of fresh troops were dispatched from France; and expeditions
were sent against the English posts around Hudson Bay to the north
and the Iroquois confederacy to the south.[18] Only a scattering of men
were added to the Acadia garrisons. But at the very moment when
Nelson seemed to have succeeded in establishing himself as middleman
and dispenser of licenses in the Acadia trade, the French government
embarked on a new policy by granting Clerbaud Bergier, a merchant
of La Rochelle, and several Paris associates the right to set up a company
to exploit the region's fisheries. Once in Acadian waters, Bergier quickly
determined to drive out what he viewed as the New Englanders' interloping vessels, and in 1684 he secured royal backing in the form of
orders that prohibited foreign traders from entering Acadia and dismissed the official, Governor La Vallière, who had authorized Nelson
to sell licenses. A new governor, François-Marie Perrot, was appointed
with instructions to drive English influence out of the colony.[19]

The precarious peace in northern waters quickly disintegrated. The
new company's harassment of English traders was followed by capture
and counter-capture of each side's fishing vessels, with some of the
English ships being carried as far away as La Rochelle for condemnation
in French admiralty courts. Bergier's hopes of establishing a profitable
monopoly were never realized; and, once in office, Governor Perrot
soon recognized that his own profit and the survival of the colonists in
his charge required a continued, if now more surreptitious, contact with
New England's merchants. But the episode revealed the fragility of
Nelson's attempts to trade across the borders of two converging empires,
each committed to a policy of closer central control and increasingly
aware of the other as the prime threat to its ambitions. Even when a
local accommodation could be arranged, with blind eyes turned in Boston and Quebec, it was still abruptly vulnerable to the ambitions of
newcomers to the game who were backed by the overriding authority
of officials across the Atlantic.

At the same time, Nelson was experiencing a similar disruption at the
hands of his own countrymen. Throughout the years after King Philip's
War, Governor Andros of New York had continued to maintain the
garrison he had placed at Pemaquid to support his claim to rule the
coastline between the Kennebec and St. Croix Rivers. Saint-Castin's
position at Pentagouet had been menaced, and at least one Bay merchant, John Alden, had been arrested for trading illegally. Andros'

replacement in 1683 by a still more belligerent governor, Thomas Don-gan, an Anglo-Irish soldier, carried this "forward" policy a step further. Dongan and his council laid down comprehensive restrictions on trade and fishing in the region. All vessels seeking to trade between the Ken-nebec and St. Croix must first register at Pemaquid; and "no one what-soever as he will answer it at his perill shall take a permitt or lycense to trade there from John Nelson at Boston or any other person what-soever, except such as are appointed or Commissionated by the Gov-ernor of New York."[20] Dongan followed up with a sharp letter to Nelson accusing him of sympathizing with Saint-Castin and the French and insisting on the validity of the Duke of York's title. Nelson's reply, as reported back to New York, was equally sharp: Saint-Castin had a good title to his lands by the French possession of Acadia. Nor, as a French aristocrat, would the baron come in and pay homage to the captain of Pemaquid fort, who was "a me[a]n person, and of noe parts" and unfit to negotiate with a gentleman of Saint-Castin's standing. Finally, beyond such niceties of title and protocol, Nelson made the practical point that any attempt to displace Saint-Castin was sure to bring his Indian allies down in bloody vengeance upon the local settlers. In a calmer letter, no longer extant, Nelson evidently explained to Dongan how London had compelled Sir Thomas Temple to surrender England's title to the French at least as far down as the Penobscot River—fifteen years later, Nelson believed that the true boundary lay even further west, on the St. George River. In reply, Dongan sneered at finding "any English gentleman to write so much for the French Interest"; expressed a pious but wholly unwarranted confidence in the capacity of English bureau-crats to draw accurate colonial boundaries; and again warned Nelson not to meddle in matters beyond his competence.[21]

The stage was set for a clash of jurisdictions, and it came in a case that would linger in the annals of European diplomacy for years to come, enshrining John Nelson's name in the memories of bureaucrats yet un-born.[22] In May 1686, the ship *Johanna* dropped anchor at Pentagouet at the mouth of the Penobscot River after a voyage from the Spanish Mediterranean port of Malaga of a little less than a month. The ship's captain and part-owner, Philip Severett, a native of the Channel Island of Jersey now resident in Portsmouth, New Hampshire, was already well known to Edward Randolph and other royal officials as an invet-erate free trader. In Spain, Severett had taken aboard a large quantity—some seventy pipes (each containing around a hundred gallons)—of wine, a pipe of brandy and two of olive oil, and some barrels and baskets of fruit. His orders were to deliver his cargo to Saint-Castin at Pentagoet, within French territory. But, as subsequent lawsuits, depositions, and diplomatic notes revealed, this was but the first stage of a more elaborate scheme with a decidedly English connection. Severett had financed an earlier cargo of wine with bills of exchange given to Gideon DeLabatt, a merchant of Fayal in the Portugese Azores, and drawn upon several merchants of Boston, including Nelson and Richard Wharton. The present venture, French officials later noted, was on the joint account of "Sieur Nelson, Watkins et consorts"; and Severett's intent from the very beginning, after landing his cargo at Pentagouet, was to send (i.e., smuggle) it in small lots down the coast to ports in New England.[23] In later years, this method of transshipment would become the classic tactic of traders who wanted to shield all or part of their cargoes from official scrutiny—coastal voyages could never be as strictly regulated as transatlantic ones. The plans for the *Johanna*'s cargo had the further advantage of using a transshipment point supposedly immune from English official interference: Saint-Castin's residence filled the function played in the following century by Spanish ports in the Caribbean and in modern times by the Canadian beach within a night's journey of a Prohibition-era United States of America.[24] In addition, Severett had passed by the coast of Acadia in the course of his voyage and had taken on some fish, perhaps to serve as a (literal?) cover story upon his return to New England.

All might have gone well—all probably had gone well for earlier ventures left unrecorded by their success—had not New York officials at Pemaquid gotten wind of the venture and determined to exercise their master's claim to control of the coastline as far as the St. Croix. Some two weeks after Severett had put his cargo ashore, Captain Thomas Sharpe, commander of Pemaquid fort and Nelson's man "of noe parts," sailed into Penobscot Bay and captured the cargo where it lay under a cover of boughs and old sails, guarded by two of the *Johanna*'s crew. Some of the goods, he discovered, had already been sold to Saint-Castin or transported back to Boston, but he seized the rest, marked the casks with the broad arrow of government ownership, and brought them back to Pemaquid. From there, they were conveyed to Boston under the supervision of John Palmer, a English-educated lawyer who held a variety of offices in Dongan's administration, including that of judge of New York's vice-admiralty court—the arena where the cargo, together with Severett's *Johanna* (also seized by the New Yorkers], would go on trial.[25]

Nelson was compelled to come forward to protect his investment, and he responded on several different fronts and levels. To New York officials, he protested the illegality of the seizure, a necessary but almost certainly futile tactic, given Dongan's desire to make an example of interloping traders, New York's claim to rule the Penobscot area, and the eagerness of Palmer and his colleagues to split the profits of confiscating the cargo. He also looked to such legal avenues and political influence as he could command in Boston to hinder the prosecution of the case. He failed to prevent the authorities there from authorizing a trial of Severett and his ship in New York, and legal suits he launched against various New York officials eventually collapsed.[26] But he did secure what proved to be valuable support from both Collector Edward Randolph and President Joseph Dudley of the Dominion of New England in the form of letters sent to London in which (echoing Nelson's words to Dongan) they described the seizure as made in territory long regarded as French and as an action likely to precipitate a French and Indian war.[27] Even Randolph opposed the New Yorkers' disruption of a region traditionally under Massachusetts' supervision, particularly when it diverted the profits of regulation into the hands of English officials other than his own.

Finally, and most audaciously, Nelson joined with Saint-Castin in appealing to the French authorities in Acadia and through them to Paris. By coincidence, the seizure of the *Johanna* occurred just as French and English officials in Europe were concluding negotiations designed to put an end to such misunderstandings. The Treaty of Whitehall, signed in the fall of 1686, reversed the old concept of "no peace beyond the line" in which international conflict in the Americas was taken to be no necessary impediment to peace in Europe. Instead, building on various local pacts concluded in earlier years, the Treaty provided for the maintenance of a state of neutrality between the two nations' American colonies even if war broke out in Europe. It contained several provisions that bore directly upon Nelson's predicament. The Treaty of Whitehall reaffirmed the terms of the Treaty of Breda awarding Acadia to France, although it was no more specific than that treaty had been in defining Acadia's boundaries. It also sought to prohibit what the diplomats seem to have viewed as the irritants of trade between English and French America and fishing in the immediate vicinity of each other's coasts.[28]

Back in Acadia, Governor Perrot could not yet have known the precise wording of these provisions, but his response to Nelson's appeal for aid was deftly pitched to take such attitudes into account. In letters to Paris, New York, and Boston, he made no mention of the cargo's eventual destination, but simply insisted that Pentagouet was in French territory, so the ship and cargo must be restored; adding in his letter to

Paris a strong testimony to Nelson's vital role in supplying the Acadians with supplies. Later, he sent a subordinate, Joseph Robinau de Villebon, on a mission to Nelson in Boston and then on to New York, to press the French case.[29] Perrot was only doing his official duty in reasserting Acadia's boundaries, but his willingness to go so far in helping Nelson was also influenced by his own unofficial trading with New England and a personal friendship so close that his son later spent several years in the Nelson household in Boston.[30]

The case of the *Johanna* had wound its way from Penobscot Bay through the provincial capitals of Boston, New York, and Port Royal, and finally entered the courts of Europe. Eighteen months after her seizure, the French ambassador and France's commissioners appointed to execute the Treaty of Whitehall submitted memorials of protest to the English Crown. At the same time, Severett petitioned for the return of his ship, which he depicted as rotting at her moorage in New Hampshire. In response, John Palmer, now in London, presented the case for the prosecution. From the royal Privy Council, the matter was referred to its Committee of Trade, to the Commissioners of the Customs, to the Lords of the Treasury, and then with unusual speed back up the bureaucratic ladder to the Privy Council again. There, in January 1688, Severett secured an order restoring his ship, an order duly honored in New England later the same year.[31] The French arguments, citing Charles II's orders to Temple to surrender his forts (including Pentagouet) were legally strong, a fact confirmed by Randolph's and Dudley's testimony from Boston. In addition, James II, threatened with invasion from Holland and insurrection at home, was anxious to remain on good terms with France.

Nelson and his associates, however, received no compensation for the loss of the *Johanna*'s cargo, and events in New England now conspired to render the political climate there increasingly hostile to his interests. Even as Palmer seized the wine, a royal governor was being chosen to supersede Joseph Dudley in Massachusetts, a governor who proved to be none other than the Edmund Andros (now Sir Edmund) who had first pressed the issue of New York's eastern boundary. Andros, like Dongan, was a military man by both training and inclination; and upon his arrival in Boston in December 1686, accompanied by a small force of British regular troops, he soon demonstrated a keen thirst to impose good order and a close obedience to the Crown on his new subjects. John Palmer and other veterans of Andros' New York administration received high positions in Massachusetts, replacing the last of the old Puritan officeholders; and over the next few months, Andros began a

CARTE
DE LA VILLE, BAYE, ET ENVIRONS DE
BASTON

sweeping assault on the underpinnings of the New England way: levying taxes without consent, challenging land titles, and withdrawing state support for the established Congregational churches. Nelson, as a loyal Anglican, must have approved of the favor Andros accorded the Church of England, a patronage that led to the building of King's Chapel in downtown Boston, the first place of Anglican worship in New England, where Nelson would later serve as churchwarden and vestryman. Socially, too, he had abundant opportunity to mingle with the new rulers of the Dominion, since Andros initially lodged at the home of his mother-in-law, Mrs. Rebecca Tailer.[32]

Yet Nelson still stood apart. When Andros replaced the old officers of the Boston militia with others drawn mainly from the ranks of the local Anglicans, Nelson was offered but refused to accept a commission.[33] There is some evidence, also, that he began to shun physically a political situation he found uncertain and distasteful. A few years earlier he had purchased, for the considerable sum of £1,400 New England money, the greater part of Long Island, at the mouth of Boston Harbor—a narrow and in parts craggy strip of land two miles long and a quarter broad, jutting out northeast from the southern shore, athwart the main channels leading into the harbor, and with a protected anchorage. There he owned a house and dock. Judging by French records that took to referring to Long Island as "Isle Nelson," he used it as a depot for his trade, one closer than Pentagouet but similarly shielded from prying official eyes.[34] Perhaps he was again responding to the pattern set for him by his uncle's way of life, for Sir Thomas Temple had for a time owned Noddle's Island in the harbor, closer to town (and the present site of Logan Airport). For much of the rest of Nelson's life, Long Island would become the gentleman's landed retreat, the "squiredom," that Temple had not lived to enjoy. Another, more contemporary and commercial, model might have been the man who bought Noddle's Island from Temple, the rich merchant (and adept political chameleon) Samuel Shrimpton, accused on several occasions during the 1680s of using his island to outfit pirates and engage in illegal trade.[35]

Facing page. A French map of Boston Harbor, drawn in 1693 by cartographer and engineer Jean-Baptiste-Louis Franquelin in preparation for a naval expedition against the town. Long Island, at the harbor's mouth, is identified as "Isle Nelson," complete with house and dock. From A. L. Pinart, ed., *Recueil des Cartes, Plans, et Vues Relatifs aux États-Unis et au Canada, New York, Boston, Montréal, Québec, Louisbourg (1651–1731)*. (*Courtesy of the Boston Public Library*)

From Boston, Nelson continued to trade with Acadia, and his vessels were undoubtedly among the small fleet of English ships that reports from Port Royal complained were reaching Acadia during these years, with the lucrative connivance of the colony's military leaders. Nelson was still known to be a man possessing ties and influence with the French: when Samuel Sewall's brother lost a fishing vessel to a French privateer in the summer of 1687, Sewall promptly wrote to Nelson "to see, if Brother might have his Ketch again."[36] Andros' response to the capture, however, and to reports that the French were seeking to reassert their control over the fisheries, was strictly official. Rather than using Nelson as intermediary, as Governor Bradstreet had done in 1682, Sir Edmund dispatched his lieutenant governor, Francis Nicholson, another English soldier, on a mission to Port Royal. Nicholson was no more successful than Nelson had been in meeting the leading French officials, although he did secure assurances at a later date that English fishermen would not be molested, provided that they did not land in Acadia to dry their catch.[37]

Andros also intervened in another area vital to Nelson's interests by tightening his government's control of the Dominion's eastern boundaries. Early in 1687, these boundaries had been extended to include the land between the Kennebec and the St. Croix formerly claimed by New York; Andros and his council now drew up plans to regulate trading in the region and expel any settlers of doubtful loyalty to the Crown. Behind policy lay self-interest: as Randolph sourly noted, Andros had brought a number of his old New York subordinates with him to Boston, and several, including John Palmer, had laid out large land grants for themselves around Pemaquid. Saint-Castin, already alarmed by the seizure of the *Johanna*, abandoned his attempts to remain isolated from the growing storm and appealed directly to Quebec for aid to resist the English advance. With thirty soldiers and sufficient funds, he promised, he could enlist four hundred Indians in Pentagouet's defense.[38] Before aid could be sent, and while Saint-Castin was away in Canada proving his new loyalty by aiding the French campaign against the Iroquois, Andros led a raid on the baron's trading house at Pentagouet and seized its contents as hostage for Saint-Castin's submission to the English Crown. From this incident, Nelson told English officials a decade later, arose "the Indian War, with which we have ever since been infested."[39] In reality, it was only the most dramatic of a series of incidents that finally cemented what the English had long envisioned (and so helped to create)—an offensive alliance between the French and the Abenaki. A succession of skirmishes between English settlers and local Indians around Casco Bay, during which hostages were seized and cattle slaughtered, escalated into open warfare.[40] Critical of what he regarded as the mishandling of the situation by his subordinates on the spot, Andros was nonetheless drawn into defending the frontier settlements. By the end of 1688, he had mobilized over five hundred troops and stationed them in forts and garrisons east of the Merrimack.[41]

To the north, in Canada, meanwhile, the French authorities were launching an offensive of their own, designed to strengthen Acadia's borders and reduce its dependence on New England. Missionaries were dispatched to proselytize among Saint-Castin's Indians; a frigate stationed in Acadian waters to expel intruders; encouragement given to the shipping of supplies to the colony; and substantial reinforcements of men and munitions furnished for the French garrisons at Port Royal and Chedabouctou. A new governor, Louis-Alexandre des Friches de Meneval, arrived in Acadia from France with strict instructions to revive the region's local industries and agriculture and to exclude all foreign traders and fishermen. Even as Andros and his superiors in London reasserted the English title to the lands as far east as the St. Croix, Meneval laid plans to construct a fort far within these bounds, at Pentagouet.[42]

On both sides, by the last months of the 1680s, the lines of battle were fairly drawn. An uneasy peace was giving way to open warfare, local accommodation to confrontation directed and fuelled by metropolitan policy and resources. On land, the way stood open to a renewal of the bloody border conflict of a dozen years before; at sea, commerce withered under the attacks of pirates and privateers—one such raid by a crew of Englishmen aided by French and Flemish renegades swept through the French fisheries at Chedabouctou in August 1688 and intercepted most of the ships sent to bring supplies to Acadia, including a valuable cargo imported by Saint-Castin.[43] In such a situation, those who, like Saint-Castin and Nelson, had sought, in Edward Randolph's phrase, "to live indifferent" to international conflict, found their room for maneuver abruptly curtailed.[44] Saint-Castin, aggrieved by his losses and wooed by Quebec for the sake of his friendship with the Abenaki, could easily turn to stand alongside his former brother officers in the ranks of the French offensive. Nelson had no such role to play, nor any comparable influence to barter for his support. To the contrary, as the Boston moderates who had helped install the Dominion had already found to their cost, the Andros regime scorned to seek the approval of its subjects or create a local base of political support. In the spring of 1688, New York and New Jersey were added to the Dominion, forming a single government stretching from Maine to Delaware Bay. At its head, observers noted, Andros became more than ever "safe in his New Yorke confidents, all others being strangers to his councill." Obedience, not participation, was his watchword, and the only role likely to be allotted Nelson was that of scapegoat, as one accused of fanning the flames of war by trading with Saint-Castin and his Indians.[45] One way out lay across the Atlantic, in the hope that what London had created, London might also be persuaded to bring to heel. Nelson must have watched with interest as a succession of New Englanders, among them Richard Wharton, Increase Mather, and Samuel Sewall, set sail for England to plead their own and their country's cause at court.[46] A letter to Nelson from his London uncle, Sir Purbeck Temple, thanking him for gifts (including a set of prodigious antlers) and assuring him a welcome should he come to England, suggests that Nelson had begun to mobilize his Temple relatives in hopes of retrieving his own deteriorating position.[47] But by the time that Sir Purbeck penned his reply, in mid-March of 1689, his nephew in Boston already knew that a political earthquake had struck Europe with a force that would surely transform the situation in America: blessed by Providence and a Protestant wind, Prince William of Orange had invaded England and toppled the rule of Andros' sovereign, James II.

IV

REVOLUTION AND REJECTION

The bloodless, Protestant, constitutionally decorous, and hence, in English eyes, ever-to-be-revered-as-Glorious revolution of 1688 that overthrew James II brought lasting changes to John Nelson's Atlantic world. In England, William of Orange assumed the throne, but under the terms of a constitutional settlement that led towards an enduring and fruitful balance of royal and parliamentary authority. On the larger European stage, the events of 1688 cemented a diplomatic coalition intent upon curbing the overweening ambitions and militant Catholicism of "that Great Leviathan," Louis XIVe of France. Two centuries in which England and France had been more often allies than enemies gave way to a century and a quarter of bitter rivalry and war. In North America, likewise, the Glorious Revolution transformed the intermittent frictions of adjacent colonial expansion into a violent clash of imperial ambitions not resolved until England's conquest of French Canada in the 1760s. For Englishmen in America, the image of the mother country would assume a new reality and significance as they found themselves inextricably swept up in Europe's worldwide contest for supremacy.

In the first months after William's invasion of England, however, the situation as seen from across the Atlantic caused more confusion than rejoicing. Well into March of 1689, many colonists were still uncertain

of the fate of William's invasion, let alone its ultimate consequences for
James's rule. Should Englishmen overseas rise in revolt as their com-
patriots seemed to have done, in the conviction that tyranny must be
resisted and in hopes of shaping a local settlement? Or did loyalty and
prudence counsel patience and a wait for orders in the belief that final
authority derived from the Crown no matter whose head it adorned?
Better, perhaps, to remain in suspense than to risk suspension as a
traitor.

The colonists of New England faced a particularly sharp dilemma.
Nowhere else in America had Stuart policies, in the shape of Andros'
autocratic regime, brought so abrupt and threatening a break with cherished political and religious practices. Even before news of the upheaval
in England, the towns around Boston were rife with discontent. Yet,
long years of Puritan rule had ingrained so deep a respect for established
authority that even the imposition of a royal governor had provoked
nothing stronger than lamentations. Protest against such arbitrary practices as Andros' levying of direct taxes without consent had subsided in
the face of a few exemplary prosecutions. To all outward appearances,
New Englanders were prepared to suffer in silence and wait for relief
by way of the petitions being presented against Andros by Increase
Mather and his allies in England. A wholesale reversal of Stuart policies
would be too good to be true. Once before had come accounts of James's
overthrow, by the Duke of Monmouth in 1685, only to prove false.[1]

In this delicate calculus of caution and courage, reliable information
would tip the balance. As Ian Steele has shown, definite news of both
William's landing and his accession to the throne reached Massachusetts
later than it did most of the other American colonies.[2] Not until early
April of 1689, when a ship from Nevis in the West Indies brought to
Boston copies of the Prince's Declarations issued in the course of his
invasion, was there formal confirmation of William's landing—a fact
Governor Andros immediately sought to suppress.

But John Nelson already knew much more than this. Ten days earlier,
on March 25, he wrote a breathless and excited letter to a unidentified
correspondent in Acadia. He told of "the Greatest Revolutions that
perhaps ever befell Europe." With the "Ould Quarell of Religion"
revived in England, the Prince of Orange had invaded in alliance with
"the Protestant partie" and won a complete victory over King James.
The king had "fled but was Taken, and is now said . . . "—at which point
of high suspense the letter's next section is missing, lost, or (like many
other personal records of these overly "interesting" times) cautiously
destroyed. So far, Nelson's news was of the vintage that had reached

Barbados and Philadelphia in February. It had travelled on up the coast to New England, perhaps, by means of the private channels of mercantile communication that often outstripped the official posts.[3] In a further page, however, Nelson boldly strove to turn the new circumstances to his own advantage. He enclosed letters for two of his commercial correspondents around the Bay of Fundy, Guillaume Bourgeois and "Mr. De Chaudfours," one of the three Damours de Chauffours brothers settled on the St. John River, and asked for any intelligence of Acadian men and affairs that would help "to renew my former Correspondence."[4]

The letter reveals both Nelson's strength and weakness as an international observer—his keen perception of how upheaval in England would call into question Governor Andros' authority, coupled with an overly optimistic faith that heightened national rivalries in the Old World would not spill over to hinder a revival of trade in the New. More important, it points to why Nelson played so prominent a role in the Boston drama that followed a few weeks later—the revolt that overthrew Andros and the Dominion of New England. The events of that day of April 18, 1689, remain shrouded, both by the understandable reluctance of participants to set down on paper what amounted at the time to treasonous rebellion, and by the subsequent myths that gathered around their success. The most probable scenario, as later described by Cotton Mather, is that a number of leaders from the days of charter rule were prepared for a possible uprising but had hoped to avoid it. Once it had begun—with the seizure at daybreak of the officers of the royal frigate moored in Boston harbor, the mustering of local militia, and the besieging of Andros and his subordinates in the fort bordering the harbor— then Mather and his allies, as "some of the Gentlemen present," stepped in to direct "the ungoverned *Mobile*" with the aid of "a *Declaration* accordingly prepared." This document denounced Andros' arbitrary ways, hailed the Prince of Orange's enterprise, and proclaimed New England's readiness to wait peacefully for orders arriving from England.[5]

This scenario, of spontaneous mob combustion quenched by the powers that used to be, presented to the world a politically convenient and, for the most part, accurate picture of resistance to tyranny tempered by deference to a traditional order. Yet it also glossed over the immediate circumstances of the uprising and the unusual character of its military leadership. A mutiny among the soldiers stationed out on the eastern frontier brought matters to a head; and it was another victim of Andros' "forward" policy in that region—John Nelson—who suddenly emerged as leader of Boston's rebel militia. Nelson, "at the head of the soldiers," directed the siege of Andros in the fort and co-signed and then presented the demand for its surrender. Later the same day, his troops cut off a dramatic attempt by the garrison to escape by boat to the frigate; and after Andros' surrender, Nelson was put in charge of the fort and the governor's imprisonment there. He was also a founding member of the "Council for the Safety of the People and Conservation of the Peace" formed to administer the colony's affairs.[6] Years later, a report to France's Intendant of Commerce portrayed Nelson's leadership as crucial to the revolt's success: without him, it was said, a few volleys from Andros' garrison would have scattered the Bostonians "like young partridges."[7]

This was sudden notoriety for a man who had hitherto neither sought nor attained any political prominence in his home community. Moreover, the two other leaders—David Waterhouse and John Foster—identified by contemporaries as "young Captains" who took initial command of the rebels, were remarkably similar to Nelson in background and interests: youthful, English-born, members of Boston's merchant community and its Artillery Company, but not freemen or previous holders of political or civic office. Like Nelson, too, both were involved with trading to the east, with the Indians and Acadia.[8] Other elements helped touch off the blaze, notably a group of deserters from the royal frigate who pursued their own vendetta by seizing the ship's officers as the latter came on shore. Once the uprising was well under way, more-traditional leaders appeared along with hundreds of militiamen from towns around Boston. In retrospect, Andros' autocratic ways and his reliance on outsiders and intimates to do the work of government had undercut his regime's legitimacy and laid abundant kindling for revolt. But it can fairly be argued that Nelson and his confederates were the crucial link between general discontent and private grievances on the one hand and full-scale, politically directed revolt on the other. Standing outside the old Puritan establishment, they did not share its obsession with good order or its willingness to wait upon events. Nor could they expect to be prominent in the kind of government likely to be restored if Andros were peacefully set aside as a result of solicitations in London. To the contrary, they had personal reasons to precipitate a confrontation and an ensuing confusion from which their trading interests could profit. Raised with England's chaotic politics and bred to habits of adventure and decision by their ventures beyond Boston, they were intellectually prepared to step forward as leaders in a moment of confusion—and sufficiently informed of events in Europe to take the risk.[9]

New political groupings often come to the fore amid the confusions and opportunities of a revolution; sometimes, as in Paris in 1791 and

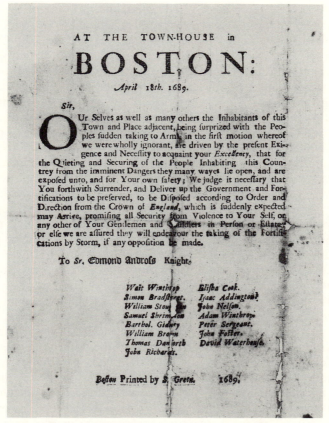

AT THE TOWN-HOUSE in

BOSTON:

April 18th. 1689.

Sir,

OUr Selves as well as many others the Inhabitants of this Town and Place adjacent, being surprized with the Peoples sudden taking to Arms, in the first motion whereof we were wholly ignorant, are driven by the present Exigence and Necessity to acquaint your *Excellency*, that for the Quieting and Securing of the People Inhabiting this Countrey from the imminent Dangers they many wayes lie open, and are exposed unto, and for Your own safety; We judge it necessary that You forthwith Surrender, and Deliver up the Government and Fortifications to be preserved, to be Disposed according to Order and Direction from the Crown of *England*, which is suddenly expected may Arrive, promising all Security from Violence to Your Self, or any other of Your Gentlemen and Souldiers in Person or Estate; or else we are assured they will endeavour the taking of the Fortifications by Storm, if any opposition be made.

To *Sr.* Edmond Andros Knight.

Wait Winthrop	*Elisha Cook.*
Simon Bradstreet.	*Isaac Addington.*
William Stoughton	*John Nelson.*
Samuel Shrimpton	*Adam Winthrop.*
Bartbol. Gidney	*Peter Sergeant.*
William Brown	*John Foster.*
Thomas Danforth	*David Waterhouse.*
John Richards.	

Boston Printed by *S. Green.* 1689.

Broadside issued on the day of the uprising in Boston, April 18, 1689, calling on Governor Andros to surrender. The first ten signatories had all served as charter magistrates or Dominion councillors. Nelson's name heads a group of five Boston merchants without previous political experience. (*Courtesy of the Massachusetts Historical Society*)

Moscow in 1917, they establish themselves in power. More often, however, and especially in the English-speaking world, tradition and habit regain their hold. Such was the case in Boston in the aftermath of April 18. The Council of Safety appointed to run affairs took shape as a coalition of new and old, with Nelson, Foster, and Waterhouse sitting alongside several more-established merchants, a brace of Winthrops, and a number of former charter magistrates; including one, Simon Bradstreet, first chosen to that office fifty-nine years before. The Council's declared policy was that expressed in the Declaration issued on April 18; of awaiting orders from England and hoping for a restoration of the legally vacated charter with larger additional powers. In the days that followed, however, the Council faced relentless pressure from an aroused public opinion intent upon eradicating all vestiges of the Dominion and returning forthwith (and without English authorization) to the strict letter of charter rule. The Council was compelled to enlarge its membership with representatives from outlying towns and then to summon two successive, popularly elected conventions. But neither of these conventions would acknowledge the Council's legal authority to govern: the only proper rulers of Massachusetts, each insisted, were those men, on or off the present Council, who had accepted the post of magistrate back in 1686. Late in May, and after prolonged debate, the Council gave way and agreed to a resumption of charter government as it had existed three years before, with the octogenarian Bradstreet as governor.[10]

To the modern eye, this seems a peculiar kind of revolution—the representatives of the people, overriding their leaders' advice, vote to restore an *ancien régime*. For Nelson and his confederates, it amounted to a blunt repudiation. Within a few days of the uprising, indeed, many of those who had readily followed Captain Nelson through the streets of Boston had begun to question his commitment to the revolutionary cause. Throughout his life, Nelson found it difficult to muster a convincing show of vindictiveness towards defeated adversaries or rivals; and what was now viewed as his unduly courteous supervision of Andros as prisoner (reinforced by an episode in which the former governor came close to escaping dressed as a woman, only to be betrayed by the men's shoes peeping out from under his disguise) caused his removal as commander of the fort. His successor was warned to be more severe: "otherwise they will Nelsonize him."[11]

Nelson's standing also suffered, less directly, from his affiliation with Boston's Anglican community. Many Church of England men had accepted office under the Dominion, and they were among the first to be swept into prison along with Andros and others of his "Evil Instruments" on the day of revolutionary judgment. Released, many were again rounded up as the usual suspects in a hysteria that swept Boston the following month in the wake of reports that an outbreak of fire was the result of arson. For years to come, part of the revenues of the Anglican

King's Chapel would be given over to replacing shattered windows.[12] Feeling against members of the town's mercantile community was less virulent and more selective. But since few had held office in the old charter government, it was disproportionately the merchants who were pushed out of their once-dominant role in the Council of Safety by the public insistence on a return to charter rule. Thirteen of those displaced, including Nelson, Foster, and Waterhouse, eventually signed a grudging pledge of allegiance to government by charter. They promised their support, provided that previous guarantees of protection to Andros and his colleagues be honored and that the colony await "the direction we expect from the Crown of England." Two of the thirteen were thereupon added to the body of charter magistrates, but Nelson, Foster, and Waterhouse were not among them.[13] Having served the new government's turn, they were cast aside.

Plainly, Nelson and his confederates had hoped for a solution that would stop short of a blanket reinstatement of the old Puritan regime. In part, their position rested upon the belief shared by others at the time that the charter was legally defunct and could only be revived with English authorization. More generally, they feared that a reversion to charter rule would shoulder them back out of the political limelight and begin a new round of internal divisions and confrontation with the Crown just as William's accession offered a chance for a balanced and lasting settlement.

Through the summer months of 1689, these fears steadily became more real. By comparison with the strict public order maintained in the Bay Colony before the onset of the Dominion, something akin to anarchy now reigned. Following the flight or withdrawal of the frontier garrisons established by Andros, Saint-Castin and the combined forces of the eastern Indians began a series of devastating raids reaching as far west as Dover, New Hampshire. Once more Massachusetts' Maine settlements lay in ashes. A conciliatory proposal to compensate the Frenchman for the losses inflicted on him by Andros came to nothing; and attempts to counter the enemy's assault were crippled by a widespread reluctance to enlist or pay taxes for the support of an indecisive and possibly illegitimate government. Even in Boston itself, the magistrates' authority was called into question as their orders for the release of former Dominion officials were forcibly opposed by noisy crowds.[14] At sea, pirates and French privateers ravaged coastal trade while the royal frigate appointed for guard duty lay in Boston harbor, immobilized by the confiscation of her sails. A group of merchants, Nelson among them, petitioned for the ship to be allowed to sally out, only to have the magistrates' agreement overridden by representatives fearful that the plan would open the way for some form of coup to reverse the revolution.[15]

The result was a splintering of the uneasy coalition pieced together by the April uprising—a parting of the political ways. As charter magistrate and deputy governor Thomas Danforth observed in a midsummer letter to Increase Mather in London, "sundry of those gentlemen and merchants that were very active in this matter on the day of the revolution" had now—"missing of what they expected"—become wholly disenchanted with the course of events.[16] Most suffered in silence; some (as in Salem) pledged loyalty while urging negotiation with England; but others began to work actively to undermine the tottering regime. Several leading citizens of Charlestown precipitated an immediate confrontation (and their own imprisonment) by denying the authority of the new government; a larger group pursued the more indirect but, as Danforth angrily acknowledged, ultimately more threatening course of petitioning the English Crown directly for aid and intervention. A string of petitions began to circulate for dispatch across the Atlantic to London—from settlers under attack on the eastern frontier, from Anglican leaders in Massachusetts, and from several of the port towns around the Bay, including one from "divers gentlemen, merchants, and others of Boston."[17] Several called for the Crown to reunite New England and set it under the command of a single executive, although one allowed more limited powers than those abused by Andros.

John Nelson signed several of these petitions and helped orchestrate their dispatch: his uncle, Sir Purbeck Temple, was enlisted to present one in person to the secretary of state responsible for colonial affairs.[18] In effect, Nelson had assumed the role of spokesman and leader for what amounted to a new political grouping, of men whose horizons had been raised by the experience of the Dominion and its aftermath beyond the provincial boundaries of New England. Some, in Danforth's scornful phrase, were "factors and strangers"—traders or first-generation settlers in New England whose lives, like Nelson's, had already brought them into contact with the dangers and opportunities of an outside world. Others had awakened to a need for stronger and more unified government as the horrors of border warfare burst around their ears. All looked to England to guarantee a more protected environment for territorial and commercial growth. By contrast, the great majority of New Englanders remained as yet—like Danforth himself—too insulated from foreign attack, too convinced of the dangers to godly rule posed by closer ties with England, and too wedded to an agrarian and isolationist cast of mind to see any need for change. In their eyes, the petitioners, far from offering a solution, were a key part of the problem as the very species of people—speculators, traders heedless of English commercial regulation, and ambitious office-seekers—whose venturings over the wall around the Puritans' carefully cultivated garden had embroiled New England in its present troubles.

Nelson, therefore, was not alone in his discontent. As usual, however, he was also pursuing plans of his own. He had resumed trading in eastern waters: Count Frontenac, returning to Canada for a second term as governor, made landfall at Chedabouctou Bay in September 1689 after fifty-two days at sea and found there a ketch owned by Nelson and captained by a French Huguenot, carrying a cargo of coal. Nelson, Frontenac informed Paris, was notorious for trading with the Indians as well as committing "autres pirateries" along the Acadian coast.[19] But Nelson was already laying plans to cover such interloping with a veneer of political legitimacy. In midsummer of 1689 he wrote to Sir Purbeck Temple and to his father Robert Nelson in London of his hopes to revive the proprietorship that his uncle (and their brother) had held. Presumably he held out to them, as inducement beyond the ties of kinship, the possibility that Sir Thomas Temple's debts to them might at last be repaid. To judge by his father's actions and Sir Purbeck's reply, their responses were significantly different. Robert Nelson discouraged his son from coming to England to press his claim and urged him to undertake a plundering expedition in the Cromwellian style of the 1650s. Robert applied to the Crown on his own behalf for letters of reprisal, citing his and Sir Thomas Temple's ancient losses, but never pursued the matter further.[20] Given John Nelson's lifelong record of courteous dealings with his adversaries, and his denunciation of those who acted differently, this scheme probably completed the alienation of father and son. Sir Purbeck, by contrast, warmly encouraged his nephew to come to England. A cousin, Sir Richard Temple, a commissioner of the Customs and member of Parliament, had promised to use his good offices to get Nelson what he desired. All could be done "with littel charge were you but heer," even to "the government of the Place in chefe as my brother Sir. T. Temple had, but without your presence your friends cannot serve you."[21]

What followed, however, served only to show how difficult it was in the late seventeenth-century Atlantic world to concert plans across an ocean's breadth. By the time Sir Purbeck's answer reached Boston, nearly a year after Nelson's letter, circumstances had changed to such a degree that the quest for a revived proprietorship seemed both impolitic and superfluous. In England, the return of Andros and his subordinates from imprisonment in Boston to a cordial reception at court showed that colonists who had overthrown royal government in King William's name could no longer expect ready acceptance of their actions in London or corresponding political favors. Triumphantly acquitted of charges of misgovernment, Sir Edmund and his former lieutenant governor, Francis Nicholson, were soon headed back to America as the newly appointed royal executives of Virginia and Maryland. And, so far from contemplating the creation of new proprietaries, Crown officials were working to eliminate those few that remained in the hands of such as the Calvert family and William Penn. Nor were they likely to favor a colonist—Nelson—now accused by the indefatigable Edward Randolph of engaging in illegal trading in Virginian tobacco.[22]

Back in New England, meanwhile, the tide of war engulfing its northeastern seaboard had already opened a way for Nelson to press his aims by more direct and locally focussed means. As early as the summer of 1689, desperate to stanch the steady hemorrhage of men and resources into fruitless expeditions and beleaguered garrisons, the Massachusetts leadership had begun to consider means—"if the Nutrallity in the plantations . . . do not continue"—to carry the war into the enemy's country and strike at what they now perceived as the root of all their miseries, the French settlements in Canada.[23] One branch of this strategy aimed at winning the aid and friendship of the formidable Iroquois confederacy centered to the west of New England below Lake Ontario. Long a terror to France's Indian allies, the Iroquois had just demonstrated their power by a devastating raid on the French settlements around Montreal. Ambassadors were dispatched to treat with the confederacy, and in the fall a contingent of New England troops was added to the garrison of Albany, the New York outpost that was the key point of diplomatic contact with the Iroquois and a vital barrier to any French invasion down the Hudson River.[24]

A second part of the plan, promising more certain relief, envisioned a direct assault—bypassing Maine—on Acadia or even Quebec, the citadel of French power. From past experience, the first was judged to be the easier prize. It was also the more pressing irritant, since two French frigates out of Port Royal had recently cut a swath through Salem's fishing fleet, drawing anguished calls for action from the town's leading merchants. A meeting of the commissioners of the Confederation of New England, the body that for half a century had concerted the region's internal self-defense, likewise urged measures that would strike beyond New England and against the French. In December 1689, the Massachusetts government published England's declaration of war against France and voted to seek volunteers to participate in an expedition against Acadia.[25]

This was a remarkable and—as it turned out—enduring turn in the Bay Colony's history, towards a full participation in the clash of European empires. Not for another century would Massachusetts escape from a position in the front line of transatlantic conflict. Seeking to reassert its founding Puritan identity and escape from local difficulties, it found itself enlisting in—and hence, for years to come, shaped and disciplined by—a far larger contest, defined by broader, national loyalties. For Nelson and his allies, the fragile state of mind and body politic in which Massachusetts entered this contest offered a chance to recapture some part of the initiative they had lost after leaving the Council of Safety. The call for volunteers to serve against Acadia acknowledged the reality that the restored charter government was as yet too weak in resources and authority to prosecute the enterprise on its own—for months its very existence had depended on loans from sympathetic citizens.[26] There seemed no alternative but to contract this public venture out to the private sector.

Nelson responded to the December vote with a speed that suggests that he had played a part behind the scenes in its formulation. Within three weeks, he submitted a lengthy argument to the assembled council and representatives. His prime purpose was to overcome the traditional New England reluctance to participate in military action that might seem to take the offensive and hence be adjudged unjust, an issue that had in the past prompted sharp debates within and among the various Puritan colonies.[27] His reasoning was both philosophical and pragmatic: a defensive stance has failed and offers no better hope to come; "the common Rules of Prudence" teach that "it is much better to prevent and meet an evil than to Attend or Wait it"; and now is the time to strike before the French can strengthen their position in the spring. Finally, by such an expedition, "we render our selves servisable to the crowne" and promote the honor of England and the Protestant religion.[28] He advanced no specific proposals as to how or even where an attack should be directed; but he offered, on behalf of "Divers private Gentlemen," to undertake the enterprise at their joint personal expense under the supervision of a committee appointed by the government.

In response, the Massachusetts representatives immediately voted to encourage an expedition against Acadia, offering any "Gentlemen and Merchants" who would prosecute it a loan of two of the colony's armed sloops, the right to any plunder taken, and the profits from future trade with the region. Nelson and six others were named to an advisory com-mittee.[29] As scholars have noted, the committee's makeup reveals a coalition. Four of its seven members—Nelson, John Foster, Nathaniel Oliver, and John Alden—were Boston merchants; all save Alden former members of the Council of Safety and all except Oliver longtime traders with Acadia. The three other members—Bartholomew Gedney, Benjamin Browne, and Charles Redford—were among the merchants of Salem who had appealed for help the previous fall against the French attacks on the town's fishing fleet.[30] Plainly, any expedition under this leadership would be designed, not just to damage the enemy, but to recapture Acadia's lands and seas for particular commercial interests. Equally evident in the committee's subsequent report, however, was a canny reluctance to rush in where the state had feared to tread. At least five hundred men would be needed, and it would be "most convenient" for the whole scheme to be a public venture and charge. If not, then beyond the aid, plunder, and trading profits already promised, two further concessions were necessary: one or both of the colony's sloops should be fitted out to guard the English fishery off Acadia, and—an obvious legacy of the fate of Sir Thomas Temple's proprietorship—the undertakers of the enterprise must be promised reimbursement if Acadia were taken from them before their investment could be recouped.[31]

The merchants' demand for what might be called, in the parlance of modern defense contracting, a no-risk, cost-plus guarantee plainly disconcerted the Massachusetts leadership. Two weeks later, the council and representatives spoke of the "absolute necessity" of an expedition, yet went no further than to repeat the original offer of a month before, omitting any mention of the additional concessions Nelson and his associates demanded.[32] There the matter rested, as precious time ebbed away. Finally, two disasters and the threat of others brought matters to a head. Smarting from the Iroquois raid of the previous summer and as convinced as Nelson of the futility of remaining on the defensive, the French had likewise determined to carry the war into the enemy's country. Late in February, Boston received news of the brutal destruction of the town of Schenectady, near Albany, by one French and Indian war party, and, in mid-March, of the devastation wrought by a second war party on the settlement of Salmon Falls in New Hampshire. Graphic tales arrived of scores of Protestant settlers gruesomely butchered or taken captive. A third war party was reported—accurately—to be on its way to attack the remaining English outpost at Casco Bay.[33]

Word of the Schenectady disaster blew new life into the expedition against Acadia. "Just about dinner time" after the news had arrived, wrote Samuel Sewall, "Mr. Nelson comes in and gets me to subscribe 100. [pounds] to the Proposals against the French. I thought 'twas time to doe something, now were thus destroy'd by Land too." A second diarist, Benjamin Bullivant, recorded a widespread expectation that Nelson would be made "generalissimo" of the expedition, "as the fittest person for the enterprise."[34]

But it was not to be. Instead, the days that followed further changed the Bay Colony's strategic horizons in ways that, coupled with an upswing in its government's confidence, worked only to diminish Nelson's role. Letters from the Crown in London had already undercut the colony's dissidents by endorsing the authority of the restored charter regime. New taxes were levied on the strength of this legitimacy, and the representatives meeting in the latest of what had for the past seven months been styled a "Convention" finally ventured to designate themselves a fully fledged "General Court" in the manner of the old charter government.[35] One fruit of this increased assurance was a formal decision on March 12 to prosecute the Acadia expedition as a public and not a private venture. A new committee was appointed to oversee its preparation, consisting, not of merchants, but of magistrates plus Major General Fitz-John Winthrop and a newcomer to the colony's politics recently returned from London, Sir William Phips. By then, too, in the wake of Schenectady's destruction, the question of the expedition's commercial profits and losses seemed trivial compared to its promise—glowingly depicted in a mid-March sermon by Cotton Mather—as part and prologue of a larger interlinked design embracing all the northern English colonies.[36] In response to calls from New York and their own western borders, Massachusetts leaders joined with their neighbors in planning a coordinated assault by land and sea on the main French settlements along the St. Lawrence River. The capture of Port Royal would serve, in Governor Bradstreet's phrase, to "gain some reputation" with the Iroquois, and the route up New York's Hudson River now seemed a plausible if circuitous way to secure the shores of Massachusetts.[37]

By the middle of March, therefore, Nelson's efforts to revive the expedition had succeeded, but at the expense of his own role in the venture. Far from making Nelson "generalissimo," Bullivant angrily recorded, the "Country Deputies said he was a Merchant & not to be trusted." One of his associates in the January proposal, Bartholomew Gedney of Salem, received the post, only to be supplanted two days later by Penn Townsend, a wine merchant and provisioner and one of Boston's representatives in the General Court. Two days later still, on

March 22, "Sir William Phips offers himself to go in person." Townsend promptly resigned and Phips was appointed in his place. Nelson was offered the place of deputy commander but, noted Bullivant, "refuseth with scorn & contempt."[38]

As this revolving door of appointments suggests, personalities also played a part in the final outcome. Nelson had done as much as any man to enlarge his fellow colonists' strategic vision, but in their eyes he remained too tainted by past history and present politics to be allowed the lead in its implementation. It was not just, as Bullivant had suggested, that he was a merchant; for others who lived by trade—Gedney, Townsend, and those such as Elisha Hutchinson and Samuel Shrimpton among the magistrates—still won colony-wide positions of trust. Rather, his opposition to charter government, disdain for political maneuvering, and plain preference for trading over warring with the likes of Saint-Castin all set him in a category apart. Even so, he might have remained the indispensable man had he not been eclipsed by the equally strong but utterly different personality who suddenly stepped forward to usurp the place he had felt to be his—Sir William Phips, destined to be a deadlier enemy than any he would meet in the ranks of the French or Indians.

A dozen years older than Nelson, Phips had grown up in rural obscurity on the Maine frontier. His early life remains shrouded in the myths spun by Cotton Mather's obsequious biography, but he burst into transatlantic fame and fortune in the mid-1680s by recovering several hundred thousand pounds' worth of treasure from a Spanish wreck in the Caribbean. Feted by his English backers and knighted in 1687 by an appreciative James II, Phips spent the next three years restlessly navigating between England and New England in search of the respect and office appropriate to his hard-won status. Spectacularly self-made but ever seeking to make more of and for himself, Phips possessed the kind of personality that is continually driven to validate itself through confrontation: his career through the 1680s and beyond was marked by a string of episodes in which, under cover of upholding some recently assumed authority and regardless of ideology, he picked face-to-face quarrels with opponents ranging from restless crewmen and rival treasure hunters to magistrates of the old charter government of Massachusetts.[39] Seething from a frigid reception by Sir Edmund Andros after he turned up in the Dominion in 1688 with the purchased office of provost-marshal-general, Phips took refuge with Increase Mather in London, where he worked for Andros' recall and then for restoration of the old charter. Back in Boston by 1690, he appeared to the inex-

Sir William Phips, first royal governor of Massachusetts under the Charter of 1691. A portrait attributed to Thomas Child, in the possession of the Gardiner family. (*Courtesy of Mr. Thomas Gardiner*)

perienced colonists to be an ideal candidate for command—visibly aggressive, more than ready to take charge, honored in England and yet a native son. His newly forged alliance with the formidable father-and-son team of Increase and Cotton Mather was now sealed by instant initiation into the Massachusetts elite: compressing into a few hours what mere mortals took half a lifetime to achieve, Phips was named freeman of the colony, commander-in-chief, and Major General one day, and received baptism and full membership in the Mathers' Boston North Church the next. A few weeks later, he was nominated and then elected a magistrate.[40] Glamorous, vindinctive, and flung up against Nelson both by their accidental rivalry for the Acadia command and by his frontier-bred suspicions of the town gentry who traded with New England's enemies, Phips would shape the course of the next eight years of Nelson's life.

The two men's enmity erupted both during and soon after the ensuing expedition against Port Royal. Untroubled by any merely mercantile concern for preserving Acadia's trade and fisheries, Phips saw his task as one of inflicting as much damage and extracting as much plunder as possible. Sailing at the end of April, 1690, with a force of over seven hundred men, he intimidated Governor Meneval and his outnumbered garrison into surrendering Port Royal upon promise—according to the French account—of the protection of private property and safe-conduct of the garrison back to French soil. Phips and his men immediately violated these terms, and spent days pillaging the settlement, desecrating its church and seizing anything movable down to the old clothes off the settlers' backs. The plunder, Phips was careful to inform readers of the printed journal of the expedition, was gathered into "Mr. Nelson's Storehouse" in Port Royal. There, too, the chaplain attached to the expedition preached a sermon to the assembled marauders.[41] After detaching parties to raid and destroy around the Bay of Fundy and up the Atlantic seaboard as far as Chedabouctou, Phips returned to Boston bearing with him Meneval, the French garrison, and one of Saint-Castin's daughters as prisoners. He made no effort to hold onto or make use of his conquests save for exacting an oath from a handful of the Acadian settlers that they would be loyal to England and send back reports to the Boston government.

Nelson's contempt for the conduct of this exercise in retaliation burst out in his espousal of the cause of Phips's captives. Beyond his own passionate belief that pledges of personal behavior, once given, were inviolable, he could point to the Massachusetts leadership's insistence in planning the expedition that Port Royal's defenders should be allowed to surrender upon terms. In addition, Phips had doubly violated his word by taking into safekeeping Governor Meneval's personal belongings—a remarkable collection ranging from wigs, silk garters, and four lace-trimmed nightcaps, to a set of silverware and a large quantity of hard cash—and then claiming them as spoils of war. The matter hung fire over the summer while Phips was employed in leading another and larger naval expedition up the St. Lawrence River to attack Quebec. Here his luck finally ran out, as poor coordination between the land and sea forces, false expectations, and his own strategic ineptitude produced a humiliating repulse that plunged the northern colonies back into division and debt.[42]

Phips returned to Boston in no mood to be accused of dishonorable conduct towards an enemy; and when, in late November, Meneval and Nelson (in whose house the French governor had taken refuge) won a hearing before the Massachusetts magistrates, a furious row ensued. "Very fierie words between Sir William and Mr. Nelson," recorded Samuel Sewall, one of the councillors. "When Sir William went out seemed to say would never come there more, had been so abus'd by said Nelson, and if Council would not right him, he would right himself." Meneval, doubtless at Nelson's suggestion, got permission to leave for England to press his claim, only to find himself hauled from the ship in which he was preparing to sail by an armed party of Phips's supporters and, on Christmas Day, thrown into prison. He then swore out a writ against Phips, to Cotton Mather's vast indignation at a Frenchman's being permitted due process. The embarrassed council—intimidated, Meneval charged, by Phips and his mobbish "canaille"—stepped in and cancelled the writ but ordered Phips to make restitution of at least the plundered personal effects, backing up their action with a private letter from Governor Bradstreet. Sir William grudgingly returned a portion—only one-fifth, Meneval later claimed—of the money seized and a few clothes, but then departed to rejoin Increase Mather in London—a place, presumably, where purloined trappings might suffice to disguise even Sir William as a gentleman.[43]

Phips's retreat allowed Meneval to leave for France, and Nelson to revive his schemes for a more measured and constructive approach to Acadia. In the months following the English raid, the region had been left in limbo. Meneval's lieutenant, and now his successor as governor, Joseph Robinau de Villebon, had returned to Port Royal soon after the raid only to conclude that its defenselessness required him to reestablish French authority from a base inland at Jemseg, fifty miles up the St. John River. From there, too, in touch with Quebec by the overland route, he could better carry out the French Crown's instructions to work in close cooperation with the mainland Abenaki Indians in waging "continual and violent war" against the English. For the moment, however, Villebon deliberately made no attempt to force the French coastal settlements around the Bay of Fundy to reject contacts with New England.[44]

The Massachusetts government was no better able to assert its authority over Phips's conquests. Deep in debt and popular discontent, it again looked to private merchants to initiate public policy. John Alden of Boston made four voyages to Acadia in the twelve months following June 1690, one in the fall being authorized for the purposes of reporting on conditions there, furnishing supplies (save for ammunition) to the settlements, and obtaining the redemption of English captives now in Indian hands.[45] The last may have served to allay public resentment at renewed commerce with the enemy, and it had acquired some legitimacy from Phips's exchange of a number of captives during the expedition against Quebec. But it was already, as it would be for many years to come, an excuse and cover for surreptitious trade. Other New Englanders dealt with the region through Acadian intermediaries, in a twilight world of Anglo-Frenchmen willing to promise both sides allegiance and information—one of Nelson's trading vessels, for example, was captained by an Acadian, Jean Martel, who was also Governor Villebon's son-in-law and a partner of Acadia's leading privateer preying on English shipping. Another frequent visitor from Port Royal, Abraham Boudrot, purchased his freedom to correspond with the Boston Huguenot merchant Andrew Faneuil with reports sent back to Villebon.[46] The hazards and shadowy nature of such voyages were typified in an account of 1693 that told of a friendly reception given to a Boston ship in one part of the Bay of Fundy, followed by a murderous ambush, killing six crew-members, in another: "what voyage they have made I know not, they being very cautious in speaking."[47]

Perhaps in the hope of bringing order to these uncertainties, and certainly with the aim of turning any such order to their own advantage, Nelson and five other "undertakers" submitted a new set of proposals to the Massachusetts General Court in the summer of 1691. One of the five was Nelson's old ally, John Foster; the others—James Taylor, Edward Bromfield, Elias Heath, and Jose Appleton—were likewise Boston merchants but with broader political connections, Bromfield being a friend of the Mathers, and Appleton part of the powerful Appleton clan based in the Essex County community of Ipswich. Taylor would later serve for more than two decades as the province treasurer.[48]

Together this group offered to re-fortify Port Royal and maintain a small garrison there at their own expense, providing they were granted a monopoly of trade with Acadia for five years or until its disposition by the Crown. There was no mention of any guarantee against loss of the kind that had stymied the project of the previous year. In effect, the undertakers proposed to set up a privileged trading company of the kind that had begun the colonization of Virginia and Massachusetts. Rather than importing settlers, however, it would establish trading posts similar to those once run by Sir Thomas Temple and resembling on a small scale the "factories" maintained in Asia and Africa by such great enterprises as England's East India Company. An unsigned and undated memorandum to the Massachusetts council accompanying another draft of the proposals suggests that what emerged had involved hard bargaining: it protested against a proffer of less generous terms, stressed the costs and hazards the undertakers would be assuming at a time when the state itself could do nothing, and insisted upon the power to appoint their own candidate—Colonel Edward Tyng—to command in Port Royal and supply him freely with stores and ammunition.[49] One concession made in return—in order, in the words of a printed broadside of June 4, "to prevent all misrepresentations of Monopolizing or pursuing private interests"—was to permit others to share in the monopoly and pursue their private interests if they came forward within three weeks. By later accounts the eventual shareholders in the "company" numbered some twenty or twenty-two, each subscribing £46; a list provides the names of ten who joined the original six. Among them were Nelson's old associates James Lloyd and David Waterhouse. Others included the veteran Acadian trader John Alden and his eldest son, John; Andrew Belcher and Benjamin Alford, two of Boston's wealthiest merchants; and, signed on his behalf by Nelson, "Mr Mortell"—seemingly the Jean Martel who was Villebon's son-in-law, joining a project to impose English rule on his fellow countrymen.[50] Their chosen commandant, Colonel Tyng, was one of the few New Englanders with extensive experience of frontline military command, having commanded garrisons in Maine under both the old charter and the Andros governments.

Armed with the General Court's grudging approval of the scheme, Nelson and his colleagues sought for ways to smooth its course. They secured an official commission for Tyng to command and govern Port Royal. In addition, they pressed for negotiations to be reopened with Saint-Castin, Nelson's old associate and the man seen as the key to any resumption of commercial relations with the eastern Indians. In return for a nominal allegiance to England, he would be allowed to remain among his Indians and receive supplies from Boston, with a guarantee of his safety should he wish it.[51] Both Governor Bradstreet and Nelson wrote to Saint-Castin to this effect, adding a plea for his cooperation in the return of prisoners held by the Indians. Saint-Castin's response, however, foreshadowed the failure about to engulf the whole scheme: while returning a civil answer pointing out that the English colonists were themselves holding captives (such as Meneval's garrison) that they were in honor bound to return, he also forwarded copies of the correspondence to Quebec with his own much more belligerent analysis. The Bostonians' humble tone, Saint-Castin noted, revealed their country's "extremely low" condition and their stark fear of further Indian attack. Their proposals for local negotiations were simply an attempt to detach France's Indian allies, something he would oppose to the utmost. Plainly, Saint-Castin was in no mood to desert his newly proved French loyalty.[52]

In retrospect, Nelson and his colleagues badly misread the whole situation. In the twenty years since Acadia's cession back to France, they had become accustomed to believing that there was still room to operate within the intermittent frictions of Europe's American empires: they failed to realize the degree to which the pressures of formal warfare, coupled with Acadia's exposed position, had raised the stakes and risks, doubly so for a venture planned—and perceived by the enemy as planned—with both a military and commercial purpose. Too many to trade unobtrusively, Nelson and his confederates were too few to fight; Villebon showed the better strategic sense in leaving Port Royal, like some small Caribbean island, open to passing forces with its settlers free to make what compromises they could. The years to come would show that only prolonged and costly commitment by metropolitan governments would suffice to take and hold Acadia in the new, post-1689 world of warring European empires.

Finally, and again in hindsight, one must wonder what made Nelson decide to embark with the expedition as it took shape in Boston in the late summer of 1691. In the nine years since his father-in-law's death, he had seemingly abandoned such voyages in favor of managing his own and the Tailer enterprises, sending others to trade on his behalf. He was now more than ever paterfamilias: his mother-in-law, Rebecca Tailer, had died in the smallpox epidemic that was another legacy of Phips's failure in Canada, his wife's remaining brother was still underage, and he and Elizabeth were now the parents of four infant daughters.[53] Perhaps his new partners insisted he lend his experience to the expedition as a price of their involvement. Perhaps, too, Nelson felt a need to salve his humiliation at Phips's hands the previous year by showing in person how dealings with Acadia should be conducted. Finally, he may have seen it as a last chance to tread in his uncle's footsteps and refurbish some remnant of Sir Thomas' seigneurial power. One piece of evidence suggests a plan to spend a winter or longer in Acadia, as in his youth: before leaving he entrusted his old friend James Lloyd with a power of attorney over his affairs.[54]

Whatever his dreams, the reality proved to be a bitter awakening. Late in August of 1691, Nelson, Tyng, the two Aldens, and some twenty men set sail for Acadia in one of Andrew Belcher's ketches. After a further, fruitless attempt to enlist Saint-Castin's aid, they arrived in Port Royal, where they quickly accumulated a substantial cargo through trade—seven hundred and sixty beaver skins, one hundred and forty elk hides and several hundred sea otter, muskrat, and other pelts—to a value (it was later estimated in France) of 4,751 livres; some £400 in New England money.[55] But their stay in Port Royal was cut short when its inhabitants told them that they were unable to protect those come to be their garrison from attack by the local Indians—a sardonic comment on the expedition's weakness. Nelson and the others resolved to try their fortune trading around the Bay of Fundy. Unfortunately, however, the French Crown had decided back in April to reassert its authority in Acadian waters. A swift-sailing frigate, the *Soleil d'Afrique*, had been sent out to carry Governor Villebon back from a brief stay in France, with instructions that he retake Port Royal.[56] Arriving there shortly after the English had left, the frigate preceded them to the mouth of the St. John River. There, in the late afternoon of September 22, upon news of the English ship's approach, the frigate emerged from concealment behind a point of land and forced the ketch to surrender. Nelson, Tyng, the Aldens, and their men were brought ashore. The elder Alden was sent back to Boston on parole, upon his promise to return with French prisoners for exchange and with a ransom for the ketch. Nelson, as the greatest prize, was dispatched overland on an arduous fifteen-day journey on foot and by canoe to Quebec under the escort of Villebon's brother.[57] He would not see Boston or his family again for nearly seven years.

V

FROM QUEBEC TO THE BASTILLE

In the years before the events of 1689, John Nelson's captivity would have been brief. Prisoners were costly to keep, and, if not kept securely, likely to escape and thereby lose their value as bargaining chips in diplomatic negotiation. Kept too long, they would return with valuable information about their captors upon their release. Moreover, the laws of war—grounded in a mutual recognition of the wisdom of refraining from doing unto others what you would not wish, if captured, done unto you—had provided since medieval times for a regular system of exchange. Prisoners could derive a certain pride as well as a sense of their precise status from finding out who and how many of the enemy were deemed their equivalent. Nelson was certainly not seen as lacking such status or as one whose past activities required his being surrendered— as North American captives occasionally were—to personal or tribal vengeance. "He is," wrote Governor Frontenac's secretary back to France, "a gentleman of merit and intelligence; possessing influence in Boston where his friends have always been opposed to those of Sir William Phips. He has ever distinguished himself by kind treatment of the French, as well in peace as during the War and to him M. de Monneval, Governor of Port Royal, is indebted for his liberty. In like manner he may anticipate every civility that can be extended to a prisoner."[1]

Frontenac, a veteran soldier-courtier steeped in the intricate etiquette of Louis XIVe's Versailles, was as good as his word. A French officer and journal writer, Louis-Armand de Lom d'Arce de Lahontan, who spent the winter of 1691–1692 in Quebec, found Nelson—"a very gallant Man"—lodged in the governor's own house and treated "with all manner of civility." Lahontan was at that moment being pressed to marry the governor's goddaughter: the young and, by all accounts, highly accomplished daughter of Mathieu Damours de Chauffours, a member of Frontenac's Sovereign Council and father of the same Damours brothers who had traded with Nelson in Acadia. The New Englander's credit must have stood high even in captivity, for after Lahontan had stalled for four months, Nelson was able to host a grand dinner for the couple and the cream of Quebec society at which he undertook to provide a thousand écus (some £250 in English money), doubling the lady's dowry, on the day that the marriage took place.[2] Not to be outdone, Frontenac in his turn offered the young officer trading licenses and preferment worth another seven or eight thousand écus. But the footloose Lahontan declined to be drawn into what he depicted as a conspiracy by married men to reduce him to a similar condition—and the dowry went unclaimed. Through the winter and well into the following summer, nonetheless, Nelson retained all the status of an honored guest, at a charge to the colony's treasury of four livres a day—twice the pay of an army lieutenant. As a prisoner on parole—having given his word as a gentleman not to escape—he was allowed free rein to wander accompanied by a single guard within the town and citadel of Quebec, and to meet with other English prisoners, a number of whom (it was later testified) he aided with the remaining funds at his disposal.[3]

The very honor accorded Nelson, however, marked a reason why his captivity dragged on: he had become, in French eyes, too central a figure in the English war effort to be released, a man who knew and felt too much. Even before Frontenac's return as governor in mid-1689, plans were afoot for a blow against New York—"l'entreprise de Manathe," the Manhattan project—that would bisect the English colonies and sever their alliance with the Iroquois.[4] Delayed from year to year, the scheme grew to include a bombardment or invasion of the Boston region; and throughout the time that Nelson was in French hands, maps were being drawn, distances calculated, and past visitors to New England quizzed for information in preparation for the assault. A memorandum of 1697

envisioned the main invasion force disembarking in the sheltered anchorage behind "l'isle de Nelson" and marching on Boston overland
while a diversionary force of Canadians and Indians disembarked at
what is now Logan Airport and attacked from Charlestown at low tide.[5]
To return a prisoner who had been permitted to become so familiar
with the everyday affairs of the French high command would be to
disclose these plans; close acquaintance over the winter, moreover, had
convinced Frontenac that the New Englander was now too committed
to the cause of combatting all things French to be set free. Nelson could
not be coaxed back into the ambivalent and even pro-French political
position he had occupied a decade before. To the contrary, as Frontenac
informed his superiors in Paris by the fall of 1692, "he is so full of zeal
for the Prince of Orange's party, and for his religion, and so strongly
impressed with the justice of his claims on Port Royal and Acadia
through an uncle of his that it is highly important not to allow him to
return to Boston."[6] Whether out of vanity or a swelling patriotism,
Nelson had inflated his captors' opinion of his position in New England
to the point that it precluded his release.

A further reason for his prolonged detention and that of the others
taken with him lay, not in Quebec, but in the incompetence, if not
treachery, of his fellow countrymen back in Boston. The elder John
Alden had been released upon his promise to return by the end of 1691
with the remainder—some sixty soldiers—of Meneval's Port Royal garrison for an exchange of prisoners. He failed to arrive at the St. John
River until the following May and brought only six men, leaving behind—as Governor Villebon was informed—others who wished to return. Alden capped his bad faith by taking a French vessel under cover
of Villebon's safe-conduct and then, after dropping off the six soldiers
on a nearby island, fleeing the scene with two Acadians sent to help in
the exchange, leaving the enraged Villebon to write a bitter denunciation
of his actions to Boston.[7] Alden may have acted more out of a combination of caution and opportunism than out of a deliberate intent to
break his word and abandon his companions, given that one of those
he left in captivity was his eldest son. But he was a hard-bitten realist
of a type quite unlike his fellow venturer, John Nelson. Mark Emerson,
another English captive in Acadia, reported that Alden could have
ransomed him on one of his trips there but refused, saying he had come
not to redeem captives but to trade. Emerson's redemption came at the
hands of Nelson, passing by on his way to Canada as a prisoner.[8]

As Alden sailed back to Boston, moreover, a turn occurred in New
England politics that could only redound to Nelson's disadvantage: Sir

William Phips returned in triumph as the Crown-appointed governor of Massachusetts under a new charter granted by the king. Nelson had achieved the goal he and others had sought in their petitions to England, only to find the new government entrusted to virtually the same leaders as had run the old and with the addition of his mortal enemy as governor. Worse, Phips and Increase Mather had managed to shape the wording of the new charter in a way that effectively swallowed up Nelson's claim to Acadia in a larger political consolidation. Through the fall of 1691 in London, Sir William had advanced a variety of schemes for settling the eastern seaboard and exploiting its natural resources. English officials, impressed with its potential as a source of timber for the Royal Navy and brought to believe that "Nova Scotia" could be claimed for the Crown, had agreed to incorporate all of Acadia, together with Maine and the former Plymouth Colony, within the bounds of the new charter.[9] A greater Massachusetts had come into being, outstripping even the aspirations of its merchants; but it was one that Nelson could only watch from afar.

The effect of Phips's success on Nelson's fate was soon apparent. Old Governor Bradstreet had done his best to see fair play in the ebb and flow of private passions. Phips had a far more partisan view of the uses of authority, and as governor he was not about to help free a man who had attained him of dishonorable conduct before his peers and was sure to pursue the challenge (Meneval having left Nelson a power of attorney and the necessary documents) should he return.[10] Phips had every reason to keep his rival away from Boston as long as possible.

Mere inaction would have sufficed, particularly as Massachusetts now writhed in the grip of the communal panic known to history as the Salem Village witchcraft trials. By the summer of 1692, hundreds were in prison or under suspicion. Among the victims was John Alden, singled out as a witch for his reputed sexual as well as commercial connections with New England's enemies. "There stands Alden," cried one of his adolescent accusers; "he sells Powder and Shot to the Indians and French, and lies with the Indian Sqaues, and has Indian Papooses." With his well-honed talent for getting out of tight corners, Alden broke prison and escaped prosecution.[11]

Even amid these distractions, however, Phips found an opportunity to make his enemy's situation still more precarious. It arose when Nelson, in a daring piece of espionage, smuggled back to Boston a letter of August 1692 in which he told of a French force of men and ships being readied to sail for a rendezvous in Penobscot Bay and a raid on the New England coast. He also described several meetings in Quebec with Saint-Castin's father-in-law, Madockawando, during which Nelson's ability to speak the Abenaki chieftain's language had enabled the two of them to open negotiations for peace on the eastern frontier, right under the noses of their French hosts. Nelson excused his "broken manner of writing" by explaining that only in bed could he evade surveillance; and he asked that an ample reward be paid to his letter's bearers, two French army deserters who were accompanying a small party of Dutch and Englishmen escaping from Canada to New York. Outdistancing a hot pursuit, the group reached safety and the English outposts in the Hudson valley late the following month.[12]

At no point did Nelson mention his own hopes for release, except to ask that his letter be kept secret lest "by the escape of some prisoners, the report will come hither greatly to my damage." In a note to Phips just after the receipt of Nelson's warning, Massachusetts provincial secretary Isaac Addington likewise urged that Nelson's role be kept secret lest it do him hurt.[13] But their words only seem to have served as inspiration to Phips for what he now proceeded to do. Soon after the French deserters' arrival in Boston, it was decided—by Phips alone, Nelson later charged (and no formal record of the decision appears)—to dispatch them back into French territory, to Acadia, with instructions to kidnap Nelson's old trading partner, Saint-Castin. Two Acadians were sent with them as guides: Jean Serreau de Saint-Aubin and his son-in-law, Jacques Petitpas, recently brought back to Boston with their families by a Massachusetts raiding party.[14]

For the motives behind this extraordinary scheme, we have only two somewhat later statements for (in effect) the prosecution and the defense, by Nelson himself and by Phips's gray eminence and biographer, Cotton Mather. Nelson, writing after four further years of imprisonment (and before his return to New England), was sure that he was the intended victim and Phips the villain: having prolonged Nelson's captivity by his dishonorable refusal to return the Port Royal garrison, Sir William had then, with "foolish and malicious Contrivance," resolved "to betray me unto the french" in revenge for the episode involving Meneval. "Judging noe way more readie or certaine, then to Discover unto the french the intelligence I had sent," Phips had deliberately sent back the two deserters to the place, Penobscot Bay, where Nelson had warned that the French forces would arrive.[15]

Fifteen years later, Cotton Mather sat down and drafted a letter (printed in full in the Appendix) to an unknown "worthy friend" who, it appears, was willing to act as his intermediary with Nelson in resolving "that Gentlemans Displeasure at me." It was vintage Mather, if unusually defensive in tone: garnished with learned circumlocutions, twittering into polysyllables at points of maximum embarrassment, and leavened with several affecting descents into self-pity. Phips being long dead, Mather passed most of the letter excusing his own role. He had indeed chanced to be with the governor when the latter was briefing the two deserters, but "I had nothing to do either in proposing the motion or projecting the method of what was then done." Hence he had no part in any "Design to betray and expose Mr. Nelson." Nor, he believed, had Phips any such aim—"but my present Business is only to answer for myself." Mather did acknowledge that he had played a role in preventing the return of one of the Port Royal garrison sought by the French. But the man had abjured Catholicism, and Nelson himself would not have wished him to be sent back to death as an apostate. No one, Mather concluded, had a higher regard for Nelson's "Generous Actions" than he, and he called on heaven and "scores of witnesses" to testify to the tears and prayers he had offered up on Nelson's behalf "with all possible Honourable particularity" during the latter's years of captivity.[16]

Whatever the extent of Mather's complicity, it was plainly Phips's scheme, although Mather argued (and with better immediate knowledge than Nelson) that the governor's council had given the plan their blessing. Perhaps Lieutenant-Governor Stoughton was too busy presiding over the trials of the accused witches—four more were hanged in the last week of September—to notice the danger threatening Nelson, his niece's husband. Phips's plan could be justified on grounds of public policy as a cheap, if ruthless, way of severing a crucial French link with the eastern Indians; those suspicious of Phips's motives (and they were already numerous in Massachusetts) could also note that it served his personal purposes, rain or shine. If successful, it struck at one of Nelson's French friends and cleared the way for Phips to develop his plans for land, fur, and lumber dealings along the eastern coast. If a failure, it would probably result in the exposure of his rival's espionage and perhaps tar him with the brush of plotting against Saint-Castin.[17]

In the event, the scheme failed almost as soon as it had been launched. Phips had retained the families of the two Acadians sent as guides with the deserters to serve as hostages for their behavior. But the Acadians were made of sterner stuff—the elder, Saint-Aubin, had killed a man paying undue attention to his wife some thirty years before—and during the voyage from Boston they overpowered the two deserters and handed them over to the French forces they found gathered in Penobscot Bay.[18] The court-martial that followed had an imposing panel of judges—Saint-

Castin, the intended victim; Pierre Le Moyne d'Iberville, in the first flush of his career as the greatest colonial soldier of his time and fresh from ravaging English settlements as far afield as New York and Hudson Bay; Denys de Bonaventure, the officer who had captured Nelson twelve months earlier; and another young Canadian destined for military distinction, Jacques Testard de Montigny. The journal Iberville kept as commander of the expedition records the prisoners' fate. They resolved, he wrote, to show "les sauvages" how they treated deserters and traitors, "d'en faire un exemple sur la frontière." On November 4, after a week's interrogation in which the two men confessed Nelson's role in their flight from Canada, they were taken out and ceremoniously executed by the breaking of their skulls—"la teste cassée." Recogizing that he had lost the element of surprise, Iberville then abandoned his attack on the settlements in Maine. Saint-Aubin and Petitpas were awarded five hundred livres for their services and to redeem their families from captivity.[19]

Back in Quebec, meanwhile, Nelson's part in this drama had already cast a chill upon the hospitality he had been receiving. As a prisoner, his espionage could hardly be adjudged treasonous or dishonorable— quite the contrary, as chivalrous French officers acknowledged—but it plainly put an end to his status as the governor's houseguest. As it happened, Frontenac had just received a letter from Minister of Marine Count Pontchartrain in Versailles specifically cautioning against allowing so much freedom to Nelson, whom Pontchartrain judged to be the most spirited and capable of those seeking to attack Canada.[20] In a reply penned just hours before the deserters escaped with Nelson's letter, the governor had airily dismissed the danger; a confidence that must have rung hollow as Iberville reached France and told why he had abandoned his attack. At the same time, however, Frontenac had broached what now served as a way out of a thoroughly embarrassing situation. In warning against Nelson, Pontchartrain had also reversed his previous instructions: the New Englander, he declared, was no longer exchangeable for the remaining soldiers of the Port Royal garrison, since the latter's detention was unlawful by the terms of Meneval's capitulation to Phips. In that case, Frontenac replied, it made no sense to keep Nelson in Canada, since there were no other prisoners in English hands for whom he could be exchanged: he, along with Edward Tyng and the younger John Alden, whom Villebon had recently sent up to Quebec, would be put aboard the next available ships and transferred to France for safekeeping.[21] No sooner said than done; and by January 1693, after a midwinter passage down the fast-freezing St. Lawrence and across the

North Atlantic, John Nelson was back in Europe for the first time since his childhood, reaching harbor at the Atlantic port of Brest, France, before being sent south down the coast to the naval base of Rochefort.[22] Migrants to America often returned to the mother country to display their success or settle down for their old age: if Nelson had dreamed of such a voyage, his storm-tossed return as state prisoner must have assumed all the trappings of a nightmare.

A still harsher fate awaited him in France. Nelson was in the mid-Atlantic by the time that word of the miscarriage of Iberville's expedition reached Quebec. Once ashore, however, he—and all who were in any way connected with his stay in Canada—felt the full force of official displeasure. Convinced that the New Englander's espionage had ruined the previous year's offensive and compromised the future defense of Quebec, Louis XIV[e] and his ministers launched a farflung search for all who might have been his accomplices. In Quebec, a Dutch woman thought to have assisted in the deserters' escape was taken up and closely questioned; in Paris, a larger fish was swept into the net when a leading Canadian merchant visiting France, Mathieu-François Martin de Lino, was arrested and cast into the fortress-prison of the Bastille. De Lino, fluent in several languages, had served Frontenac as interpreter in Quebec, and hence had come into frequent contact with Nelson during the latter's stay. Moreover, his travels seemed to match up with evidence taken from the two deserters before their execution suggesting that a French merchant was going to France to spy on Nelson's behalf.[23]

Versailles showed its concern by entrusting de Lino's interrogation to one of the most powerful men in France and the creator of Paris' first municipal police force; Gabriel Nicolas de La Reynie.[24] Through intense questioning over several days, the young merchant stubbornly maintained his innocence. He had known Nelson well and had been present, by Frontenac's command, whenever the English prisoners met together. He had watched as the king's lieutenant at Quebec, François Provost, "squeezed the thumbs" of one of these captives to elicit information about the two deserters after their flight. But Nelson, de Lino attested, spoke perfect French and was well able to pursue his own plans without the help of others. La Reynie quizzed him closely about possible Huguenot associates and ransacked his papers for evidence of communications in code. But he felt bound to report that there was insufficient evidence to justify further action against de Lino. In Canada, likewise, the trail ran cold—the Dutch woman had aided the two deserters but without knowing their intentions.[25] De Lino may have inadvertently let slip some of the information passed on to New England—

Nelson later recalled that he had heard of the French plans through an "undersecretary."[26] But if any official was to blame for the debacle, it was clearly Frontenac, who in seeking to prime the pump of his prisoner's knowledge and cooperation with generous treatment had instead allowed Nelson to turn this strategy to his own purposes.[27]

Deprived of any subordinate scapegoats, Versailles officials unloosed a flurry of orders regarding Nelson, Alden, and Tyng. Infuriated by reports that some of the remaining Port Royal soldiers in Boston had been sold into servitude in Barbados, they let it be known that the three English prisoners would never be released until the whole garrison was returned. All such prisoners would henceforth receive the same care—or lack of it—as their counterparts in English hands. Tyng and Alden were shipped back up the coast to the great port of La Rochelle. The center of Protestant power in France until its capture by Catholic forces in 1628, the city contained the headquarters of the principal commercial companies trading with Africa and America, including that established by Bergier to exploit Acadia's fisheries ten years before. Tyng and Alden now followed into the company's custody the cargo of furs they and Nelson had collected around the Bay of Fundy, to serve as compensation for the company's heavy losses at English hands. There the unfortunate Tyng, "thro want & hard usage . . . dyed Miserably without any Assistance."[28] Alden survived until the payment of a ransom of twelve hundred livres—about £100—allowed his return to New England in the mid-1690s. He seems to have forgiven his father's less-than-paternal part in his long absence, for the elder Alden passed his last years before his death in 1702 at his son's Boston home.[29]

For Nelson, an equally cheerless but still special treatment was reserved. Branded "un homme très dangereux" likely to subvert anyone he came into contact with, he was sent a hundred miles inland to the royal fortress of Angoulême, there to be kept—the king commanded—from all communication with the outside world.[30] At the stroke of a pen, Nelson was cut adrift from the life of his seaborne Atlantic community. As he passed into Angoulême, he must have glimpsed from the town's cliff-topping ramparts the view still spectacular today, stretching far to the north and west across the valley and vineyards of the Charente. There lay the sea, beneath the horizon. But this was not to be the easy confinement of Quebec. The castle of Angoulême guarded the city's landward flank, facing east towards the forests of the Limousin and the foothills of the Dordogne. Once within its walls Nelson would have been kept within its most formidable defenses: the great eighty-foot keep, or donjon, built by the Lusignan family in the thirteenth century, or the adjoining round tower added a century and a half later, both so massive that they would survive even the chateau's post-Revolutionary transformation from royal fortress to republican town hall.[31]

Through the spring and much of the summer of 1693, Nelson was under heavy guard, as dead to the outside world as the legendary "man in the mask" then beginning his third decade of secret confinement at Louis'[e]'s XIV command. Alexander Dumas would weave a famous novel around this figure, who was rumored to be the king's brother or double; Nelson's imprisonment, too, would become the stuff of legend—immured in a hole behind an iron grate, the story ran, he was resurrected by the casual curiosity of a passerby who then conveyed news of his existence to England.[32] Samuel Drake, the nineteenth-century author who wrote a historical novel based loosely (very loosely) on Nelson's life, depicted his hero undergoing gruesome tortures before smuggling out a message hidden in a bread roll and being rescued by the love of a young French girl (Drake's Nelson having shed a wife and a dozen years to play the part).[33] The truth was less gothic but more revealing of Nelson's unchastened spirit: after some months of the closest confinement, he managed to bribe one of his jailers to pass a letter "to some Gentlemen in Paris to whom I had formerly bin Servisable in their Necessities," who in turn persuaded Versailles to permit an easing of his imprisonment.[34] One of these gentlemen was surely former governor Meneval, now back in Paris and still mindful of Nelson's help and hospitality two years earlier. Another may have been Simon-Pierre Denys de Bonaventure, the captain of the ship that had captured Nelson, since he later claimed to have lent Nelson during the latter's captivity the large sum of five thousand livres.[35] Whatever arguments these "Gentlemen" used, they must have pointed to the illogic of victimizing the very man who had fought hardest for honorable treatment of French prisoners.

In July 1693, therefore, Pontchartrain gave orders for Nelson to be permitted greater freedom. He could eat with the officers of the chateau's garrison and send out, under censorship, such letters as he wished. Furthermore, he would be allowed to leave France once the twelve-hundred-livre ransom to the Acadia Company was paid and once he had posted what amounted to a bail bond for fifteen thousand livres more. The bond would be forfeit should he fail to secure the return of both the remainder of the Port Royal garrison and the son of former governor Perrot, likewise detained in Boston.[36] If not technically involving an exchange of prisoners, the proposal made the soldiers' return a prerequisite of Nelson's full liberty. It also paid him a twofold tribute—

to his sense of honor in expecting that he would hold himself bound by its terms, and to his presumed ability to engineer the soldiers' return where all other means had failed.

The stage seemed set for Nelson's release. But two more years would pass before he left Angoulême, years that must have heavily chafed this "most restless spirit"—Frontenac's phrase—kept from his natural element of the sea.[37] The problem lay in meeting—or, alternatively, re-negotiating—Pontchartain's proposals. Little help could be expected from Massachusetts while Phips remained in power, and Nelson looked for friends closer at hand—to his fellow traders in the Atlantic mercantile community. If he approached his English relatives for help, it was without any visible success. His father remained estranged; Sir Purbeck Temple was now an old man on the verge of death; and his more distant but politically well-placed cousin, Commissioner of Customs Sir Richard Temple, whom he had sought to cultivate back in 1689, took no part in his release. Only another cousin on his mother's side, John Paschal, offered any assistance, and then more by chance than by design. Paschal moved in political circles—he would soon win a seat on the board of commissioners appointed to dispose of prizes taken by England's Royal Navy—and he learned of Nelson's plight, he told his cousin, through a conversation at the Lord Mayor of London's table during a civic banquet. With further information obtained from Nelson's old ally, David Waterhouse, now back in England, who showed him one of Nelson's "melancholly" letters from prison, Pascal then solicited at the Admiralty and with the commissioners responsible for the exchange of prisoners on his cousin's behalf.[38]

Paschal's efforts, however, were only part of the more concerted campaign for Nelson's release begun by his fellow traders some months before. If not yet recognized or run as a formal lobbying group, those who described themselves in their petitions as "gentlemen and merchants trading to New England" had nonetheless emerged as a coherent "interest" at Whitehall by the early 1690s. Their primary concerns were economic—for the security and prosperity of North Atlantic trade—and at a time when war with France had imposed a host of restrictions upon shipping, they were in frequent attendance upon royal officials to co-ordinate the dispatch of convoys and advise on matters of policy.[39] Yet commerce was not their only bond: many, like Waterhouse or Samuel Sewall's London cousin and correspondent, Edward Hull, had at some point lived in New England or retained kinfolk and business partners there. A number had taken sides along with emissaries from New England in the lively Whitehall debates that accompanied the overthrow of the Dominion and the granting of the new Massachusetts charter.[40]

Nelson's friends now used these established channels to plead his cause. A petition submitted while he was still in Canada pointed out that the French were refusing to release any captured New Englanders until the Port Royal garrison was returned, and asked for Phips to be instructed to release his prisoners.[41] Other petitions followed as word arrived of Nelson's and Alden's confinement in France. The faithful Waterhouse, with two other merchants, rendered an account of the prisoners' sufferings and pledged security for their release. Striking to the heart of the French demands, he and Elisha Hutchinson, a member of Phips's council who was now in London, submitted sworn testimony that all the French prisoners had left Massachusetts "for England and other places."[42] Soon afterwards, in August of 1694, Nelson's and Alden's own petition to the Crown was presented at Whitehall, backed by the signatures of forty-nine merchants and visiting New Englanders.[43]

Between these efforts and the prisoners' release, however, stretched long months and a succession of obstacles. Viewing Nelson and Alden as prisoners of war, the Privy Council and its committee, the Lords of Trade and Plantations, referred their case to the commissioners appointed to deal with the exchange of prisoners; only to find that the French viewed the two as excluded from the normal categories of exchange. Throughout 1694 and into the following year, amid the larger task of exchanging hundreds of captured sailors, the correspondence between each side's negotiators grew increasingly vituperative. Nelson and Alden were prisoners of state, not of war; neither they nor Mr. Cox, an English diplomat held at Dunkirk, nor even a captured niece of the Archbishop of Canterbury could be released; the colonies were not included in the treaty of exchange; and where precisely was the remainder of the Port Royal garrison? Their case became entangled in issues ranging from the petty—the nationality of the vessels used to send back prisoners, to the tragic—the fate of the English and Irish sailors captured while serving in French vessels and executed on charges of high treason.[44] French officials now refused to repatriate an English garrison that had surrendered at Hudson Bay on terms similar to those of Port Royal; and each side stored up important prisoners to be held hostage for those of the other—a brother of the great French privateer Jean Bart and a certain Chevalier de Pomerade were deemed equivalent to Cox and Nelson.[45]

Ultimately, two developments pried open the prison gates. On the

English side, Nelson and his allies reluctantly accepted the terms out-lined by Pontchartrain and made arrangements for the required fifteen-thousand-livre bond. It was financed through the Huguenot connection that so often lay behind Anglo-French commercial dealings in these years: Abraham Duport, a La Rochelle merchant, issued the bond, while Waterhouse and others pledged their credit to his brothers, Messrs. Stephen and Simon Duport in London, to indemnify him against any loss. By the terms of the bond, Duport promised to go to prison in Nelson's place or pay fifteen thousand livres—some £1,250 in New Eng-land money—if Nelson did not secure the repatriation of young Perrot and the Port Royal soldiers within eighteen months of his being allowed to leave France.[46]

In Versailles, meanwhile, French officials turned to advancing Nel-son's release on bond as part of a larger scheme to use him as a diplomatic intermediary. In the years following his capture, the fortunes of war in North America had swayed back and forth, with attack and counter-attack ranging as far afield as Newfoundland, Hudson Bay, and the Caribbean. At the summit of affairs, Louis XIV[e] and his ministers pressed with undiminished zeal for new and more glorious campaigns to be launched against New England and the Iroquois. Farther down the chain of command, however, at the level of balancing the books and preserving some remnant of French colonial trade, others looked for ways to set some limit on the war's destructive effects. Among these people were France's intendant of commerce, Jean-Baptiste de Lagny; and Charles-François Duret, Marquis de Chevry. Each was familiar with Acadia's plight and Nelson's career—de Lagny as Pontchartrain's deputy in colonial affairs and author of several crisp letters to Whitehall about Nelson's case, and Chevry as a director and then president of the Acadia company to which Nelson and Alden were paying ransom. Meneval may also have had a hand in their plans, for he had worked with both men and owed his appointment as governor of Acadia back in 1687 to Chev-ry's patronage.[47] Their scheme also harked back a decade in seeking to reactivate the treaty for neutrality in America negotiated between France and England in 1686. Judging this too delicate a matter to be raised at the official level—France refused to open any negotiations that might acknowledge William of Orange as king, and England declined any that did not—de Lagny and Chevry hit on Nelson as a man of known experience and reputed influence who could broach the topic in London.[48]

In the summer of 1695, therefore, when Nelson at last re-emerged from the gates of Angoulême, his destination was Paris and the Bastille.

French officials might have been less eager to meet with him had they known that their irrepressible prisoner had been whiling away the last months of his greater liberty in Angoulême by dabbling in a little more espionage. The mid-1690s in France were a time of mounting political discontent and, in the countryside, widespread famine. As Nelson told the story, Frenchmen "distinguished both by quality and place" positively flocked to him to complain of life under Louis XIVe, and several were willing to carry discontent to the point of treason. Back in Quebec, the unfortunate de Lino had found that mere contact with Nelson led to an assumption of guilt. His successor, the secretary to the governor of Angoulême appointed to assist the prisoner with his letters, was induced to take the extra step of offering to act as an English agent. With this aid, and circumventing the censorship imposed by Versailles, Nelson managed to forward an entire cipher system and its key to the Earl of Portland, one of William of Orange's principal advisers. Portland, in turn, encouraged him to recruit more informants to send back intelligence of French activities. The French secretary had by now removed to a similar post under the intendant of Brittany. He offered, if suitably funded, to establish himself as a spy in the French naval base of Brest—a particularly useful location in view of London's preparations for a landing nearby to attack the port. The attack, when it came, failed, with heavy casualties, the French having their own ring of informants well placed within the English court. Moreover, Whitehall and the secretary were unable to agree on whether the necessary funds should precede any information, or the information, the funds. But plans for activating what might in modern parlance be called the Nelson Network were still alive long after its spymaster had reached England.[49]

Meanwhile, Nelson arrived at the Bastille at seven o'clock in the evening of August 29 and was assigned a single-occupancy room on the ground floor of the Chapel Tower—just across the courtyard from that occupied by de Lino during his interrogation two and a half years before.[50] Despite the Bastille's fearsome reputation, many of its (mostly aristocratic) prisoners lived in comparative comfort, receiving visitors and attended by servants; among the previous occupants of Nelson's cell were the Duc de Biron and the Prince de Rohan. Conditions were far more tolerable than those in Paris' four other main prisons such as the terrible La Tournelle, the purgatory from which inmates passed into the hell of service in the king's galley fleet. Nelson was given liberty to exercise in the courtyard of the Bastille, and special arrangements were made for him to receive de Lagny and other visitors.[51]

Over the next few weeks, Nelson recalled, he had "divers discourses"

Passport issued to John Nelson, November 30, 1695, permitting him to leave France. The signatures are those of King Louis XIVe and his Minister of Marine, Louis Phélypeaux, Count Ponchartrain. (*Courtesy of The Houghton Library*) with Chevry and de Lagny deploring the destruction wrought by war in North America. Much of it, they diplomatically (and wholly inaccurately) agreed, was due to the machinations of the Indians on both sides. Peace could return if governors in the various colonies were allowed to establish local zones of neutrality. From Nelson's perspective, New England's finances, its ravaged border communities, and Boston's trade with Acadia would all benefit from a cessation of hostilities. Yet French officials also saw material advantages for their own side. A "local option" neutrality would help unhinge the English alliance with Canada's most damaging enemy, the Iroquois; it would discourage raids on Acadia and its fisheries; and, in the long term, it might edge Massachusetts, that "espèce de Republique," towards reasserting its old autonomy from England, dividing France's foes.[52] It made sense to make peace where France was numerically and strategically weakest and war where she was strong. And any reduction in the charge of Canada's defense would help fight France's more immediate opponents in Europe, especially at a moment—even as Nelson arrived in Paris—when William's Anglo-Dutch-German army in Flanders was achieving its one great victory of the war by capturing the barrier fortress of Namur.

De Lagny and Chevry, therefore, had no difficulty in obtaining Pontchartrain's approval of their proposals. By late September, Nelson was suggesting that he be assigned a ship to bring back the rest of the Port Royal garrison. With a self-possession bordering on impudence, he also asked for eight days' freedom before his departure to tour Paris and its sights. Just at that moment, however, fresh dispatches arrived from Canada telling of Frontenac's plans for a further offensive. With them came a group of Indian chiefs sent over to be awed by the power and majesty of Louis XIV[e]'s France. Now, it seemed, was not the moment to seek peace. Nelson, it was argued, was still too dangerous a man to be released. Ultimately, after a debate in council, Louis and his ministers agreed to postpone any further talk of a neutrality; Nelson, however, since he had fulfilled his side of the negotiations, could not honorably be kept from attempting to fulfil his bond.[53] On December 10, 1695, three years after his arrival in France, a chastened Nelson promised to leave the country and make directly for Flanders without any tourist stops on the way. On the same day, early in the morning, he was taken by carriage to board the stagecoach leaving for Mons on the French frontier. Eleven days later he secured a passport to cross the Channel from the English envoy in Brussels.[54] Fittingly, this first English face was also that of a cousin several times removed—Robert, son of the Sir Charles Wolseley who had been Sir Thomas Temple's

All these weaknesses would in time be overcome—by peace, a Protestant succession, the erosion of English Jacobite sentiment and French military might, and the emergence of the Bank of England—but for the moment they shaped and limited what Nelson or any other newcomer to England's turbulent politics could hope to achieve. His first task was not of his making: to fulfil the terms of the bond that had permitted his release. This alone was reason enough to delay a return to New England. Within a few weeks of reaching London, however, he took up a second, self-imposed task, one first forged in Boston but newly honed by his years in captivity—a resolve to bring the old English world to the aid of the new in an effort to turn back the rising tide of French power in North America. Over the next two years, his work would leave a significant imprint on English colonial policy. In seeking to neutralize Nelson and, through him, colonial conflict, Versailles officials instead propelled their former hostage to a position where his knowledge and talents could do French interests enduring harm.

In his first task, discharging the bond, Nelson could feel that circumstances had already turned in his favor. Late in 1694, Sir William Phips had been recalled to London to answer a broad array of charges of misgovernment. There, early in the next year, he had died of his encounter with an English winter, the one opponent even a Phips could not overpower. It was several years before his successor as governor took up his post, and in the interim, executive power rested in the competent and conciliatory hands of Lieutenant-Governor William Stoughton, Elizabeth Nelson's uncle. Stoughton favored Nelson's cause by accelerating the ransoming and exchanging of prisoners; in particular, after repeated denials that any of the Port Royal garrison remained in New England, five were found, separated from the families they had established since their capture, and returned to Canada.[2] This drastic action was not wholly for Nelson's benefit: without it, New Englanders found, French officials at the other end of the exchange would in turn refuse to send back the many English captives in Canada, often taken as children and converted to Catholicism, who pleaded to remain with their French or Indian families and masters.[3] As in modern times, the return of prisoners and hostages was a much more complex and emotionally wrenching problem than it seemed on the surface. At some point, too, the son of former governor Perrot made his way back to France from his detention in Boston, satisfying another condition laid down in Nelson's bond. Throughout 1696, however, French officials continued to hold out for a further accounting of the Port Royal garrison, bringing Nelson ever closer to the bond's eighteen-month deadline after which he would have to return to prison or sacrifice the fifteen thousand livres.[4]

If, as Nelson came to believe, Versailles was deliberately trying to keep the bond hanging over his head, he showed himself conspicuously unwilling to be intimidated. Within days of his arrival in London, he was out and about at the city's Royal Exchange, the center of mercantile life designed by Sir Christopher Wren as part of London's reconstruction following the Great Fire of 1666.[5] There, on the Exchange's "New England Walk," he encountered many of the traders who had under-written his petition for release. From their experience of the ways of Whitehall, he could plan the best way to present his case to officialdom. To judge by his strategy, he quickly appreciated that to approach the body already familiar with his case and other colonial matters—the committee of the Privy Council known as the Lords of Trade and Plan-tations—would be, for the present, a waste of time. Held to account for many of the problems afflicting English commerce—inadequate trade protection, foreign interloping, and the instability of public credit—the committee had also become the subject of a contest between king and Parliament over which branch of government should take such matters in hand. For the moment, something approaching a vacuum existed in the usual channels; and Nelson turned instead to the king's principal secretary of state, Charles Talbot, Duke of Shrewsbury. A man much admired by contemporaries of both sexes for his good looks, strong conscience, and casual charm, Shrewsbury was a reluctant politician continually pressed into service by the king and as often pleading bad health in an effort to retreat to his country estates. In early 1696, he was at the height of such power as he cared to exercise. As Pontchartrain's English counterpart—namely, the minister ultimately responsible for the dispatch of colonial business—Shrewsbury offered the best avenue through which Nelson could hope to obtain the ear of government.

The New Englander clearly hoped and even expected that his record would merit the personal attention of England's ministers. Had he not consulted with the highest levels of government in Boston, Quebec, and Paris? But he was neither the first nor last colonist visiting London to discover that American matters ranked far down the list of affairs con-sidered important at court. In a memorial to Shrewsbury drafted in late January, Nelson solicited an interview in which he promised to lay out issues vital to England's prosperity and the security of her American colonies. He dangled the bait of his ability to secure intelligence from his ring of agents in France. More darkly, plucking the chord of anti-Catholic hysteria never far below the surface of late seventeenth-century

English life, he promised to expose "certaine Jesuitts and Emissaries" who had recently entered England.[6]

To the duke, however, Nelson must have seemed just another in an interminable procession of the "projectors" for which the period was famous: each striving to float a company, market an invention, mine a precious metal, or sniff out a conspiracy, and all for England's greater glory and an incidental profit. By such standards, Nelson's propositions were short on both specifics and the promise of private advantage, a bad sign, since a robust patriotism was all too often the last refuge of the impoverished projector. Shrewsbury had heard it all before. Pleading his customary "indisposition,"he sent word through his secretary and agent in London, James Vernon, for Nelson to submit his full proposals in writing. Curtly regretting his inability to secure "that access which otherwise I might have hoped for, and happily might been of use," Nelson set to work.[7] Yet history has reason to bless Shrewsbury's indifference, for it drew from Nelson a remarkable outpouring of opinion and information, one of the period's few substantive English assessments of the forces underlying the contest for power in North America.

Nelson began with a brief and, in the circumstances, modest account of his long familiarity with Canadian and Acadian affairs. Surprisingly (although in keeping with his disavowal of personal advantage), he made no mention of Sir Thomas Temple, nor of his own claim to Acadia. He told of the contacts he had made while in Angoulême and their promise for conveying intelligence of affairs in France. But he then turned to his main purpose; to explain how the French had achieved a threatening predominance in North America, and how England could learn—and therefore save English America—by their example. His first point would be repeated over and over again by historians of comparative American colonization. "The great and only advantage which our Enemies hath in those parts," he argued, "does arise chiefly from the nature of their settlement which contrary unto our plantations who depend upon the improvement of lands and trading upon the seas, their's of Canada has its subsistence from the trade of furs and Peltry with the Indians." In consequence, the French had made a virtue out of the necessity of cultivating the Indians by means of gifts, pensions allotted to leading chiefs, bounties paid on scalps, and the encouragement of their own young men to fight alongside Indian war parties. Especially effective in recent years, Nelson believed, had been the French tactic of bringing Indian leaders from different tribes across to Europe for a firsthand look at French power, to such effect that even England's traditional allies, the Iroquois, were now turning to France or neutrality. The fatal effects of losing such allies would be felt from New England to Carolina, for "we may lay it down as a maxim, that those who are masters of the Indians will consequently prevail in all places where they are neglected as we have too much done."[8]

For England to save the situation, it must adopt French methods. A tour of the city of London, the newly arrived Nelson believed, would soon convince Indian leaders of England's greatness. In the colonies, governors must regulate all dealings with the Indians to ensure their being conducted on just and equal terms—"love and inclination" would come only when "a full trust and dependence can be obtained." Much more could be done to counter the success of French Catholic missionaries in making themselves "masters of the consciences of the heathen," and Nelson spoke in scathing terms of the misuse of the funds first collected in mid-century for the conversion of the New England Indians, funds designated for the propagation of the gospel but too often diverted for commercial purposes.[9] To spiritual aid must be added military assistance, and Nelson urged that colonists such as the hunters around Albany who were willing to accompany Indian war parties should receive every possible encouragement.

Finally, Nelson identified English America's fundamental weakness as "the number and independency the one from the other of so many small Governments," all following their different interests and refusing to help their fellows. Were the northern English colonies from New York to Massachusetts to be united, then they would outnumber the French in Canada fifteenfold. Given naval help from England, they could turn from "a bare defence" to the conquest of Canada. Warming to this prospect, Nelson held it out to Shrewsbury as the only advantage that England could expect to gain from the present war; and he suggested the wealth, at least £200,000 a year, that a English monopoly of the fur trade would bring. Phips's ill-planned repulse should not deter a further attempt. Moreover, now was the moment to act, for Versailles had shelved the plans for a neutrality that he and de Lagny had discussed in the Bastille in favor of a full-scale descent led by the formidable Iberville upon what the French well knew to be weak and divided English colonies.[10]

Some of these themes, particularly the need for a stronger and more concerted defense of the northern English colonies, had been heard before at Whitehall. But Nelson's memorial stands out from others of its kind in several respects. It was exceptional in its calm comparative assessment of the French and English experience in America and its suggestion that the latter could learn much from the former. In decided contrast to most contemporary New England writings, it presented the Indians, not as fiendish savages to be swept away, but as autonomous peoples to be wooed and won through persuasion and collaboration—as powerful and essential players in the contest to control North America. The memorial sounded a familiar note harking back to the days of Andros' Dominion of New England in urging a renewed union of the northern English colonies. But it gave this strategy a novel twist by suggesting, in language William Pitt would echo sixty years later, that England would profit most by preserving a stalemate in Europe and committing its resources to expanding its colonial empire.

Yet novelty has never been a coin of great value in English politics, and the memorial as a whole showed Nelson's inexperience in the task of spurring a man like Shrewsbury into action. It oscillated awkwardly between episodes in Nelson's personal odyssey and a series of sweeping generalizations; its central theme, that France had much to teach England in colonial affairs, had scant appeal at a time when King Louis and all his works had become political anathema; and it put forward no coherent plan of action to implement the changes it advised.

Above all, in an era when English colonial policy was predominantly shaped by the search to advance particular interests, Nelson's memorial was far too casual in its account of what financial benefits his reforms would bring, and to whom. Significantly, this was the one area in which Shrewsbury bestirred himself to seek more information, evidently with the passing thought that he and other investors might finance a conquest of Canada. Nelson responded with a second, shorter memorial in which he clothed his generalities with what he hoped would be some alluring financial flesh. With Canada conquered and its lands granted to the investors in the enterprise, he informed the duke, duties on the trade in furs and other goods would bring "your Lordships" some £18,000 a year, along with lesser sums derived from leasing out or operating other aspects of the country's commerce.[11] A few moments' reflection, however, would have told Shrewsbury that this was no great prize for so large a project, in view of the preparations and military forces required. It could not be carried through by private investors alone, and a government called on for aid was not likely to relinquish any conquests into private hands. Greater returns could be gained, Phips-like, from recovering sunken treasure, or from sponsoring privateering ventures. Only a few months earlier, in fact, Shrewsbury and several other leading English politicians had secretly agreed to back such a venture proposed by one Captain William Kidd. Though this particular scheme would turn sour, bringing its backers into political hot water (and Kidd to the gallows for piracy), it and others like it were still a far better investment than the full-scale expedition needed to conquer Canada.[12]

As spring passed into summer, Nelson must have realized that nothing more could be expected from Shrewsbury's direction. Across the Channel, Versailles still refused to discharge his bond. In his lodgings at "Mr. Habbard's house on Garlick Hill"—a tiny street in the heart of the City, southeast of the still-unfinished St. Paul's Cathedral and a few steps short of Southwark Bridge—Nelson must have seethed with impatience to find himself, as it were, once more imprisoned; physically free, yet helpless to shape his own destiny.[13] Slowly, however, circumstances in Whitehall began to change in ways that allowed his expertise to be brought into play. In May of 1696, King William had finally cut through the prolonged debate over the respective spheres of Crown and Parliament in superintending commercial and colonial affairs by appointing a new body of commissioners for the purpose, the Board of Trade.[14] Like its predecessor, the new Board was charged with gathering information and forwarding reports and recommendations. Unlike the Lords of Trade, however, it was not a committee of the King's Privy Council and so lacked the direct ties with executive power that came from overlapping membership with the Council. Time would reveal the inherent weakness of this advisory role, as expertise lacking authority flagged by comparison with authority lacking expertise. For the moment, however, the exceptionally competent (and high-salaried) body of commissioners appointed by William gave a new energy to London's involvement in American affairs. By September, they had begun a full-scale investigation of conditions in the northern colonies, prompted by complaints from agents sent over from New York that French pressure on its frontiers was endangering the alliance with the Iroquois. At the agents' suggestion, John Nelson was summoned before the Board to expound on French plans and ways they might be countered.[15]

On September 16, 1696, therefore, Nelson took a boat up the Thames to the Board's new quarters in Whitehall (just refurbished under the direction of Sir Christopher Wren) and delivered a long "discourse" on his experiences and the state of French settlement in Canada. A week later, at the Board's request, he submitted his testimony in writing, set down in two memorials.[16] The first repeated almost word for word what he had submitted to Shrewsbury seven months before.[17] The second was entirely new, a closely argued plan for the reduction of Canada. Its opening pages suggest how much more often Nelson must have voyaged there than the surviving evidence documents, for they were cast in the form of sailing directions up the St. Lawrence River to Quebec, describing the more difficult passages and estimating the population of the principal settlements. Nelson then gave an overview of the lands, recently wasted by Iroquois raids, that lay upriver as far as Montreal. Overall, he computed, Canada's total white population could not exceed two thousand families and a thousand soldiers—an estimate roughly corresponding to modern calculations of some thirteen to fourteen thousand men, women, and children by the end of the century. And not only were these inhabitants spread out along three hundred miles of a river often difficult to navigate, but as many as five hundred of the colony's best men were always off trading among the Indians a thousand miles distant from Quebec. Hence Canada could not resist a simultaneous, two-pronged English assault, on Montreal by land and Quebec by sea. This was already a familiar plan of attack: broached thirty years before, adopted by Phips and the New Yorkers in 1690, it would remain the staple English strategy until its final success in the English conquest of 1759.[18] In Nelson's version, two thousand English and Indians by land and the same number by sea would suffice. More novel was his suggestion of how to complete the task. Rather than continuing to profit from the dispersion of French settlement, as his initial strategy had suggested, final victory would be achieved by frightfulness, by ravaging Canada's crops and farms and driving the inhabitants to take refuge in Quebec where, he optimistically proclaimed, "hunger in a fortnight's time will contrive the Surender."[19]

Nelson's memorials plainly impressed the Board by their breadth of vision and depth of personal knowledge. On the day after they were read, Sir Henry Ashurst, the agent for Massachusetts who happened to be present on other business, was closely questioned about his association with the fund for missionary work among the New England Indians, the fund Nelson charged was being misused.[20] A week later, on September 30, the Board approved and forwarded to the council governing England during the king's absence at war in Flanders a long report on the defense of the northern colonies, drafted by one of the Board's most distinguished members, the aged philosopher John Locke. It repeated point by point—and sometimes word for word—Nelson's advice in the memorial first given to Shrewsbury on ways the Indians could be won over to the English cause, even down to inviting their leaders over for a firsthand encounter with the sights and sounds of London. Building on Nelson's criticisms of the colonists' disunity, as well as those submitted by the New York agents, Locke's report recommended the appointment of a captain general to coordinate colonial defenses.[21]

A further indication of the Board's regard for Nelson came in the form of a friendly letter from an expert in gauging Whitehall's prevailing winds—Nelson's old rival from Dominion days, Edward Randolph. After service as surveyor-general of the customs in the tobacco colonies around the Chesapeake, Randolph had been in London for the past year, prodding his superiors to take action against the illegal trading he found rife throughout the colonies. His testimony, coupled with Parliament's concern for the state of English commerce, had already resulted in the passage of a new Navigation Act greatly extending royal supervision of colonial trade. Thereafter, he became a frequent attendant at Whitehall as he battled colonial agents and proprietors to establish a new hierarchy of Crown-appointed law officers in America to implement the Act. [22] Throughout, as in past years, Randolph drew on the powerful support of William Blathwayt, clerk and secretary to the Lords of Trade for twenty years, nephew of the Thomas Povey who had helped finance Sir Thomas Temple, and now a dominant member of the new Board of Trade.[23]

Indeed, it was as Blathwayt's emissary that Randolph wrote to Nelson, inviting him to Blathwayt's house to discuss "your services and sufferings and your capacity to serve the crown." Nelson was also bidden to call on John Povey, the husband of Blathwayt's stepsister and his longtime associate in the Plantations Office.[24] Judging by Nelson's subsequent letters, praising Blathwayt as the only man in England with a perfect knowledge of colonial matters, he kept at least the first appointment and thereby forged an alliance of convenience that benefitted both men in the months ahead.[25] Each had more immediate goals than a conquest of Canada. Blathwayt had long shared Nelson's apprehension about the military weakness of the northern English colonies, a concern he had emphasized in pressing for the creation of the Dominion of New England back in the 1680s. He also had clients in office in America, particularly Governor Benjamin Fletcher of New York, whom he was seeking to shelter from the rising tide of Whig power in Whitehall. Out of England at the king's side when Nelson had appeared before the Board, Blathwayt wanted to meet this star witness face to face.

Nelson, for his part, had come to share Blathwayt's long-held belief that the Crown must exert a closer supervision of America in general and New England in particular. If not yet—and never to be—a royalist in Blathwayt's bureaucratic mold, he now accepted that no single colony or body of adventurers could turn back the French in the northeast without some greater measure of royal backing. And he, too, had personal interests to resolve, in the form of the bond for which Versailles would soon demand its pound of flesh. On this matter it was probably the resourceful Blathwayt who proposed a new variation on an old theme to force Versailles towards a compromise. For years, the fur-trading posts around the frigid shores of Hudson Bay had oscillated between French and English control, in an epic of tiny armies beset by starvation, scurvy, treachery, and the lottery of whose forces would arrive first each season. At the beginning of September 1696, the French garrison left in York Fort by Iberville after his capture of the fort the previous year was in its turn forced to submit to an English expeditionary force. Taking a leaf out of Sir William Phips's book, the English commander violated the terms of the surrender and brought the garrison and its leader, Gabriel Testard de La Forest, back to England. At the Board's suggestion, Nelson applied to have La Forest held as a hostage for the return of his bond.[26] In the meantime, he prepared for the worst, should this tactic fail. His old ally David Waterhouse held bills of exchange payable by the English treasury for a thousand pounds worth of materials supplied to Royal Navy vessels in New England waters, bills likely to remain unpaid for years, given the chronic disarray of the royal finances. Playing on Whitehall's sympathy for his plight, Nelson represented the money as crucial for discharging his bond and won a recommendation for its early payment.[27]

These personal matters, however, were overshadowed by grim news from Boston. The irrepressible Iberville, in yet another of his lightning thrusts, had captured the Royal Navy frigate *Newport* and then the fort at Pemaquid, rebuilt by Phips to be the key to New England's eastern defenses. Frantic letters arrived from Massachusetts bewailing its "despairing Condition" and seeking royal aid in almost every conceivable form—military stores, more frigates, orders to compel other colonies to send help, Crown-funded garrisons in Acadia, and a conquest of Canada, that "Fountain from whence issue all our Miserys."[28] Called before the Board of Trade for his opinion, Nelson proposed constructing forts along the line of the Kennebec River and striking at Canada's economic lifeline by intercepting the annual convoy returning home to France, a scheme he had already shared with John Locke. But it was Nelson's more general remarks at this November 20 meeting, and their political implications, that captured the Board's attention. There was not a man in New England, he declared, "capable of Military Command, not an Engineer, nay not a Soldier that had ever seen the face of an Ennemy except the Indians." Led by Blathwayt, Board members resolved to submit a report to the Crown on the state of New England "according to Mr. Nelson's discourse." It urged that, should the captain general for the northern colonies recommended in their September 30 report not be appointed, a governor with military experience should be sent forthwith to Massachusetts with powers to mobilize all forces throughout New England.[29]

The military emergency, in fact, coupled with the spur of Nelson's testimony, forced English officialdom to confront a number of inter-related political problems that had perplexed Whitehall ever since the collapse of the Dominion. At their core was the long-standing dilemma of how the northern colonies could best be brought to present a united and effective military front at the least possible cost to the Crown while preserving their separate political identities. A variety of schemes whereby the governors of Massachusetts and New York could exercise command of the militia of their more protected neighbors or require specified quotas of men in time of need had all proved ineffective. Further complicating the matter after Phips's death was a prolonged debate over what kind of government should be created for his successor. One of Shrewsbury's Whig followers, Richard Coote, Earl of Bellomont, had won appointment as governor of Massachusetts in the spring of 1695. But both the earl's status and his debts led him to seek a more credit-worthy position; and he was soon named to rule New York as well, an arrangement with the added advantage of displacing Governor Fletcher, a Tory appointee. Soon afterwards, Bellomont further cemented his ties with his new province by joining Shrewsbury and New Yorker Robert Livingston in support of Captain Kidd's privateering expedition.[30]

Bellomont's departure for America, however, was long delayed: by his absence in Ireland, by the administrative reorganization of 1696, and because the new Board of Trade was itself divided over the wisdom of setting the two colonies under one governor as a solution to the problems of their defense. Indeed, the two reports that followed Nelson's September and November appearances before the Board were themselves evidence of this division, with the first showing Locke's preference for the appointment of a military generalissimo without any political regrouping; and the second, Blathwayt's opposition to the haphazard joining of two widely separated colonies unless it was accompanied by a wholesale reorganization on the lines of the Dominion of New England.[31]

Yet both politics and policy required a solution, and Nelson now cast his new influence with the Board behind a middle way—a confederation of the northern colonies that stopped short of consolidation. On February 1, 1697, he presented a memorial from "the Inhabitants, Traders,

Proprietors, etc. of the North parts of America." Of its twenty-eight subscribers, eleven had supported his and Alden's petition for release two and a half years before. The memorial deplored the public and private losses incurred by French attacks, and urged that all the northern English colonies be set under a single governor in such a way as to preserve to each its civil rights, properties, and customs. Admitting the "great confusions" of the period of the Dominion, the memorial insisted that these were not the consequence of uniting the colonies but of the arbitrary way the Dominion had been framed and governed.[32]

In advocating union for defense without the consolidation that threatened tyranny, the memorial closely resembled the one Nelson had helped forward to Whitehall from Massachusetts seven years before.[33] In London as in Boston he spoke for a group of moderate royalists, an "Atlantic" interest that sought cooperation without coercion, regulation without reconstruction. Others remained mistrustful of any form of renewed political intervention orchestrated from London: two subscribers to the memorial, including the Massachusetts agent Sir Henry Ashurst, withdrew their names lest it lead to a new governor with excessive power in civil affairs; and twice as many "New England traders" as Nelson had been able to muster came forward to sign an April memorial asking merely for various forms of military assistance to be sent to New England. Representatives of the smaller colonies adjoining Massachusetts protested that the appointment of an all-powerful governor would erode their cherished autonomy.[34]

Nelson's middle way, however, became the path adopted—with reservations—by Whitehall. By mid-March the Board had recommended, and the king had agreed, that Bellomont be appointed governor of Massachusetts, New York, and New Hampshire, with power as captain general to command assistance from the militias of Connecticut, Rhode Island, and the Jerseys. Nelson could hardly take all or even the major part of the credit as policymaker, for other, more potent, political forces—Shrewsbury's backing, Bellomont's needs, the consortium backing Kidd's venture, and the plain necessity of rallying colonial defenses— all dictated a similar solution.[35] Nor was Bellomont given civil authority over the smaller colonies of Rhode Island and Connecticut, a power that Nelson seems to have favored but advocated only in general terms. The end product was the weakest possible form of confederation consistent with supporting Bellomont's dignity and debts, an arrangement abandoned after the earl's death in office in 1701. Nelson's contribution was less in shaping the result than in alerting Whitehall to the broader strategic context of the problem and in providing a covering rationale for a politically convenient but (as Blathwayt had anticipated) ineffective solution.

In the meantime, as Bellomont's government took shape, Nelson's memorials and his frequent attendance upon the Board of Trade seemed only to have whetted that body's appetite. By mid-March, he was again at Whitehall to remind the Board of the plan he had broached with John Locke the previous October for attacking Canada's trade with France. Ships of an expedition being readied to recoup the damage inflicted by Iberville on the English settlements in Newfoundland could intercept the supply fleet coming from La Rochelle at the mouth of the St. Lawrence River. The Board forwarded the plan to Shrewsbury's fellow secretary of state, Sir William Trumbull, who discussed it with the king, but to no effect.[36] More fruitful—and testimony to the impression made by Nelson's expertise—was the Board's decision, a week later, to seek his advice on the status of England's claim to Acadia.[37] Peace was in the air—secret negotiations had begun even as fighting continued in Flanders—and English officials were anxious to be fully armed for the conference table. Port Royal had fallen to Phips, but the French could argue that, since Nelson's capture, English authority there had been but a shadow government. Across the Bay of Fundy, by contrast, Governor Villebon had preserved French control of the lands around the St. John River. Unless all Acadia were ceded to England, therefore, the negotiators must stand ready to reach agreement—or agree to disagree—on its boundary with New England, whether this lay (as the French maintained) along the Kennebec or (as the English argued) further east on the St. George or St. Croix rivers.

Nelson returned a twofold answer. In mid-April he brought to the Board of Trade an account of the current English position in Acadia. Through the 1690s, the French authorities had allowed their fellow countrymen in Port Royal and nearby settlements to subscribe oaths of allegiance to England in the hope of avoiding further attacks on the region. Nelson now cited these as evidence that England could lay claim by right of conquest and possession to all the coastline from east of Cape Sable around to Chignecto in the Bay of Fundy. Simultaneously, perhaps apprehensive that the peace might provide for the return of all wartime conquests, he submitted a more general petition to the Lords Justices ruling England in William's absence. In it he recounted Sir Thomas Temple's claim to Acadia and Nova Scotia by virtue of the grants from Sir William Alexander and Charles de la Tour, the losses Temple had suffered from the Treaty of Breda, his own inheritance of his uncle's title, and Acadia's inclusion—"by surprise"—in the charter of Massachusetts. For the protection of England's interests "as well as the proprietie of your Petitioner," he asked that his information be forwarded to the king.[38]

Yet even as Nelson seemed to be settling into a role as Whitehall's resident expert on northern American matters, his own affairs were approaching a crisis. Fifteen months after leaving the Bastille, he was no nearer to convincing French officials that he had fulfilled all the terms of his bond, despite the return of Meneval, young Perrot, and the five soldiers of the Port Royal garrison. His lifeline out of prison had become a tether. Soon the bond's deadline would elapse and Nelson would face either a return to captivity or economic ruin on top of all his years of hardship. In Whitehall, he was still fighting to have La Forest, the French officer captured in Hudson Bay, kept hostage to bring pressure to bear upon the French. Neither La Forest nor the powerful Hudson's Bay Company (whose directors included Secretary of State Sir William Trumbull) saw why they should be dragged into the dispute; the French threatened a further round of reprisals; and Nelson had to lobby frantically to keep his strategy alive.[39] Late in May, a glimmer of hope appeared for both men when an offer was made for the return of Nelson's bond; only for the matter to be again deferred. By then, however, Nelson was no longer in London to present his case. As weary of paper fetters as of iron bars, he had embarked on a desperate strategy to make or break his case: defying London's restrictions on overseas travel in time of war, let alone its prohibition of private dealings with the enemy, he had crossed the Channel to Holland to plead his cause face to face with the French diplomats negotiating the treaty of peace.[40]

Several legends have grown around Nelson's career, and the most colorful embroiders this episode. More than a century later, his great-grandson, United States senator James Lloyd, recounted a family tradition that King William himself had advised Nelson that the war's end made it needless for him to return to France to discharge the bond. Upon Nelson's saying he intended to go, "the king, with some warmth, repeated, that it was unnecessary, and forbade him to do it. 'Will your majesty then pay my bonds?' was asked. '*No!*' said the king. Then Nelson replied, 'Please God I live, I'll go!' " a phrase his proud descendant adopted for the family coat of arms and emblazoned on the side of his carriage—to the mystification of his fellow New Yorkers.[41]

Like many good legends, the story does not entirely fit the facts, for William was abroad in Flanders all that spring and summer, the war was still in progress, and Nelson did not return as far as France. Nonetheless, the two may have met earlier or in Flanders, and the story embodies two traits remarked on by Nelson's contemporaries: his obsession with meeting personal obligations and his headstrong resolve to shape events before they could shape him. Contemporary evidence reveals that he did take a few precautions. Towards the end of his mission, and before returning to England, he wrote to disclose his activities to Blathwayt, whose expertise in colonial matters and position as King William's private secretary during the Flanders campaigns might serve to shield him from official wrath. At some point, he also disclosed his plans to Edward, Lord Villiers, England's ambassador at The Hague and one of the diplomats empowered to negotiate peace with the French.[42] But in the context of the troubled 1690s, he was still taking a startling risk. The nation was abuzz—and Whitehall's paperwork glutted—with stories of plots to assassinate the king, high officials in treasonous contact with the exiled James, and foreigners lurking purposefully in English seaports. Only a few months earlier, the beheading of the convicted traitor Sir John Fenwick on London's Tower Hill had furnished both public entertainment and a pointed reminder of the cost of trafficking with enemies of the state.

Of the details of Nelson's mission, little survives beyond his own sparse testimony. He sought, as always, to cut through official delay by appealing directly to those in power, and he may have devised his strategy upon learning that the leading French diplomat at the formal negotiations begun in May at Ryswick in Holland, close to The Hague, was François de Callières. Callières stood high in Louis XIVe's favor and would soon become his principal private secretary; more important for Nelson, he was brother to the governor of Montreal in Canada, a man with whom Nelson enjoyed, he told Blathwayt, "a very good acquaintance."[43] Callières and his fellow negotiators, of course, were dealing with infinitely more complex matters than the status of Acadia or the fate of a single English prisoner. The war had involved every European power on battlefields spread across the globe. Still unresolved was the momentous question it had begun with—the disposition of the vast realms of the ailing and childless King of Spain. By Nelson's account, however, the Frenchman found time to discuss his case. What emerged was an appropriately diplomatic solution: Callières would intercede for the return of Nelson's bond if the latter in turn would draw up and carry back to England proposals for creating a state of "local option" neutrality in America, such as Nelson had discussed with Chevry and de Lagny in the Bastille back in 1695. Late in June, as he waited in Rotterdam, Nelson at long last received back his bond. The next day, triumphant, he took ship back across the North Sea on the packet boat to Harwich.[44]

He soon felt the consequences of short-circuiting the diplomatic process. Back in London, the Lords Justices ruling in the king's absence were in a fractious mood, convinced of their deliberate exclusion from what was going on across the Channel. Indeed, the great number of countries represented, the complexity of their demands, and the shifting fortunes of an ongoing war had combined to stall the peace negotiations; William was trying secret channels to break the deadlock; and, as Whitehall officials suspected, relative underlings like Blathwayt, working at the king's side, knew much more than they about events.[45] The news sent back by Ambassador Villiers of Nelson's sudden interjection in the proceedings was one more straw in the wind—a man of a distinctly checkered past with no diplomatic credentials and a known associate of Blathwayt was for some reason being allowed to treat directly with the French. Writing back to Villiers, Secretary of State Trumbull agreed that Nelson, "who seems to be an ill Man," warranted investigation. On the evening of July 1, soon after his return to London, Nelson came before the Lords Justices of England sitting with other members of the Privy Council—a duke, a viscount, five earls, three commoners, and a primate (the Archbishop of Canterbury). There, following his admission of his meetings with Callières, he was committed to the custody of a king's messenger "upon suspition of high treason for corresponding with the King's Enemies." In his coat pocket was found the proposal for a neutrality, and officers were sent to search his lodgings for further "Treasonable and Dangerous Papers."[46]

For six weeks, Nelson remained in custody and under suspicion, confined to the house of King's Messenger William Sutton near Soho Square. Adding insult to injury, he was charged seven pounds and three shillings in fees for his own committal. At first, proceedings were begun for his prosecution, for those in power were angered and perplexed. Particularly harsh was James Vernon, Shrewsbury's man of affairs, who had received Nelson's various proposals and talked with him several times during 1696. "He is a man I have seen before," Vernon reported to a friend on the day after Nelson's arrest, "but could never tell what to make of him. They say he is 'very knowing' in what concerns the northern parts of America, where he has lived a long while, if he was not born there, and is the owner of a considerable plantation. He has suffered a long imprisonment in France, for they were of opinion he was capable of doing them a prejudice in these parts. I know not whether, for that reason, they may not have taken some pains to gain him." Why, Vernon wondered, was he constantly corresponding with France, and why were his bonds now returned to him so that he would be at liberty to accompany Governor Bellomont to New England? The French were not usually so generous with their favors. "The man," Vernon concluded, "has talents enough to be a proper tool in their hands. If he be not a renegade and spy, he carries a good many marks of it. I think we can now expect no good of him, and therefore care will be taken he do us no hurt."[47]

The prospects looked bleak: Nelson was too true to be good, a man so out of the ordinary in experience, adversity, and initiative as to seem an enigmatic and hence suspect figure to official minds. Nor, perhaps, had he shown the necessary penitence when called to account: challenged in the Privy Council to explain his "strange presumption" in meeting with Callières without authority, Nelson, true to form, showed more concern about the case of La Forest, the French officer due for release now that he had regained his bond.[48] As the days after his arrest passed, however, tempers began to cool and allies to appear. The Board of Trade, under pressure to supply the diplomats with full information on the state of American affairs, had already shown its confidence by commissioning Nelson to prepare a full report "with all possible dispatch" on changes in colonial boundaries since the 1667 Treaty of Breda, a task that Nelson accepted despite his confinement.[49] From Flanders, Blathwayt sent a letter of explanation; and, decisively, it emerged that the king, though dubious of the value of a treaty of colonial neutrality, was willing to discuss it in order to incline the French to other concessions. Whitehall officials began to realize that Nelson was an eccentric individualist acting for reasons of his own, and that he had not compromised the negotiations in ways that merited formal prosecution. His arrest had been a sufficient vent for their irritation, enough to demonstrate their concern.

Late in July, Nelson petitioned to be heard or released. He also sought aid from the new head of the senior branch of the Temple clan, Sir Richard, who had succeeded to his father's baronetcy earlier in the year. Sir Richard solicited Secretary Trumbull and Edward Southwell, a clerk to the Privy Council, on his kinsman's behalf and expressed his expectation of a happy conclusion, provided that Nelson "carry it as fair as you can towards all in power."[50] Nelson seems to have dutifully bent his stiff neck, for on August 13, 1697, the Privy Council, after administering "a severe reprimand," ordered his discharge. The Council, reported Vernon, "found more of indiscretion and presumption in the undertaking than either malice of [or?] French inclination."[51]

Nelson, surely, was now free to return to New England and his long-suffering wife and daughters. Why he tarried another six months, passing up the chance to leave with Governor Bellomont in the fall, remains a minor mystery. His father was close to death, and Nelson may have felt a belated twinge of filial duty; one that fell on stony ground, to judge by the terms of Robert Nelson's will.[52] More likely, he came to feel that he could do New England and himself greater service by staying until the terms of peace were finally resolved. The formal treaty finally signed in September 1697 at Ryswick echoed that of Breda thirty years before in providing for the return of all American territories to their prewar ownership and status. Precisely where the prewar boundaries lay, however, remained the task of a joint commission. Here, once more, the Board of Trade welcomed Nelson's expertise. In October, it deemed his offer to provide a memorial on Acadia "very acceptable," and two weeks later he submitted a lengthy analysis of matters that the English commissioners should consider in settling New England's eastern borders.[53]

In Nelson's eyes, three issues were of paramount importance—the fisheries, relations with the Indians, and the establishment of procedures to avoid future misunderstanding and conflict. He feared the treaty's restoration of Acadia to the French would encourage them to exclude all English fisherman both close to land and out on the high seas. Citing his uncle's practice back in the 1660s of allowing high-seas fishing but charging a £5 fee to all boats "making or drying of their Fish on the shoares," he pressed for a similar compromise to prevent conflict and protect so valuable an English trade. Likewise (although in much vaguer language), he warned against French encroachment on the Indian lands "on the backside of our Plantations," particularly those lying between New York and Canada, an encroachment that endangered English "Traffick with the Natives." Lastly, he suggested that the northern colonies would never be free of mutual suspicion and conflict until some procedures could be established to remove jealousies and adjudicate disputes. Local governors should be permitted "to send or cause to reside with each other such person or persons as they shall see meet" to negotiate points of dispute and bear witness that each side was keeping faith.[54]

Viewed in the context of Nelson's career, the memorial clearly aimed to promote English interests in a way that would also advance his own.

It resurrected the French proposal for a local neutrality, but in language that avoided mention of the word that had just raised so many hackles in Whitehall. It kept alive the tradition of handling matters according to the ways of Sir Thomas Temple. And it brought into a single focus many of the different facets of Nelson's past—his long-standing involvement in Acadia's fishing and Indian trade, his service as French agent during the early 1680s in selling fishing licenses, his negotiations with Quebec, and his ambition to act as middleman and merchant-adventurer between New England and New France. One feature of Nelson's years in London that undoubtedly recommended him to English officials (and certainly set him apart from other colonists then treading the corridors of Whitehall), was that he never directly solicited for office or some other token of personal advantage. Small wonder the worldly James Vernon "could never tell what to make of him."[55] Between the lines, however, Nelson was promoting himself, but in subtler fashion, by seeking to define the terms of trade and international relations in ways advantageous to his own particular talents and experience. Disdaining political position himself, he sought to shape a situation where politicians would be led to favor what he could best offer.

The memorial also helps explain what otherwise seems inexplicable: Nelson's casual statement upon submitting it to the Board of Trade that he was off to France "on his own private occasions" and would send back from there any further information "that can be for the advantage of England."[56] True, the conclusion of peace had removed the barriers to travel on both sides of the Channel, and Nelson now took care to secure official permission for his journey. A note written to John Locke reveals that the aged philosopher had commissioned him to bring back a parcel of books from Paris.[57] It may be that Nelson, recalling the French government's rejection of his impudent request to see the sights of Paris upon his release from the Bastille, had resolved to spend a Christmas in Paris at last. More probably, however, his central purpose was to refresh his contacts there, both official and unofficial, and to discover whether his advice offered in London meshed with any measures planned by Versailles. Might the way now be open for him to become New England's "resident" in Quebec, in the manner of the renowned merchant-ambassadors—Jenkinson, Roe, and Harborne—who had set the pace of English commercial expansion into such regions as Russia, India, and the Levant? Or, less fancifully, could he at least revive the trade that New England merchants had enjoyed with Canada and Acadia before the events of 1689?

Whether or not such thoughts inspired Nelson's visit to Paris—and the case rests more on supposition than evidence—the visit's outcome suggests that they met with, at best, only unofficial encouragement. In a letter sent to the Board of Trade from Paris in early December, Nelson made no further mention of his hopes to apportion the fisheries and permit the adjudication of disputes. Instead, he reported that the French intended to claim the Kennebec as Acadia's western border; a claim that, once admitted, would be as "fatall and irreparable" a blow to English interests as the surrender of Acadia thirty years before. Indian enemies would be encouraged and precious lands and timber lost. At the least, the French must be brought to accept the boundary accepted in Sir Thomas Temple's time, at the St. George River forty miles farther east. As for the fisheries, nothing but a vigorous assertion of traditional English rights would suffice. From hopes for compromise and cooperation, Nelson retreated to the belligerent nationalism of his first months in London.[58]

Amid these disappointments, we can at least imagine Nelson passing Christmas in Paris with his old friend Meneval, eight years after he had spent the same season trying to extricate the former governor of Port Royal from Phips's clutches in Boston. If so, they must have vied with each other in relating the trials of their respective captivities. One Canadian friendship that Nelson certainly renewed was with Pierre Le Moyne D'Iberville, fresh from yet another conquest of the English forces in Hudson Bay and recalled to France to prepare an expedition to the mouth of the Mississippi River. Together, the two men paid a visit early in the new year to the home of Nicholas Toinard, John Locke's principal correspondent in Paris and, like Iberville, a warm admirer of Nelson's exploits. Toinard was a keen collector of information about America and he relished, he told Locke, the company of two such celebrities and the adventures they related. But there were no more formal negotiations. By February 1698, Nelson was back in London, after a tempestuous winter crossing of the Channel that left all his baggage, including the books destined for John Locke, waterlogged. Take care to dry the books, he told Locke, and "I hope you will rather receive satisfaction from my escape which was great than be concerned about your Damage."[59] By then, too, he was at last on the point of leaving for America, perhaps by way of the fleet that set out each spring for New Hampshire's Piscataqua River to bring back masts and other stores for the Royal Navy. Five and a half years after his arrival in Europe, he left it as quietly as he had come, never to return.

a friendship later sealed by the marriage of Lloyd's eldest surviving son to John and Elizabeth Nelson's daughter Rebecca.[3]

Nelson returned to a Massachusetts formally restored to peace with France by the Treaty of Ryswick but still disturbed by border clashes with the eastern Indians. Its new governor, the Earl of Bellomont, had reached New York earlier in the year, only to remain in that factious corner of his three-province government until the following May, leaving Boston's government in the experienced but increasingly palsied hands of Lieutenant Governor William Stoughton. Eager to receive and honor Bellomont (an Irish peer known for his belligerent Whiggism), frustrated Massachusetts legislators were reduced to debating the form and meaning of the coat of arms with which the earl sealed his letters from New York.[4]

With Stoughton's patronage, Nelson quickly resurrected the very issue that had precipitated his abrupt departure from America—the vexed question of Massachusetts' ties with Acadia. Indeed, the first surviving record of his return to America found him already reimmersed in eastern waters, as if unable to resist their call. Whether by splendid irony or a keen sense of occasion, he reached the mouth of the St. John River in mid-September of 1698, reentering his old commercial world at the very portal through which, seven years earlier almost to the day, he had descended into the purgatory of imprisonment. To complete the symmetry, his hosts at the St. John River were the same two officers, Governor Robinau de Villebon and frigate captain Denys de Bonaventure, who had trapped and captured him back in 1691.[5] By Villebon's account, Nelson's main cargo was news and correspondence, and his intention was to voyage farther north, as far as Quebec. But the winter was already closing in. In Quebec, old Governor Frontenac lay dying. By late October, Nelson was back in Boston and at work drafting a report, to be shared with Massachusetts officials and with London, on French intentions and their consequences for New England's relations with Acadia.[6]

As Nelson recognized, these relations had survived his absence, even during the open warfare of the 1690s. From Boston, wily traders like the elder John Alden, or Huguenot merchants with ties to both sides like David Basset, Gabriel Bernon, Andrew Faneuil, and Pierre Baudouin (founder of the famous Bowdoin family) had used the exchange of captives or special licenses to skirt official embargoes and keep the lines of commerce open. The Acadians were equally active on their own account. With Governor Villebon unable to govern the colony with any degree of rigor, many were quite willing to trade and sail under English colors in moments when they felt most in need of the Bay Colony's supplies. Even the redoubtable Saint-Castin, it was said, had at one point taken an oath to live as a neutral and not to bear arms against the English. And with Pemaquid dismantled, the baron soon resumed a regular commerce with New England.[7] Poor harvests in Acadia during the last years of the century further increased this dependence, although sceptical French officials preferred to blame the colony's scarcities on its settlers' passion for hunting, Indian trading, and idle debauchery "dans la profondeur des bois" instead of honest agricultural toil. Part of the problem, however, lay in officialdom itself; for word continued to filter back to Paris that Governor Villebon was as active as his predecessors in turning a (bribed) blind eye to illegal trade and using his official position to conduct his own commercial ventures.[8]

Nelson had no reason to disturb this interwoven network of accommodation, assuming that he could regain some share of the action. But with his sense of the larger international context sharpened by his years in Europe, he argued that immediate action was essential lest peace be the ruin of this small prosperity. From a sight of Villebon's instructions and from a letter the governor had sent to Boston, Nelson knew that French officials were determined to return to their interpretation of the letter of the 1686 Treaty of Neutrality, one extending Acadia's boundaries west to the Kennebec and so far out to sea that it would cripple New England's fisheries.[9] Already, French patrols were back at their old game of seizing English fishing boats found in offshore waters. The matter was doubly urgent since, as Nelson pointed out, it was certain to be on the agenda of the Anglo–French commission set up by the Treaty of Ryswick to adjudicate American disputes. Back in Boston, in a volley of letters to London, Nelson urged "vigorous and resolute measures" against French "pretensions and innovations" that he presented as part and parcel of a larger imperialism. What France sought in America, he told the Board of Trade, paralleled its designs on its European neighbors; not just New England's interests but those of the whole English nation were at stake, because of the value of North America's forests and fisheries for England's balance of trade. Among the letters, sent by way of his London cousin, John Pascal, was a personal appeal to William Blathwayt as the one man in England with enough knowledge of "the Affairs of America" to rebut French claims at the conference table. Lieutenant Governor Stoughton added official endorsement of Nelson's arguments, and the Massachusetts General Court prepared an address to King William that rehearsed them in more sonorous and apocalyptic language.[10]

For a few weeks, Nelson stood at center stage, prompting and shaping his province's policies. In late November, he presented a petition to the General Court that told of his imprisonment and of his labors in gathering French captives to procure his release and redeeming Englishmen held by the French. The Court voted him the thanks of the province and a payment of a hundred pounds, symbolic reparation of the kind that the Court would later pay to victims of the Salem Village witchcraft trials.[11] In London, the Board of Trade responded to the appeals from Boston by digesting Nelson's memorials of the past two years into the centerpiece of a massive summary of England's territorial claims in North America.[12]

The months that followed, however, brought, not a new chapter of Anglo–colonial cooperation, but a reprise of the pattern of earlier years. The Anglo–French commissioners in London wrangled into the new century over Acadia's boundaries—at one point, the French offered to accept the line of the St. George River in return for a moderation of English claims in Hudson Bay.[13] But the matter was no closer to a resolution when Louis XIV[e]'s resolve to secure the Spanish throne for his grandson plunged the Atlantic world back into war in 1701.

In America, meanwhile, as in the early 1680s, signs of a local accommodation emerged from behind the official exchange of irreconcilable positions. Villebon was keenly conscious of his colony's exposed and dependent position; he applied to Paris for authority to revive the old licensing system so that English boats fishing out of sight of land could purchase permission to come onshore for supplies or to cure their catch. Such an arrangement, he argued, would produce a useful income for Acadia's government. It would give both sides an incentive to maintain good order in the fisheries at the expense of the pirates and renegades who menaced the coastal settlements.[14] The governor did not wait for a reply before opening channels to New England: with his garrison reduced (as he informed Paris) to a diet of shellfish, he wrote an urgent letter to Nelson in the spring of 1699 requesting a cargo of wheat and other supplies. Payment would be in the form of "good peltry" and a permit to fish. Nelson himself would be welcome: "I hope we may see you heere in a short time, when I hope our new wine may be arrived to assure you with our glasses in hand that we are, Sir, your most humble servants." In a postscript, Villebon conveyed his respects to "Madam Nelson and your daughters," enclosed a letter from young Perrot "who was inconsolable in not seeing of you last yeare," and enquired whether Nelson could extract from Sir William Phips's widow some last pieces of Port Royal plunder—Villebon's army service records.[15]

The letter reached Nelson just as the Earl of Bellomont, gout-stricken and unable to walk, finally entered Boston to assume his governorship in a lavish ceremony attended by vast crowds and punctuated by the music of drums, trumpets, cannon, and fireworks. Showing a greater respect for royal authority than he had in the time of Andros, Nelson applied to the earl and his council for permission to export the grain. In June, after the council had debated Acadia's plight, he was authorized to send the cargo.[16] But there is no evidence that he accompanied it or ever got a taste of Villebon's new wine. One surviving document suggests a plan to take advantage of any new licensing system: late in 1699, the selectmen of the town of Hull granted Nelson a site on the southeastern corner of Boston Bay, two miles from his Long Island home, where he could construct "wharves, warehouses, and other houses convenient for the promoting of the fishing trade." The venture would probably have been run by Captain Sylvanus Davis, a veteran soldier and Indian-trader who had recently retired from a stormy career on the Maine frontier to live in Hull and enter Nelson's employ.[17] If so, the enterprise was still born—and Davis died in 1703. Moreover, although official circles in Paris were surprisingly sympathetic to Villebon's licensing scheme, the resumption of war with England made its formal acceptance impossible.

Nelson had known Bellomont back in London, and, once reac-quainted, he quickly responded to the earl's request for advice on New England's eastern affairs. He drafted a lengthy memorial setting out the background of the Acadian boundary dispute and his reasons why En-glish claims could not reasonably extend beyond the St. George River. We must, he told the governor, both guard against and yet endeavor to befriend the French in Acadia; in like manner, the eastern Indians could be wooed with fair trading and English missionaries—"our neg-ligence herein has been both scandelous and fatall."[18] Later in the fall of 1699, he joined with Sylvanus Davis in a second memorial endorsing the policy just enacted by the General Court of government control of the Indian trade coupled with a ban on private trading. While the policy drew on earlier attempts to regulate relations with the tribes, it repre-sented the first sustained attempt by any of the English colonies to use and subsidize Indian trade as an instrument of diplomacy. Along the eastern frontier, from the Merrimac to Casco Bay, was established a network of officially supervised and financed "truckhouses" for trade, equipped with resources ranging from blacksmiths ready to mend the Indians' weapons to ministers eager to repair the damage wrought by popery on their souls.[19] In time, this strategy would succeed in drawing the tribes bordering New England into a new dependence on English ways and resources. In light of Nelson's long-standing insistence on the importance of weaning the Indians from French influence, it seems reasonable to assume—in the absence of proof—that the development of this policy so soon after his return from England embodied his advice and perhaps his handiwork. Two years later, he was chosen as one of four commissioners sent to Casco Bay to negotiate on matters of trade, religion, captives, and peace with six Abenaki leaders.[20]

At the turn of the century, therefore, Nelson's reputation stood high in both Boston and London. The Board of Trade still cherished his memorials; Massachusetts leaders praised his expertise and sought his endorsement of their policies. Back in the 1680s, his efforts to trade and mediate between French and English America had left him politically isolated and vulnerable to popular suspicion. In the aftermath of 1689, however, his embrace of a more militant English patriotism had brought him into growing harmony with his fellow colonists, as they in turn began to perceive both the scale of New England's travail, and the necessity of English diplomatic and military aid for its resolution. Boston's turn to seek such aid revealed the change that war, a Protestant succession, and a common enemy had wrought in the old hostility between Bay Colony and Crown; it also gave a new importance to the services of those, like Nelson, deemed experienced in the ways of the powerful on both sides of the ocean and able to act as agents and intermediaries on the colonists' behalf. Whitehall, for its part, had already shown its readiness to reward New Englanders willing to solicit for office.[21] Had Nelson put himself forward, given his political and family connections in both Old and New England, he might well have gained some political post in London's gift, a vice-admiralty judgeship or command of a province annexed by conquest, perhaps even the governorship of Massachusetts, left vacant by the deaths of Bellomont and Stoughton during the spring of 1701.

Such possibilities, however, were never put to the test. Instead, during the early years of the new century, Nelson steadily withdrew from public affairs and back into private life. In part, no doubt, he found his political effectiveness still hobbled by his lingering reputation as an outsider and free spirit. To judge by the number of Boston and Salem merchants

---

Facing page. John Bonner's map of Boston, 1722. John and Elizabeth Nelson owned houses on Hanover Street, a site just below the Mill Pond on the map and now occupied by Boston's new City Hall, and on Merchants' Row, adjoining the Town Dock and close to what is now Faneuil Hall. (*Courtesy of the New York Public Library*)

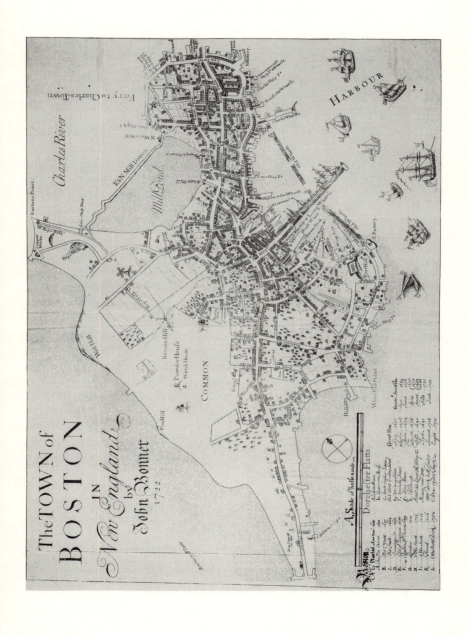

elected to Governor Bellomont's council, the old popular prejudice against mercantile involvement in politics had largely disappeared. But not only was Nelson a particularly suspect kind of merchant, he remained an Anglican in a political world dominated by Puritan Congregationalists and a man seemingly too familiar with French men and measures for his own or his country's good. He would never win elective office. Nor, on the other hand, would he turn aside to seek it: for all his emergence as a public figure, he acquired neither the commitment to public life that kept men like William Stoughton and Samuel Sewall Massachusetts magistrates for most of their adult lives, nor the passionate thirst for political power that drove exiled Dominion official Joseph Dudley to solicit ceaselessly through the corridors of Whitehall until his eventual return in triumph to his native land in 1702 as Bellomont's successor as governor of Massachusetts.

Whatever Nelson's political limitations, both imposed and self-imposed, he had always been able to plunge back into the waters of eastward trade that had been his world since boyhood. Now even this central current of his life began to slacken, as age (he was nearly fifty), past hardships, and a renewed domesticity turned his course back within more constricted horizons. Late in 1699, he and Elizabeth sold the two houses they owned in downtown Boston, on the "Long Back Street" below Beacon Hill and on Merchants' Row by the Town Dock, and took up what became permanent residence on their Long Island estate out in Boston Harbor.[22] Domestic cares took on new meaning as Elizabeth bore two sons to add to the couple's four daughters, sons whose names—Temple and Paschal—honored the family's transatlantic rather than provincial kin. Even the proffer of an official position could not shake Nelson's resolve to stay and cultivate his island: though named to the 1702 commission for justices of the peace in Suffolk County and to almost every subsequent commission for the next three decades, he was never recorded as having taken the oath of office and his name never once appeared among those of the justices listed as presiding over the Court's regular sessions in Boston.[23]

Nelson's withdrawal both from public life and from the prying eyes of Boston society make it difficult to assess how quickly he completed his refashioning from Captain John Nelson, frontier trader, to John Nelson, Esquire, country gentleman of leisure. Long Island remained a fine spot at which to offload a few surreptitious cargoes before completing Customs formalities in downtown Boston. But circumstances seem to have accelerated Nelson's disengagement from trade. His old ally and drinking companion, Acadia's Governor Villebon—Nelson's friendliest enemy—died in the summer of 1700, to be succeeded by a tough old soldier, Jacques-François Monbeton de Brouillan, who scorned ties with the enemy in favor of refortifying Port Royal. Another longtime trading partner, Saint-Castin, left for France the following year, where he excused himself from charges of dealings with the English only to become so entangled with French lawyers over the disposition of his family's estates and titles that he was compelled to remain there, a free spirit held fast in parchment bonds, until his death in 1707. In the meantime, war once again disrupted commerce with the eastward, as Governor Dudley retaliated against French and Indian raids on Maine and northern Massachusetts with seaborne expeditions that ravaged the settlements around the Bay of Fundy, and, in 1707, unsuccessfully besieged Port Royal. As for the Indian trade, Nelson could hardly attempt to revive it without contravening both the new laws forbidding such commerce and his own expressed support for the truckhouse system run under government supervision. His only known involvement with Acadia in these years resembled not so much a commercial venture as a gentleman's satisfaction of a debt of honor: in 1706, Denys de Bonaventure reported that Nelson, to whom he had lent five thousand livres during Nelson's imprisonment in France, had sought to repay the debt by sending him a cargo of cloth and hardware valued at thirteen hundred livres (about £100 New England money), a cargo he—Bonaventure—had then retailed to his fellow Port Royallers at so modest a profit (fifteen percent) that he hoped Paris would bless the enterprise.[24]

This is not to suggest that trade to the eastward ceased. But as the hand of government came to dominate the collision of empires in America, such commerce increasingly became the preserve of merchants with good political connections who could take advantage of such ostensibly official occasions as the exchange of prisoners and diplomatic correspondence—a circle in which Nelson had never cared, and had certainly ceased, to move. As Bonaventure scornfully noted, some traders were deliberately arranging for prisoners to be doled out in small numbers in order to increase the number of passports issued for voyages that could serve as a cover for trade. Yet Bonaventure's own younger brother, Louis Denys de la Ronde, had just returned from such a voyage, and a mission to Boston the previous year by another French officer, Augustin de Le Gardeur de Courtemanche, which was launched with the aim of resurrecting the old scheme of a neutrality in North America, had quickly sparked charges that its real purpose was a revival of private trade.[25] The situation flared into open scandal in Massachusetts in 1706 when six merchants with close ties to Governor Dudley were imprisoned and heavily fined by an enraged Massachusetts General Court on charges of trading with the enemy in time of war.[26]

Nelson was not completely divorced from these events. He appeared as an expert witness in a case involving the quality of a cargo of beaver skins brought from Acadia; and he joined nearly fifty other Massachusetts merchants in protesting the release of a notorious French privateer operating out of Port Royal. With John Alden, Jr.—his former fellow captive in France—he came to the aid of Samuel Vetch, one of the merchants charged in the trading scandal, with a deposition presenting the ingenious but implausible argument that the Acadian Indians Vetch had dealt with were not hostile to England and could be viewed as English subjects by reason of Sir Thomas Temple's patent.[27] But that was the limit of his involvement in the scandal; and perhaps the best testimony to Nelson's withdrawal from eastern trading was the fact that, at a time of what one contemporary called "a horrid combustion" about such trade, Nelson—long one of the usual suspects—was never implicated.[28]

Instead, Samuel Vetch and his associates bore the brunt of public fury; and Vetch, the man whom Nelson and Alden had defended, proved to be Nelson's spiritual successor in other ways as well, by his adoption (and with greater success) of many of the schemes Nelson had put forward in the 1690s. The son of a Scottish Presbyterian minister fiercely opposed to Stuart rule, Vetch had served in William of Orange's invasion of England and in the English army in Flanders. He arrived in New York in 1699 as a survivor of the ill-fated attempt to settle a colony of Scots at Darien in Central America. Marriage into the prominent Livingston family, together with a cargo of goods saved from the wreck of the Darien Company, set him up as a merchant in New York with dealings in the lucrative illegal trade with Canada. Moving to Boston in 1705, he swiftly became the "particular friend" of Governor Joseph Dudley, whose younger son accompanied him and the French emissary, Courtemanche, upon the latter's return to Quebec later in the year. It was these connections, along with a trading trip to Acadia the following spring, that exposed Vetch to prosecution and punishment at the hands of the Massachusetts General Court.[29]

But Vetch was a man of exceptional vision and resource. Even before his prosecution, he had sent to London a set of proposals to provide security for New England and a fresh outlet for his fellow countrymen's energies by planting a colony of Scots in Canada and additional settlements in Maine.[30] Arriving in England in 1707 to press an appeal against his conviction, he submitted a much more detailed scheme that set the plan for Scottish settlement within a proposal for a full-scale Anglo-colonial assault on French Canada. By comparison with Nelson's memorials of the 1690s, Vetch's "Canada Survey'd" was less cogent in its analysis of the nature of French Canada, the weakness of the northern colonies, and the role of Indian relations. But its central theme of how a modest investment in the conquest of a small number of Frenchmen would pay huge dividends to England and "the whole British Empire in America" was far better calculated to appeal to an official English audience. Not only, Vetch argued, would the northern English colonies be freed from the wasting attacks by land and sea that were impeding their development, but they would then be able to fill their proper imperial role of supplying provisions to the Caribbean colonies and importing English manufactured goods. The conquest of Canada would open the way for Englishmen to dominate the transatlantic trade in fish, furs, and naval stores, swelling the mother country's wealth, power, and balance of trade. Finally, Vetch drew on his military expertise to present a plausible plan of campaign. He endorsed the strategy first advanced by New Yorkers and the Iroquois in 1690 for a two-pronged attack, by land from Albany and by sea against Port Royal and down the St. Lawrence River; and, after listing and assessing French resources, he requested a precise number of English ships and regular troops to lead colonial forces in the seaborne assault.[31]

Wide-ranging in his assessment of the means and ends of his objective, Vetch also displayed a remarkable talent for winning endorsements for his plan from across the spectrum of Anglo–American opinion, ranging from government ministers in England and Scotland, to colonial leaders as far south as Pennsylvania, and even his own and Governor Dudley's political opponents in Massachusetts. He formed an unlikely but politically potent alliance with the former lieutenant governor of Andros' Dominion, Francis Nicholson, an ardent Anglican and royalist recently returned from a stormy term as lieutenant governor of Virginia. Together the two returned to New England in the spring of 1709 with news of the Crown's endorsement of the project and their inclusion in its leadership.

Vetch and Nicholson found a Massachusetts remarkably eager to admit royal forces into a share of conquering lands long jealously preserved within its own particular sphere of influence. Cotton Mather, for example, backed the project for Scottish settlement, and Samuel Sewall, his dreams troubled by menacing flocks of Frenchmen, endorsed a royal takeover of Acadia.[32] But the next two years revealed the practical impediments to turning enthusiasm into achievement. Through the summer of 1709, hundreds of colonial troops mustered in Boston and north of Albany, only to find that the promised forces from England never arrived. In the following year, after more lobbying by Vetch and Nicholson, a smaller force did appear and, with colonial assistance, easily won the surrender of the small French garrison of Port Royal. Vetch was left as governor over the new Crown Colony of Nova Scotia. Finally, in the summer of 1711, a full-size force of English troops and warships reached Boston, embarked several colonial regiments, and set sail for Canada, only to encounter shipwreck and disaster in dense fog at the mouth of the St. Lawrence River. Almost half a century would pass before the English finally conquered Quebec.

These were projects that Nelson had spent much of his life—and a portion of his liberty—trying to advance. Yet his involvement in them was minimal. Echoes of his ideas emerged, most strikingly when five Iroquois leaders were brought to Boston to inspect the assembled troops and when four more Iroquois were escorted to London in 1710, where they became the sensation of the spring season and helped reinforce the colonists' pleas for aid. By comparison with Nelson's argument for such visits ten years before, however, their effect was less that of impressing the Indians with England's might than of convincing Englishmen of the strength and glamor of the colonial cause.[33] One report listed Nelson as a volunteer for the Canada expedition planned for 1709; but if so, he left the field to his brother-in-law, William Tailer, who commanded one of the two Massachusetts regiments present at the capture of Port Royal. Nor was Nelson among the seventy-two subscribers who lent forty thousand pounds to the province to defray the costs of the 1711 expedition.[34] Instead, the only commodity he furnished was advice: when the main English forces reached Boston in the summer of 1711, their commander, the fretful and incompetent Sir Hovenden Walker, twice consulted with "Mr. Nelson of Long-Island . . . a Person of good Sense and well acquainted with the Interest and Affairs of these parts of America," on matters concerning Acadia and the navigation of the St. Lawrence River.[35] If Walker had hoped to persuade Nelson to accompany the expedition, he failed—and the fleet entered the St. Lawrence under the guidance of pilots who led it onto the rocks.

Plainly, not even the resurrection of causes once so dear to him could lure Nelson back into public life. More than fifty years of age—an old man by the standards of the time—but with another quarter century of life left to him, he was now emphatically "John Nelson, Gentleman." He remained a frequent visitor to downtown Boston: on business, attending the Anglican services at Queen's (formerly King's) Chapel, or dining with his friends—Samuel Sewall recorded several evenings spent

Philippe de Vaudreuil, Governor of French Canada from 1703 to 1725, and correspondent of John Nelson. A portrait by Henri Beau. (*Courtesy of the National Archives of Canada*)

in Nelson's company at the home of the wealthy merchant Simeon Stoddard.[36] His business, however, now was not so much with commercial matters as with the services one gentleman could render another. There was, for example, the thankless task (one that blighted Cotton Mather's later years) of serving as executor and administrator of his friends' estates. The settlement of one such estate, that of his father-in-law's old business partner, Richard Wharton, dragged on for more than two decades, enmeshing Nelson in a string of suits and accountings, and "much inquietude."[37] Unhappily, Wharton's farflung property dealings had brought the estate into conflict with the formidable figure of Nathaniel Blagrove, one of a trio of extraordinarily contentious and politically active landowners in southeastern Massachusetts—Blagrove, Nathaniel Byfield, and John Saffin—each one locked in mortal combat with the other two. Blagrove seems to have relished and prolonged the affair because he saw it as a way of annoying Byfield, whose daughter had married Nelson's brother-in-law, William Tailer. At one point, marooned on his island and compelled to default in a suit by "the then Extremity of the Weather," Nelson had to turn to the Massachusetts General Court for special relief.[38]

Less onerous, and more gratifying, were the services that Nelson found himself able to render to old acquaintances outside New England. Over several decades, he served as a kind of unofficial French chargé d'affaires in Boston, providing funds to Frenchmen in difficulties or in the midst of negotiations, and, on one occasion, forwarding the ransom demanded for an English merchant captured by French forces in Newfoundland. When, in 1721, the English at last successfully kidnapped a Saint-Castin—Joseph, a son of the object of Phips's plot—it was Nelson who lent him money, later repaid by the Quebec government.[39]

These services led in turn to a correspondence with New France's highest official, Philippe de Rigaud de Vaudreuil, the colony's governor from 1703 until his death in 1725. It began at a level mildly embarassing for Nelson—and indicative of the entanglement of his finances following his return from Europe—as Vaudreuil politely pressed him to use the visits of French emissaries to New England to repay various sums of money he owed.[40] But subsequent letters combined broader issues with a genuine personal warmth, as when the two exchanged news of the health of the governor's mother-in-law, widow of the Pierre de Joybert de Soulanges et de Marson who had traded with Nelson from Acadia in the 1670s. Indeed, Nelson must have known her daughter, Vaudreuil's young and highly capable wife, Louise-Elizabeth, when the latter was an infant at play on the banks of the St. John River.[41]

Vaudreuil, however, had other motives for writing besides collecting debts and swapping reminiscences. Playing on Nelson's well-known interest in redeeming captives, he sought to open a line of communication to New England separate from the negotiations he was then conducting with the Boston government over its renewed border war with France's Abenaki allies in Maine. By the 1713 Treaty of Utrecht following the English capture of Port Royal, France had surrendered Acadia "within its ancient boundaries," but without these boundaries' being defined. Facing the same dilemma that had beset Sir Thomas Temple back in the 1660s, the French found new merit in the very argument that Sir Thomas had advanced (and they had then stoutly denied), that "Acadia" was only the Nova Scotian peninsula and did not include the mainland west of the Bay of Fundy. They could thereby retain their alliance with the Abenaki tribes and protect the strategic river system that covered the southern approaches to the St. Lawrence. The English, for their part, now embraced the old French definition of Acadia, which placed the Abenaki within their sovereignty; and Vaudreuil's efforts to enlist Nelson came on the heels of a famous (or, in French eyes, infamous) episode in which a Massachusetts expedition had stormed the Indian settlement at Norridgewock on the upper Kennebec, killing and scalping the French Jesuit missionary, Father Sébastian Rale, whom the English saw as the black-robed evil genius behind Abenaki resistance. Replying to Vaudreuil, Nelson firmly rejected any diplomatic role—"I stand wholly unconcerned in such matters and must refer you to what you receive from the government"—and defended English claims and conduct. Father Rale was "a principle Incendiarie in these unhapie ruptures." Yet Nelson remained eager to aid in the redemption of captives; and, looking back to the many Frenchmen who had enjoyed his hospitality in Boston, he proposed a regular exchange of such visitors as a means of reducing tensions between the two sides.[42] In another letter written in the same elegiac vein, probably to one of his old friend Robinau de Villebon's numerous brothers, Nelson cherished the memory of past "civilities" between them, deplored present discord, and looked forward to a time when their children could serve as "instruments of peace and humanity to all mankind."[43]

Nelson's high hopes for a future generation were utopian. Yet they were more than the passing courtesies of one aging man to another. For they epitomized a devotion to children and family, reconciling past and present to provide for the future, that emerged as the central theme of the last decades of Nelson's life. To some degree, perhaps, this theme's prominence is inflated by the happy accident of the survival of part of his family's correspondence for these years in the papers of the Lloyds of New York. Yet the material only adds depth and detail to the conclusion evident from other sources—that John Nelson's final and most fulfilling role was that of patriarch and paterfamilias. From following by choice and then necessity a lonely road—forsaking his English family for Boston and then his Bostonian family for England—he turned with relish and affection to the pursuit of domestic tranquillity.

The role of latter-day Abraham, surrounded by children, bondsmen, flocks, and fields, matched the pastoral circumstances of Nelson's Long Island life. His manor house, barns, and dock have long since vanished beneath successive waves of building, of Civil War–era forts and barracks, and of the hospital (once an almshouse) that now sprawls across the island. From five years after Nelson's death, however, an inventory reconstructs some of the shape and character of the family home. There were five bedchambers on the upper floor, and the lower floor centered around a "Great Room" with, among other items, two French walnut tables, twelve "turkey worked" chairs, an "umbrello" valued at ten shillings, and a huge copper or boiling kettle weighing a hundred and seventy pounds. Other furnishings that may have graced the house— mezzotint pictures; family portraits; maps of Flanders, Boston, and the world; a large speaking trumpet; and the family silver—were part of a separate accounting. Among the island's stock and crops were quantities of hay and barley; a few horses, cows, and pigs; and four hundred and twenty sheep. Communication with downtown Boston, at times when it was not imperilled by the winter ice that formed around the island, was by way of a sloop, a lighter, a canoe, and a dilapidated pinnace.[44]

To work this country estate, Nelson employed indentured servants and black slaves. Their number and functions are unclear—the same inventory of 1739 lists one young white apprentice with four years to serve and five black male slaves, ranging from Will, "very old" and valued at ten pounds, to four others—Jack, Boston, London, and Cor-idon—valued at one to two hundred pounds each. Together the six men's worth was inventoried at six hundred pounds—a little more than that of all the other livestock put together.[45] During Nelson's lifetime, how-ever, his servants take the stage more as problems than as assets—the maid, Penny, was plagued with "very Grevious fits"; Sam, "Mr. Nelson's Negro," was accused of stealing powder, shot, and clothing from a ship moored at a Boston wharf; and indentured servant William Bartell had to be rescued by Nelson from charges of cursing, molesting women, and breaking Boston shop-windows in 1721. Two years later, Bartell sued Nelson for failing to provide him with two suits of clothing, one for every-day and one for Sabbath-day wear, at the end of his term of service.[46] Through Henry Lloyd, his son-in-law, Nelson also took part in the saga of Lloyd's slave Obium (or Opium): hired out to three different masters during the 1690s, a runaway (on horseback), and placed with Nelson on Long Island, Obium then proved reluctant to return to Lloyd. Nelson, however, soothed his fears and sent him back with advice to Lloyd that flattery and good treatment were all that was needed to make him tractable.[47] Not all such problems were as humanely solved. "We have got Will and Sam with cost & trouble," wrote Nelson's daughter in 1719. "Sambo we sell and keep the other for his wife sake." This was not the impersonal gang-labor of Southern plantations, and the Nelsons resembled other upper-crust New England families of their time in using black as well as white bound labor in their fields and houses. But they were typical also in never questioning the buying and selling, the dehumanization and legalized license for abuse, that such servitude entailed.[48]

In these surroundings, and served by these anonymous lives, the Nelsons and their children created an affectionate, close-knit, and introspective family community. As the four daughters, Rebecca, Elizabeth, Mehitable, and Margaret—Beckie, Betty, Hittie, and Peggie in the family's letters—married, moved away, and had children, they were followed by their parents' fond concern. Family members gathered to assist in childbirths, paid summer visits, and took charge of each other's children. "Give my love to dear Beckie," wrote Nelson to her husband, Henry Lloyd, "and tell her that I charge her not in any wayes to interupt the Stipulations made between Peggie and us, concerning the return of Hary [Nelson's grandson], without whom we can not now Enjoye our Selves." Young Harry returned to live with his grandparents and become "the most agreable & pleasant Child in the world, Soe that you must in noe waies think of removeing him from us. . . . Give Becky a Kiss on my behalf & tell her I love her very dearly."[49] His easy modulation from "I" to "we" plainly included and yet subordinated Elizabeth Tailer Nelson—who was referred to as "your mother" and "my wife," but whose distinct opinions were never recorded. Perhaps Elizabeth, unlike her daughters, never learned to write beyond her signature. Equally plainly, however, she stood with her husband at the center of the family circle, one that paid little attention to unrelated outsiders, as the Nelsons and their kin kept to themselves, even in matters of business. Few other visitors came to the island, and then more by chance than invitation, as when Samuel Sewall stopped by on a voyage to Maine in 1717 and received some provisions from Nelson "with which Mrs. Baxter made very good Chokelat."[50]

Nelson's very devotion to family and Long Island life imposed its own particular cost. Detached from public and commercial affairs, he yet had daughters to place in marriage and sons to establish in the world at large, responsibilities to be fulfilled in ways befitting the family's station in society. Moreover, all too much of the evidence of his later years—the lawsuits pressing him to fulfill his obligations, the retrenchment to Long Island, and the plaintive note sounded in some of his letters—suggests that his old prosperity never fully recovered from the burdens imposed by his capture and release.[51] Paschal Nelson surely exaggerated in remembering his father as "sacrificed, vexed & ruined" by his ordeal, but his more temperate conclusion rings true: Nelson returned to find that "his private affairs were involved, mortgaged, and in Confusion, and he never retrieved them higher than to support himself and his Family properly."[52] All four daughters found husbands but, by contemporary standards, belatedly and not within the ranks of leading Boston families. Nor, it would seem, was their father able during his lifetime to pay more than part of the five hundred pounds he had pledged to each of them as dowries. The death of Lieutenant Governor William Stoughton, Elizabeth Nelson's uncle, provided an inheritance that helped defray Paschal's bills at Harvard and retired a large mortgage on the Long Island property. There were hopes that lands in Pennsylvania and a tract on the Kennebec inherited from Sir Thomas Temple could be sold to advantage.[53] By 1720, Nelson was able to assure his daughter Rebecca that "you greve too much at the Apprehension of the ill Estate of my Affaires, wherein I can safly assure you that I have in a maner gone thro' all my difficulties and am in a good prospect of makeing you in some measure sensible of it." But as his family ruefully noted in later years, their father's legacy amounted to little more than his estate, literally defined—Long Island, its fields, manor house, and flocks of sheep.[54]

Others in his circumstances might have looked to their reputation and connections for help. In a time of war and the administrative inflation it entailed, there were supply contracts to be won and positions open to those who sought them. A small-time merchant like Andrew Belcher could rise to wealth and the founding of a political dynasty; a Samuel Vetch could become an outpost governor.[55] But Nelson had never had the stomach or the ambition to be a courtier. Instead, the few and halfheartedly pressed strategies by which he tried to revive his family's fortunes harked back to his Temple heritage rather than to his New World circumstances, to a fading age of gentlemen proprietors and independent entrepreneurs.

One such strategy grew out of a reluctant involvement in province politics through his ambitious brother-in-law, Colonel William Tailer. After service at the capture of Port Royal in 1710, Tailer had left for London in the train of General Francis Nicholson, "bigg with expectations of his doing for him." And there, indeed, Nicholson's patronage had won him the position of Massachusetts' lieutenant governor, to the surprise and resentment of Jeremiah Dummer, the province's resident agent at court.[56] In terms of provincial politics, this represented a notable advance for the Anglican faction centered around Queen's Chapel in Boston. To secure the governorship of Massachusetts in succession to

Bellomont, Joseph Dudley had sworn to High Anglican heaven that he would promote the interests of Church of England once in office. With other officers of Queen's Chapel, Nelson and Tailer had backed the governor in his early political conflicts like the trading scandal by testifying to London in his favor.[57] By the time of Tailer's appointment, however, Dudley's pragmatic efforts to pose as an equally faithful member of his province's Puritan majority had brought disillusionment, to the point that some Anglicans even turned to ally themselves with the Mathers' campaign to topple Dudley from power. It was at this point that Cotton Mather conceived of mending his fences with Nelson by explaining his entire innocence of Sir William Phips's plot twenty years before.[58]

Whether this olive branch from Mather was accepted—or even extended—is unknown, but Tailer, once installed as lieutenant governor, entered into a wary coalition with Dudley that lasted for several years. In 1714, however, open warfare erupted between the two men and their respective supporters as political changes in England seemed to presage Dudley's imminent fall from power. Tailer had the backing of some Anglicans still hopeful for the appointment of a true son of their church. In addition, he and his former father-in-law, Nathaniel Byfield, had assumed the leadership of a political faction pressing for a solution to their own and the province's financial difficulties through the funding of a bank run by private subscribers rather than by the Dudleians in power. Byfield travelled to London to seek a charter for the bank and press his own claim to succeed Dudley; failing in these aims, Byfield purchased Tailer's continuance as lieutenant governor from the venal English army officer appointed as Dudley's successor, Colonel Elizeus Burges. For a few weeks, Tailer served as acting governor of Massachusetts. But Burges proved receptive to a higher offer, and in 1715 he resigned his office before ever assuming it in return for a thousand pounds sterling collected by two allies of the Dudleians, agent Jeremiah Dummer and Jonathan, the ambitious son of wealthy Boston contractor Andrew Belcher. The governorship passed to a second and much more respectable English army officer, Samuel Shute, while Tailer was abruptly displaced as lieutenant governor by William Dummer, the agent's brother and Joseph Dudley's son-in-law.[59]

Nelson had watched this complex maneuvering from the sidelines. But when the unhappy Tailer, fleeing the scene of his humiliation, set off for London once more to recoup his fortunes, Nelson stepped forward to assist his brother-in-law with a letter of introduction to the leader of the Temple clan, Sir Richard. Since the time he had helped clear Nelson of the charge of treason back in 1697, Temple's star had risen steadily. Service in Parliament and with Marlborough's armies in Flanders had led to a peerage as Lord (and later Viscount) Cobham, membership in King George I's Privy Council, and the rank of lieutenant general. For Tailer's purposes, the last was the most significant, in that he sought to show that the colonel's commission he had received for the Port Royal expedition entitled him to a permanent place in the English army establishment. In this goal, Tailer reported back to Nelson, Cobham's patronage was "of singular service, for he heartily and sincerely engaged himself in my interest & procured several of the Generall officers to be my friends." Tailer received a half-pay pension worth more than four hundred pounds a year in New England money, so that, as Nelson remarked, losing the office (and meager fifty-pound salary) of lieutenant governor "has proved much to his advantage."[60]

Nelson used the opportunity of Tailer's presence in London to advance his family's claims (through Sir Thomas Temple's Nova Scotia patent) to a share in the English conquest of Acadia. Tailer raised the matter with Cobham, and his old patron Francis Nicholson served as intermediary after Tailer's return to Boston. But the scheme met with intractable obstacles on both sides of the Atlantic. In America, the English hold on Acadia appeared so tenuous as to render any investment there a highly speculative proposition. Other, better-placed groups were already submitting claims, denouncing the Temple patent in the process. In London, meanwhile, the Board of Trade could not decide whether the lands in question lay at the disposal of the Crown (by its conquest), Massachusetts (by its 1691 charter), or one or more private claimants. The Board was keen to build up the region's population; so much so, that it offered ten pounds sterling and fifty acres of land to any white man or woman who would wed an Indian there—an agreeable turn from the policy followed in Massachusetts of offering bounties for the Indians' scalps rather than for their hands in marriage. But none of the claimants for Nova Scotia fancied themselves Saint-Castins.[61]

The final obstacle to Nelson's claim was Lord Cobham himself, who demonstrated precisely how he had amassed what would become an immense fortune by refusing to offer any help to his kinsman unless Nelson signed over to him all the Temple claims. "My Lord is in no way willing (because it does not befit his Quallity) to be Attorney for any Body upon such an affair," Nicholson unctuously informed Nelson in 1720. Were Nelson to comply and Cobham (because of his great and wholly merited influence at court) to obtain a grant, Nicholson continued, then his lordship's sense of honor and justice would doubtless make the matter "an advantage to you." Faced with so bald an extortion, Nelson balked and let the scheme subside.[62] Some years later, his second son Paschal visited England and approached Cobham once more, but without success. What might have been accomplished by a more direct and determined application was shown by the path carved through Whitehall in the early 1730s by a granddaughter of the old claimant to French Acadia (and Sir Thomas Temple's onetime partner), Charles de Saint-Étienne de La Tour. Agathe La Tour emerged from Nova Scotia and two marriages to English army officers to claim compensation for lands around the Bay of Fundy that London now wished to assign to new settlers. Such was her persistence in petitioning the Board of Trade that she was ultimately bought off with a payment of two thousand pounds, part of which went to establishing her two sons in notable military careers in English America.[63] The Nelsons and Temples, in contrast, never came close to launching so well concerted or documented a campaign. Ultimately, not long before his death, Nelson simply abandoned what he seems to have seen all along as an empty title by selling it off to a land company headed by Boston's Samuel Waldo for a hundred pounds, New England money. From a speculator's perspective, as one of them remarked, it was a bargain price for eighty million acres; from Nelson's point of view, as he laughingly reminded one of his sons-in-law, it was payment for something he had told the purchasers beforehand he had no legal right to convey.[64] Either way, it was a sad and mildly disreputable conclusion to a venture begun so bravely nearly a century earlier.

By Nelson's last years, his hopes had turned from what he could do for members of his family towards what they could do for each other and themselves. For all his obvious affection for his daughters, his patriarchal ambitions were focussed on his sons. Yet each was destined, in different ways, to disappoint him. Temple, the elder, was raised to take his father's position as gentleman trader. In the spring of 1717, he was "in business at the Dock" in Boston but not yet entered into the articles of apprenticeship that were the normal prelude to a mercantile career. With Paschal preparing to enter Harvard, their father planned to establish "a house and small familie in Towne."[65] Soon afterwards, however, Temple fell victim to the greatest single public health catastrophe that Boston has ever suffered; the smallpox epidemic of 1721, a year in which mortality in the town rose to over ten percent of its population. To add to these miseries, a virulent debate broke out between the proponents of inoculation against the disease, led by the Mathers; and those who saw the practice as highly dangerous, a view publicized by the young printers, James and Benjamin Franklin. At one point, someone threw a bomb—which failed to explode—through Cotton Mather's window with a message cursing him and expressing the hope that the device would accomplish Mather's final inoculation.[66]

Temple survived the epidemic. But as a doctor who chronicled the epidemic noted, "some who live are Cripples, others Idiots, and many blind all their days."[67] Years later, in a petition to London, Paschal Nelson recalled that his brother's illness had "greatly impaired the speech, not a little the understanding, excessively altered the Person and Temper, and disqualified the Son from any forreign Applications." Paschal's depiction seems excessive set against the brief but certainly coherent letters that Temple Nelson penned in the years following his illness. Far from being "as dead," he traded to the Caribbean, South Carolina, and along the New England coast, married the daughter of Lieutenant Governor John Wentworth of New Hampshire, and fathered three children.[68] His father's request to Vaudreuil in the mid-1720s, that the governor provide a letter allowing the Nelsons to reopen trade with the French settlements on Cape Breton, was doubtless intended to bolster his son's career.[69] Yet Temple's avoidance of his father's trading patterns, his early retirement to Long Island, and his premature death in 1739 all show that, if not incapacitated, he was unable to build upon his father's heritage.[70]

Paschal Nelson, by contrast, displayed an early independence and self-confidence quite reminiscent of his father's childhood. Harvard rather than his parents bore the brunt of his adolescent rebellion, as he enjoyed a college career "of exceptional violence" filled with drinking bouts and disciplinary proceedings.[71] This training naturally inclined him towards the military career that was in any case the customary choice of an eighteenth-century gentleman's younger son. After what he later recalled as a period of service in the British Navy, he returned to America in 1727 in the company of a newly commissioned governor of New York, John Montgomerie, who appointed him lieutenant of a military company up on that province's frontier. Pascal held this post for the next fourteen years, interspersing periods of garrison duty at Fort Oswego among the Iroquois with visits to his family in Boston and his Lloyd relatives in New York. His clear preference for family affairs (though he himself never married) probably explains why he was continually passed over for promotion. Later, after application in London, he secured a captaincy to command a company stationed in South Carolina, finally retiring to England on half-pay around 1750. There "poor Uncle Nelson" spent a last decade restlessly soliciting for office. Disdainful of further army service or a post in the Customs service, he sought a position that would show his skill in "management of the Indians," such as a command in Nova Scotia or the governorship of Georgia or New Hampshire. But his record fell far short of his ambitions. The English Temple connections he cultivated, Cobham's brother-in-law, Sir George Lyttleton, and his nephews, Richard, Earl Temple, and George Grenville, all prominent in the powerful parliamentary faction known to contemporaries as "the Cobhamites" or "the Cousinhood," were courteous and encouraging, but nothing turned up in Paschal's favor. In 1756, with the fall of the Cousinhood from power, he resolved to "quit the Scene of Expectations and Dependance and enjoy my self with my little Income among my Friends in America." Yet he never left London, and he died there three years later. He was buried at St. Martin-in-the-Fields, a few yards down the street from where his father had lived as a child.[72]

One son had begun to follow in his father's footsteps only to be felled by illness; the second had inherited his father's early rootlessness without his application, sinking into a shadow world of "Expectations and Dependance." By a strange irony, the son who would best realize the heritage that John Nelson had derived from his Temple forebears proved to be a son-in-law who was himself a Temple, a great-great-grandson of Nelson's great-grandfather. Robert Temple, who married Nelson's daughter Mehitable in 1721, had arrived in New England four years earlier. An English army officer with ambitions of becoming a landed proprietor in America, he quickly joined the wave of speculative land development in eastern New England that followed the Peace of Utrecht. His Irish upbringing gave him contacts with—and the confidence of—the many Scotch-Irish families seeking to migrate from Ulster, and during the next few years he chartered ships that settled several hundred such families in communities around the mouth of the Kennebec River.[73]

The return of frontier warfare in the early 1720s set back but did not entirely defeat these schemes; and Temple prospered to such an extent that he was able to lease the property of Noddle's Island in Boston Bay once owned by Sir Thomas Temple, and then purchase the historic estate of former Governor John Winthrop at Ten Hills on the Mystic River above Charlestown. Robert Temple's marriage to Mehitable Nelson proved well suited to advancing these territorial designs: after John and Temple Nelson's deaths, he worked hard to acquire the family estate of Long Island (it passed instead to Charles Apthorp, a nephew by marriage of another Nelson son-in-law, Henry Lloyd), and he led other

family members into association with the Kennebec Purchase Proprietors, the greatest of the land companies organized to develop the Maine
frontier. The family's claims in this region derived from a purchase by
Sir Thomas Temple passed on to John Nelson; long dormant, they were
now revived in support of a refurbished title, much as Samuel Waldo
had bought up Nelson's still-vaguer claim to Nova Scotia to add a little
instant antiquity to his neighboring speculation. "I am Much Mistaken,"
Robert Temple wrote to his brother-in-law in 1742, "If those Out Lands
Will not finally Turn Out More Valluable than the [Long] Island which
has been the Main pursuit of the family."[74] A brisk—and sometimes
brusque—man of business, Temple had perceived that the swarm of
land-hungry European migrants now reaching America offered a way
to realize the profits hidden in the maze of ancient colonial patents, a
way best followed by means of local authority, influence, and investment
rather than wearisome applications to London and vague schemes of
conquest. Once established in colonial society, moreover, Temple's family showed it could make effective use of ties with England if the opportunity arose: his second son, John, capitalized on his Grenville
connections to become lieutenant governor of New Hampshire and
surveyor-general of the American Customs between 1760 and 1774. As
such, he had to grapple with the revolt aroused by George Grenville's
Stamp Act, conflict that drove him into Loyalist exile in England. Later,
as Sir John Temple, eighth baronet, a title inherited from the English
Temples, he returned to America as England's first consul-general to
the infant United States.[75]

But all this lay far beyond the span of John Nelson's life. Through
the 1720s, he and Elizabeth continued to live on Long Island. Nelson
passed through a serious illness in the winter of 1725, and three years
later—"myself & your Mother being Growne ould and infirme" and
with the island damaged by "wonderfull Stormes"—he arranged to convey the property to their son Temple upon the latter's agreement to pay
part of its value to the other children. A rumor arose in Boston that
Nelson had been appointed the province's lieutenant governor; but instead, his brother-in-law William Tailer won back the post from William
Dummer in 1730, a belated revenge for Dummer's displacement of
Tailer fourteen years before.[76] In a last echo of matters French and
Acadian, Nelson counselled a royal official embarking upon a visit to
Saint-Castin's old haunt of Penobscot Bay and provided him with a
letter of introduction to the baron's son Joseph.[77] Early in 1732, he sat
for his portrait to be painted—at a cost of forty pounds—by the Scottish-
born and Italian-schooled artist John Smibert, recently arrived in Boston

to begin a series of commissions depicting the town's leading inhabitants. Smibert's brush portrayed a tall and sturdy man, plainly dressed save for the full-bottomed wig that framed an alert, full-featured, and intelligent face belying Nelson's nearly eighty years. Behind him, as through a window out onto his world, stretched a seascape of bays and islands; above him, in evidence of his stature, and gentility, was emblazoned the Nelson family's coat of arms.[78]

But Nelson's final days were spent, as so much of his earlier life had been, in the company of Temples, at Robert and Mehitable's house on Noddles Island. A last, short voyage carried him across the autumnal waters of Boston Bay, passing before the pointing spires of the town that had become his residence but never quite his home. "There is no Exemption from this last Ishue of Death," Nelson had written upon receiving the news of their daughter Rebecca's passing; "lett us improve the dispensations of God, soe as to be preparing our selves for this great Change." On October 25, 1734, Elizabeth Nelson died, ending a half a century's partnership. Three weeks later, on November 16, John Nelson followed her into death.[79]

VIII

"CRUSHT BETWEEN THE TWO CROWNES"

A few years before his death, in a last letter to Canada's Governor Vaudreuil, John Nelson sought permission to trade once more with French Acadia. Thereby, he noted, "I might in some measure repaire my family in the great losses I have sustained, being soe long a time as it were Crusht between the two Crownes."[1] Nelson was not a man given to lamentation or reflection: active, open, and direct, he displayed none of the anxious concern of a Cotton Mather or a Samuel Sewall for his own or his society's place in history. Yet his words, with their depiction of personal endeavor storm-tossed by larger forces, come close to encapsulating his life's central theme—the search for accommodation and response to the clash of emerging European empires in the North Atlantic world.

For it was at once Nelson's opportunity and his fate to begin his career at the moment when the scattered French and English settlements in North America moved into a new conjunction with each other and with their parent countries. During the years of their first founding by a broad diversity of groups and individuals—Puritans and Catholics, merchants and planters, fishermen and fur-traders—these settlements had remained largely isolated from each other and from metropolitan authority. By the 1660s, however, as Sir Thomas Temple and his young nephew strove to govern Acadia, France and England had turned from civil strife to an increasingly competitive quest for the profits of trade and colonial development. During that time, the boundaries of their American colonies expanded before the pressures of renewed migration and internal growth to the point of contact and, by the 1690s, collision—the start of three-quarters of a century of almost incessant warfare. In the past, geopolitical expansion on this scale had been the work of such single hegemonies as those of Rome, Byzantium, and China. The overseas expansion of early modern Europe, in contrast, was led by competing nation-states, each throwing off advance colonizations whose growth in turn embroiled them in the larger rivalry.

Out of this interplay, Nelson carved what seemed by the early 1680s to be a prosperous career. His uncle's misfortunes had warned that what London gave, it could also—through the pens of diplomats—abruptly take away. Better to trust in the local needs and contacts exemplified by Boston's trade with Acadia. This commerce, too, had to be tempered by political realities, ranging from the purely personal—like Nelson's mutually advantageous friendships with needy French officers commanding colonial outposts—to more remote and imponderable forces like the policy decisions handed down from across the Atlantic. For the moment, however, Nelson profited from the way the spaces between hitherto separated colonial settlements were contracting, becoming marginal areas of intersecting political units. Like the multinational businessman of modern times, he found opportunity in what amounted to a disjuncture between the facts of political and economic life—in this case, the imbalance between France's flimsy sovereignty over Acadia and New England's commercial domination of the region. Even when French officials bowed to economic reality and licensed the swarming of Boston's traders and fisherman, it was to the genial, genteel, and trusted Nelson that they looked to serve as middleman and broker.

But this accommodation was always precarious, and it could not withstand the mounting pressures exerted by Europe's reordering of North America's political structures. In Canada, the French Crown had already replaced the bankrupt Company of New France with a more direct and closely regulated system of royal rule, sustaining its reforms with large reinforcements of troops and settlers sent from France and an expansion of the colony's sphere of influence west to the Great Lakes and down the Mississippi. At the same time, though less dramatically, the English government's program of colonial economic regulation—the Acts of Trade and Navigation—sparked bureaucratic growth at home and political intervention across the Atlantic. By the mid-1680s, Andros'

Dominion of New England stood as stark testimony to London's determination to curb colonial self-government and bring all the northern English colonies in America under direct royal rule. The Dominion's fall in 1689 modified but by no means reversed this policy, one that persisted throughout the remaining span of Nelson's life. In his childhood, following the Stuart restoration, only Virginia, of all the French and English colonies on the North American mainland, was directly governed by the Crown. By his death, every one of these colonies had passed through a period of direct royal control, so that all of French and by far the greater part of English North America lay under the eye of governors directly appointed and supervised from Paris and London.

These changes transformed the political context of Nelson's career, and their impact was compounded by Europe's second ill-omened legacy to America during these years: the prolonged and bitter international warfare that followed the Glorious Revolution. The consequences for Nelson were exceptionally dramatic—capture, imprisonment, and a role as diplomat and suppliant on both sides of the Atlantic. Yet what happened to Nelson also took its toll, in less exaggerated form, on colonial society as a whole. All of North America's settlers—and especially those on the geographical margins now become the leading edges of clashing imperial systems—were led to accept an increasing measure of central government intervention and supervision. Only the state, at the local and ultimately the metropolitan level, had the prestige and capacity for deploying the resources needed for sustained military conflict. War, disruptive of political authority in the short term, ultimately increased dependence on the center and fostered the growth of government. Political units such as Massachusetts that had hitherto orchestrated the growth of their peripheries were compelled to cede a part of their control, and acknowledge their own peripheral status, to metropolitan authority. Colonists and governments alike looked to the center—be it Dutch William's Whitehall or the Sun King's Versailles—for office, aid, and legitimacy. In America as in early modern Europe, international conflict served as a powerful catalyst for national political consolidation.[2]

In the long term, the pressures exerted by war and royal government helped fashion an empire out of what had been a patchwork of semi-autonomous settlements. They would spell and end to such independent proprietorial ventures as those of Sir Thomas Temple. Yet their effect was seldom uniform or planned; and one lesson to be learned from Nelson's career is the extent to which he and others like him were able to play a part—and occasionally the lead—in shaping the course of events. Behind all the visible growth of royal authority in America during these years remained the crucial question of whose hand and what considerations would guide the pen that wrote the orders in Whitehall and Versailles. Preoccupied by European conflict, metropolitan officials found little time and even scantier resources for colonial affairs. English administrators, in particular, were inclined to wait upon rather than initiate events. And even when obliged to reach a decision, their knowledge of "West Indian" (i.e., North American) matters was often so fragmentary that it laid them open to the propaganda of almost any well-connected entrepreneur or office seeker who appeared on Whitehall's doorstep. As the years following 1689 were to show, there was little reason for ambitious colonists to fly in the face of royal authority as long as they could find ways to divert its power and patronage to their own account.

Nelson remained—and seemingly preferred to remain—a novice at this game. He never mastered the kind of lobbying skills shown by Mather, Vetch, or Dudley in their dealings with Whitehall. Too impatient to build a coalition, too stiff-necked to flatter, Nelson preferred the bold, individual gesture—the scheme of espionage or the dash across the Channel in 1697 to confront the peace commissioners in Holland—to the cultivation of allies in Boston or Whitehall. He was never an organization man. Yet two phases of his career reveal ways he helped shape policy on both sides of the Atlantic. In the first phase, up until the fall of the Dominion, his role was that of middleman and gadfly, inciting official action—both angry and admiring—by his commercial ventures. In the second, through the 1690s, his role became that of leader and then consultant, heading the uprising against Andros and the colonists' dealings with Port Royal, and then providing Whitehall with the rare commodity of timely and accurate knowledge of North American affairs. The last may seem trivial, but it was precious in Whitehall: decades after he had submitted his memorials, the Board of Trade still drew upon them in debating such matters as the colonies' northern boundaries and relations with the Indians.[3]

Taken together, these phases of Nelson's career shed light on the forces that guided English imperial development during these years, impelling it in some directions rather than others. England's leaders were convinced of the value of possessing colonies, but they saw their task as one of fostering the colonists' economic and political growth (and thereby the royal revenues) rather than territorial expansion. The spirit that had conquered Jamaica, Acadia, and New York in a single decade after 1654 had ebbed. "To me it appears wee have already but too much Territory abroad," wrote one official in 1689; our true interest, he concluded, "is for bare defence and the keeping of what already Wee have."[4] If there was talk of the need to augment England's "empire" in America, it more often came from colonists angling to enlist London's aid in their own defense. Nelson's life illustrates how a renewed, though still diffident, imperialism took shape and found its first coherent expression in the direction of Acadia. This imperialism grew out of the pattern of commercial ties and political involvement with the region that stretched back to the days of Winthrop, La Tour, and Sir Thomas Temple; it took on an increasing measure of state participation as men like Nelson and Phips turned from trade to military means to satisfy their varied ambitions; and it culminated in conquest and royal government after Vetch and Dudley had persuaded Whitehall that the annexation of Acadia could serve metropolitan as well as local interests.

In the event, Boston benefitted while Whitehall paid the bills. The conquest turned into a continuation of Massachusetts' dominion by other means, as Nova Scotia became part of the eighteenth-century socioeconomic realm extending from New York to Newfoundland that one writer has aptly termed "Greater New England."[5] Yet its annexation marked a turning point both in preparing the way for an English conquest of Canada and in signalling the willingness of two old and wary rivals—Boston and Whitehall—to forge an alliance of aggressive self-interest against a common foe. Considering that for years the Crown had viewed Massachusetts as the most dangerously obstreperous of all its colonies and Massachusetts had as warmly returned the mistrust, it was ironic that the only significant "imperial" expansion undertaken by either in the half-century after 1675 should have been a joint exercise.

Nelson did not share in the final conquest, and his pioneering arguments for the reduction of Acadia and Canada were overshadowed by more politically sophisticated pleadings. Nonetheless, he pointed the way and prepared the ground by his actions and information. The flag followed trade, and his was the trade it followed. At a more personal level, too, his career illustrates the shift in individual strategies that colored and accompanied these larger movements. In the years before the Glorious Revolution, Nelson's own loyalties had been more than a little flexible. True, it was an age when colonies were settled by dissidents and exiles, and when much of the work of discovery was led by men born under one flag and serving under another. But Nelson tacked before more winds than most. He cherished close ties with French officials, much warmer than any he forged with their English counterparts. His commercial ventures paid little heed to international boundaries, and his first wholehearted involvement in political affairs consisted of heading a rebellion against his own Crown's authority.

In that rebellion, however, along with most of his fellow colonists, Nelson found a renewed community of interest with his native land. A tiny handful clung to their allegiance to a deposed James Stuart: the same Thomas Dongan who as governor of New York had chastised Nelson for acting "so much for the French Interest" turned spy for the French in the wake of 1689.[6] But the huge majority joined in saluting the Revolution, that "Glorious Enterprise" that had rescued "the whole English Israel" from "Popery and Arbitrary Government." England seemed once more worthy of her children's allegiance. We should do nothing, urged Cotton Mather in a sermon delivered to the Massachusetts General Court in 1690, "but what has a Tendency to maintain our due Dependence on the authority of *England*, and to preserve and Enlarge the *English* Empire."[7]

The ensuing war with France cemented this attachment. Old and New England found common cause in defending "the Protestant interest" and "English liberties" against the great leviathan, Louis XIV[e], and his "Gallic Blood Hounds."[8] Yet even as Mather spoke, events in Massachusetts showed that he and others held quite different views of what constituted a "due Dependence" on English authority. The same sermon contained a brisk attack on the Anglican church and its "Romish worship," together with a passionate prayer that New England remain true to its old ways, "defended by Rulers that should be of our selves, and Governours that should proceed from the midst of us."[9] Here lay the grounds of the division that had already severed Nelson from the post-revolutionary government and aligned him with the dissident merchants and Anglicans petitioning London for a return of direct royal government. The character of Nelson's new patriotism, in sum, was as much a product of his enduring distaste for the old charter regime as of any new devotion for the Crown. From being a middleman between French and English power, he had moved to a more fully English but still intermediate position between the new rulers of England and Massachusetts.

Nelson held to that position after his escape from France, urging Whitehall to promote the territorial expansion and political reunification of English North America, while stopping short of the more wholehearted royalism of an Edward Randolph or a Joseph Dudley. By then, he could feel in greater harmony with the political situation in New England: as the Mathers turned to preaching the virtues of the modified form of royal government that Increase had negotiated in London, as Stoughton and Bellomont succeeded Phips, and as New Englanders as a whole perceived the value of closer ties with England in matters of defense. Gone was the stiff-necked independence of only twenty years before, when half of the assembled Massachusetts magistrates refused even to doff their hats in respect during the reading of a royal letter.[10] Nelson returned to a Massachusetts that in mind and politics had advanced to meet him. Yet, as the early years of the new century showed, Nelson remained part of a group that stood politically to the right (and geographically to the east) of the bulk of the colony's political leadership. Many of this group, like Nelson, were Anglicans at a time when the purchase of a pew in Queen's Chapel was both a declaration of political and religious loyalty to the mother country and a deliberate (and, to colonial Puritans, deliberately insulting) denial of the "New England way" as the true Protestant path. Most were merchants whose trade relied on transatlantic ties and protection. All responded to the cultural magnetism exerted by English ideals of gentility and taste. In the years ahead, this group and its descendants would furnish many of the politicians and businessmen who profited most conspicuously from Boston's political connection with England—and, ultimately, many of the Loyalists who suffered from its severance in 1776. Lloyds, Temples, Wentworths, Fitches, and Lorings were all among the descendants of John Nelson who sided with the Crown during the American Revolution.

To judge by the tone of his last letter to Vaudreuil, Nelson ended his life feeling more like a suffering loyalist than a profiteer, more a casualty than a beneficiary of empire. In part, he plainly fell prey to forces far beyond his control. The scapegoat for Phips's greed and malice, he became a pawn and hostage in a larger game of diplomatic chess. His years of imprisonment did not crush, but they diminished, his adventurous spirit, turning him inward to his years of island retirement. Yet a final judgment must strike a balance between Nelson as victim and as policy-shaper while also setting limits on his capacity to represent his time. At the last, he emerges as an idiosyncratic figure whose setbacks and achievements were as much the consequence of his own self-fashioning as of his circumstances. Hardheaded trader though he must have been to survive in the shifting currents of Acadian trade, he still cherished hopes, as in 1691, of reviving some form of his uncle's lordship, an illusion that precipitated his capture and imprisonment. Two years' attendance at Whitehall surely convinced him that, although proprietorial claims might survive in such protected areas as Maryland and Pennsylvania, there was little chance of resurrecting this form of private enterprise on the edge of intersecting empires. Yet he failed to learn the lesson that Robert Temple, in the company of other eighteenth-century speculators and contractors, would turn to his advantage—that state power could be made to serve private ambitions; that one could use government without incurring the obligations of assuming it.

Nelson failed to learn this lesson, perhaps because he always regarded government more as adversary than as ally. One reason that we know so little of his trading ventures is doubtless that so many of them were designed, like the voyage of the *Johanna* in 1686, to profit from the proximity of communities governed by different sets of commercial regulations. French and English colonial products that were supposed to be shipped to market by way of the parent country yielded higher profits when sold or exchanged directly at places like Saint-Castin's Penobscot; European goods such as the *Johanna*'s wines could likewise pay a handsome dividend. Even at this moment, no doubt, some latter-day Nelson is searching for the right location to land microchips of foreign manufacture in defiance of the prescribed protective duties. Such activities, in turn, set clear limits on Nelson's support for any form of official, and especially royal, intervention. His newfound enthusiasm in the 1690s for the expansion of England's dominion in America never extended to what Randolph or Blathwayt saw as prerequisite to such expansion: the bolstering of England's revenues, authority, and commerce by a stricter regulation of colonial trade.

In place of the laws of man—or even those of God, to judge by the resolutely secular tone of almost all of Nelson's public and private writings—the most powerful external forces shaping his personal standards and beliefs were surely his relationships with those immediately around him. His feckless but charming uncle, the French officer-officials who befriended him in Acadia, his fellow Anglicans in Boston, the grace and bearing of Frontenac—all furnished models of behavior and deportment that set him apart from the rest of his New England contemporaries. Most of the immigrants who came to Massachusetts in the 1660s after the restoration of the Stuarts became ardent defenders of the colony's Puritan ways; Nelson, by contrast, emerged a man better suited to win reward and reputation in Frontenac's New France than in Samuel Sewall's Boston. His early life displayed his daring, resourcefulness, and thirst for adventure; maturity added a chivalrous sense of responsibility to those in need of his assistance. Where Phips gratified his acquisitive instincts or John Alden steered clear of danger even at the cost of abandoning his son as hostage, Nelson rescued captives regardless of his own condition, and won the trust of his Acadian clients by his aid over and above his commercial concerns in their times of need. One of his last public appearances in Boston was in lonely support of a widow of a fellow Anglican who insisted on braving public disapproval with a formal funeral despite her husband's suicide.[11] A gentleman could do no less; but few of his contemporaries, on either side of the Atlantic, paid such practical homage to the ideal. The writer E. M. Forster once observed that, if compelled to betray his country or his friends, he hoped he would have the courage to betray his country. One suspects that Nelson's loyalties would have sent him in the same direction.

Nelson's self-characterization blinkered as well as enriched his vision. There were choices he rejected and cultural barriers he could not cross. Committed to a code of conduct that, if not a civil religion, came close to worshipping civility for its own sake, he was deaf to the passionate religiosity that still throbbed within the New England soul. Conversely, despite a life passed amid intersecting cultures, he showed not the slightest inclination to imitate his associate Saint-Castin's living of a full marginal life by adopting Indian ways and wives—the pattern that nineteenth-century imperialists would nervously deplore as "going native." His equivalent of the baron's Penobscot—Long Island—lay, by contrast, deep within the English Protestant pale, within easy reach of Boston's comfortable urbanity. And although he paid the Abenaki the cultural tribute of learning their language and urging that their leaders be courted as powerful policy-making figures, he remained as hidebound—white hidebound—as the rest of his fellow New Englanders in his depiction of Indians as pagan savages, over whose heads European gentlemen could and should reach the appropriate decisions. In protesting to Frontenac during his captivity against the payment of bounties for English captives "as Unchristian and not agreable to the custom of Nations," he was blind to the justice of the old governor's retort that the English themselves offered large sums for the scalps of enemy Indians.[12]

In the crude terms of a garnering of wealth and power, Nelson's life never fulfilled its early promise. By such a reckoning, of course, the majority of those who sought prosperity on the advancing frontiers of European empire in America found themselves, in one way or another, "crusht between the two Crownes." Countless men and women—Indian, French, and English—would perish in the eighteenth century's wars; even the redoutable Samuel Vetch, the conqueror of Acadia, ended his career in the dismal confines of a London debtor's prison. Nelson, at least, outlived his enemies and died renowned and full of years, surrounded by an affectionate family. Yet he also bequeathed something more substantial. His life pioneered and exemplified the interplay and conflict that would continue to link England and New England, France and New France in the years ahead. At a deeper, personal level, it stood as testimony to the fact that a life of striving and adventure in the new American world could be lived in a manner justly eulogized, upon his passing, as "Genteel, Enlarged, [and] Liberal."[13]

A P P E N D I X

Cotton Mather's Letter Justifying His Part in Nelson's Capture and Release

[No endorsement or addressee; all in Cotton Mather's handwriting, in draft form]

Mar. 20, 1711

My worthy friend:

It was no small satisfaction to me that you did last Night mention to me Mr <u>Nelsons</u> Willingness, that you should let me know his having been long dissatisfied at some Things in my Behavior towards him. For it gives me an opportunity, which I have long, and a thousand times, Wished for to have my Behavior therein brought under the strictest Examination in the world. I have many times heard of that Gentlemans Displeasure at me. I have often been in his way, with hopes of having some Eclaircissement of the matters which had been displeasing, handsomely introduced. I have signified unto more than one or two, how ready I was for any Interview, when or where he or they would please to assign it. I have likewise presumed so far, as to say unto the Gentleman himself (in the Chamber at the Blue Anchor) I should be glad, if he would do me the Honour of taking a glass of Wine with me at my

House. But the Good Understanding has hitherto had a Strange Enchantment upon it which, I hope, is now in a fair way to be dissolved and dispelled; and the Joy of this my Hope, turns upon the ease which it may give unto the mind of the Gentleman himself, unto whom I wish exceeding well & and all that is good; much more than on my own Account, who am so Innocent that I cannot be at all uneasy.

I don't Remember that I have heard of any more than Two dissatisfactions at me; but shall be as ready to speak unto any more, if they should be brought unto Remembrance.

The first prejudice has been, my Concerting with the then Governour of the province [Sir William Phips] to employ a French Deserter in a business at the Eastward, & this with a Design to betray, & expose, Mr Nelson by whose means the said French man was brought into the service which this count[ry] received from him.

Of this, I do solemnly Declare;

That I was in no way in the world concerned as an Adviser of the Employment which the Governour thrust upon the unhappy Deserter. I had nothing to do, either in proposing the Motion, or projecting the Method, of what was then done. All that I know, or ever knew, of it, was this; I happened to be at the Governours when he was giving this directory to the Two Blades, whereof one proved so false unto the other, as to Ruine him, and in his Ruine to do Mr Nelson a Mischief. He was pleased to tell me, what he had been doing and that it had been laid before the Council, who had approved of it. I objected unto him, That I wond[e]red the Frenchman would venture himself with such a Dangerous Companion, and that I fear'd the Consequences. He replied, That the Two Blades had come to such an Entire Confidence in one another, by their mutual conversation, & the man for whom I was afraid was not himself afraid; and so he would venture them. Then I had no more to say. But I have Now.

I must add, That as I had no Hand at all in the affayr; [*marginal insertion:* I was in no way Accessary to it; not in any sort the Contriver of it. All that ever could countenance the surmise about it was my being accidentally at the Governours House near the time it was proceeded in] so I verily believe Sr W. P. himself had not the least Intention of any Hurt unto Mr Nelson. But my present Business is to answer only for myself. And my Witness is on High, that I have ever been as free from Intending any such Harm to Mr Nelson as follow'd from the miscarriage of that affair, as any of his own Lovely Children; whom I heartily pray God, to Continue the Comfort of his Age, and the Ornaments of his Family.

I can say more than this, There never was any man, who I did upon all occasions more celebrate & panegyrize the Generous Action of Mr Nelson in sending that Frenchman from Canada to N. E. And extol the Generosity of it, in the most significant manner I was capable of. I was and am of the Opinion, that the countrey then owed to him, and this very day there are still owing him greater Expressions of Gratitude, then ever he has yett received. But we all know the pay on such obligations. However I paid all that I could in my poor way, And there are scores of Witnesses to the prayers, the Tears, the most affectionate Representations, which were offered up to Heaven from time to time on his behalf with all possible Honourable particularity, in the Time of his Captivity.

I can do no more than make this Declaration and protestation; which I am ready to do with all the solemnity that can be desired. And challenge all the people upon Earth, to bring any one Circumstance in my whole Conduct, which may be the least Contradiction to any part of it. If after this, I shall be thought a man of no veracity, I must patiently bear the Indignity, and only say, Let God be Judge!

The second prejudice has been my hindring a French Captive here, from being sent home for Mr Nelsons Redemption.

Of this, tis admirable that any one should pretend the Least Atom or Shadow of anything Blameable in me. [*Marginal insertion*: Injustice beyond an Epithet! I never did any thing, that becomes a Christian in my life, if not in this thing] I am for some Reasons Lothe to give you the story at Large; Lothe to Repeat any thing that might carry any Imputation upon persons I am not at present concerned withal. I will give it unto Mr Nelson if he please to call for it. But it is enough to say. The captive aforesaid, was one who had publicly abjured the popish Religion in the French Church at Boston. Had he been carried into France he had immediately dy'd on the Gallows as an Apostate. Mr Nelson is a Gentleman of that Honour, and that Sense of Religion, he would have chosen to have lived a prisoner in the Age of Johannes de Temporibus, before he would have seen such a thing. It would have been a Double Martyrdom; one to Mr Nelson himself. This captive was the only one of the men then scattered about the Country who was taken up, & clapt into a Close Imprisonment on this occasion: [*marginal insertion:* and the only one resolved to be sent for France, he not being shipped for Quebec] The Elders of the Fr. Church entreated me to sollicit the Lieut. Governour [William Stoughton], that things might be carried according to the Maxims and Interests of our Holy Religion. I did so, in a Letter to him, which I wish they that are owners of the L.

Governrs papers, would produce; and I would say no more. I particularly Demonstrated unto him, That there could not accrue the least Disadvantage unto his worthy Kinsman in his Captivity, by his permitting this captive to be kept in a Durance no stricter than the rest. So that if he Escaped, as a few more less obnoxious on the score of religion had done, yett his Returning such <u>port-royallers</u> (I think they were) as were found in the province, might be sufficiently affirmed. The Lt. Governour did what was desired; and there followed no Inconvenience to Mr <u>Nelson</u> from his doing what he did. If my Father had been in <u>France</u>, I would have done just as I did. And I shall give a glad Account unto the Judge of the whole Earth concerning it.

[*Marginal insertion:* You must accept my report of these things, and it is but fair that what I assert should find Acceptance with you till you find me once begin to falsify. There is a certain Degree in the Universities whereof this is one of the privileges; That the person dignified with it, may demand a greater Trust or plain Acceptance than persons of a Lower Character. I do not insist upon this, any more than I do upon some others which I might have a claim to. Allow me but the Faith which you do to any honest man in your Nayebourhood]

I cannot call to mind, anything else, that I have heard has been grievous to the mind of the gentleman who is offended at me. If in my Judgment about any Men or Things I have happened at all to differ from him, he is too wise and too much a gentleman, to make that a matter of any Offence; because in this we enjoy an Equal Freedom.

You will give me leave to make a charitable Conclusion of my Letter.

Were I sensible that I had ever done Mr <u>Nelson</u> any wrong, I would make him a more ample Reparation than he would require of me; yes, more than Monsieur <u>Placeste</u> himself could enjoin upon me. Instead of this, I am not sensible that ever I did him so much as the Least Hurt in [*ends*]

[Source: Mather Papers, American Antiquarian Society]

NOTES

PREFACE

1. John Hurd to John Singleton Copley, April 17, 1770, Massachusetts Historical Society, *Collections*, LXXI (1914): 85; *Papers of the Lloyd Family of the Manor of Queens Village, Lloyd's Neck, Long Island, New York, 1654–1826* (New York, 1927) II: 878, 889, 896, 899–900, 903 (hereafter cited as *Lloyd Family Papers*).
2. Thomas Hutchinson, *History of the Colony and Province of Massachusetts-Bay*, ed. Lawrence Shaw Mayo (Cambridge, Mass., 1936) I:321 n.; Francis Parkman, *Count Frontenac and New France under Louis XIV* (Boston, 1880), 357–359; Samuel A. Drake, *Captain Nelson: A Romance of Colonial Days* (New York, 1879).

CHAPTER I

1. John G. Reid, *Acadia, Maine, and New Scotland: Marginal Colonies in the Seventeenth Century* (Toronto, 1981), xv, 122–124.
2. Harold A. Innis, *The Cod Fisheries: The History of an International Economy*, revised edition (Toronto, 1954); John Winthrop, *Winthrop's Journal "History of New England," 1603–1649*, ed. James K. Hosmer (New York, 1908) I:46.
3. Andrew Hill Clark, *Acadia: The Geography of Early Nova Scotia to 1760* (Madison, 1968), 11–55, 238–242.

4. *Ibid.*, 71 n, 109–110, 208.
5. Henry P. Biggar, ed., *The Works of Samuel de Champlain* (Toronto, 1932) IV:28–29. Acadia's tendency to fragmentation is analyzed by Reid, *Acadia, Maine, and New Scotland*, 115; and John Bartlet Brebner, *New England's Outpost: Acadia before the Conquest of Canada* (New York, 1927), 45–46.
6. Thus the massive collections of documents published in both London and Paris: *Memorials of the English and French Commissaries Concerning the Limits of Nova Scotia or Acadia*, 2 vols. (London, 1754), and *Mémoires des Commissaires du Roi et de Ceux de sa Majesté Britannique sur les Possessions et les Droits Respectifs des Deux Coronnes en Amerique; avec les Acts Publics et Pièces Justificatives*, 4 vols. (Paris, 1755).
7. The most recent and readable account of this much-studied rivalry is M. A. MacDonald, *Fortune and La Tour: The Civil War in Acadia* (Toronto, 1983). For La Tour and Boston, see George A. Rawlyk, *Nova Scotia's Massachusetts: A Study of Massachusetts–Nova Scotia Relations, 1630–1784* (Montreal, 1973), 6–21.
8. Winthrop, *Winthrop's Journal* II:285.
9. Robert Sedgwick to Oliver Cromwell, July 1, 1654, in Thomas Birch, ed., *A Collection of the State Papers of John Thurloe Esq.* (London, 1742) II:419; Richard S. Dunn, *Puritans and Yankees: The Winthrop Dynasty of New England, 1630–1717* (Princeton, 1962), 102–104.
10. John Mason to John Winthrop, Jr., May 27, 1654, Massachusetts Historical Society, *Collections*, 4th ser., VII (1865), 417.
11. John Leverett to Oliver Cromwell, September 5, 1654, Birch, *A Collection of State Papers* II:584.
12. Rawlyk, *Nova Scotia's Massachusetts*, 25–26; Reid, *Acadia, Maine, and New Scotland*, 135–136.
13. Proceedings relative to the petition of M. de La Tour, May 29, 1656, Stowe-Temple Papers, STT Foreign Affairs, Huntington Library, San Marino; Grant to Charles de La Tour, William Crowne, and Thomas Temple, August 9, 1656, Temple-Nelson Papers no. 2, Houghton Library, Harvard University, and Colonial Office Papers, Class 1, vol. 13, no. 11, Public Record Office, London (hereafter cited as C.O.); *Suffolk Deeds* (Boston, 1880–1906) III: 22–26, 265–279; *Ibid.* IV:325–330; Reid, *Acadia, Maine, and New Scotland*, 32–33, 137. Temple's payments to La Tour, who returned to Acadia and died in 1663, are detailed in Temple-Nelson Papers, no. 3.
14. George W. Brown *et al.*, eds., *Dictionary of Canadian Biography* (Toronto, 1965–1982) I:241–242; The Case of William Crowne [1668], C.O.1/23, no. 28; Agreement of William Crowne and Thomas Temple, May 5, 1660, Massachusetts Archives, II, 506–508, New State Archives Building, Boston.
15. Temple Prime, *Some Account of the Temple Family* (New York, 1887), *passim*; Arthur P. Newton, *The Colonizing Activities of the English Puritans: The Last Phase of the Elizabethan Struggle with Spain* (New Haven, 1914), 65–66. Viscount Say and Sele, in a letter of February 1, 1657, offering to sell Thomas Temple a white horse at an excessive price, addressed his great-nephew as his "very lovinge Cosin": Temple-Nelson Papers, no. 1.
16. Agreement for carrying on a trade in Nova Scotia, [May, 1658?], C.O.1/13, no. 43. For Noell and Povey, see Charles M. Andrews, *British Committees, Commissions, and Councils of Trade and Plantations, 1622–1675*

(Baltimore, 1908), 49–60. Previous accounts of this episode have followed the editor of the *Calendar of State Papers, Colonial Series* in confusing Temple's backer, "Lord [Nathaniel] Fienes," with his father, Viscount Say and Sele, but Temple himself makes the distinction clear: W. Noel Sainsbury *et al.*, *Calendar of State Papers, Colonial Series, America and West Indies* (London 1860–1969), *1574–1660*, 489 (C.O. 1/14, no. 44).

17. Thomas Temple to [Thomas Povey], [1660]: *idem*, to Lord Arlington, March 2, 1669; *idem*, to the King, January 10, 1671, in C.O.1/14, no. 64; 1/24, no. 20; 1/26, no. 4, respectively.

18. Thomas Temple to Thomas Povey, September 9, 1658, C.O.1/13 no. 51; Thomas Bayly Howell, ed., *Cobbett's Complete Collection of State Trials* V (London, 1810), cols. 1200–1201.

19. The financial difficulties of the senior branch of the Temple family during the 1650s are described by Edwin F. Gay, "The Temples of Stowe and Their Debts: Sir Thomas Temple and Sir Peter Temple, 1603–1653," *Huntington Library Quarterly* II (1938–1939): 399–438; and "Sir Richard Temple: The Debt Settlement and Estate Litigation, 1653–1675," *ibid.* VI (1942–1943): 255–291.

20. Cotton Mather, *Parentator. Memoirs of Remarkables in the Life and the Death of the Ever-Memorable Dr. Increase Mather* (Boston, 1724), 34; and, generally, Arthur H. Buffinton, "Sir Thomas Temple in Boston, a Case of Benevolent Assimilation," Publications of the Colonial Society of Massachusetts, *Transactions* XXVII (1932): 308–319.

21. Thomas Lake to John Leverett, September 2, 1657, Mass. Archives, II, 505.

22. Temple to Thomas Povey, December 27, 1658; September 24, 1660; in C.O. 1/13, no. 59; C.O. 1/14, no. 44, respectively; *idem*, to Lord Nathaniel Fiennes, September 6 and December 29, 1659; in C.O. 1/13, nos. 71, 77, respectively.

23. Bernard Bailyn, *The New England Merchants in the Seventeenth Century* (Cambridge, Mass., 1955), 115–116; Reid, *Acadia, Maine, and New Scotland*, 139, 146; "A breviate of Sir Thomas Temple's purchase of Nova Scotia" [1669?], Temple-Nelson Papers, no. 3; Warrants to the Attorney-General, April 5, 1662, C.O.1/16, nos. 40, 42; Order of the King in Council, April 23, 1662, Egerton Manuscripts, 2395, fol. 341v, British Library, London.

24. Thomas Temple to Edward Hyde, Earl of Clarendon, August 21, 1663, *Collections of the New-York Historical Society for the Year 1869* (New York, 1870), 51–52; Proclamation of Sir Thomas Temple, March 1, 1665, C.O.1/19, no. 33; Rawlyk, *Nova Scotia's Massachusetts*, 30–32; Petition of Samuel Wilson, [1672], C.O.1/29, no. 80.

CHAPTER II

1. Joseph Foster, *Register of Admissions to Gray's Inn, 1521–1889* (London, 1889), 192; Reginald J. Fletcher, *The Pension Book of Gray's Inn, 1569–1669* (London, 1901), 357, 409; Temple Prime, *Descent of John Nelson and His Children*, 2nd ed. (New York, 1894), *passim*; *The Herald and Geneal-*

ogist IV (1867): 12. The arms of the signet ring used by John Nelson in New England and depicted in his 1732 portrait (or, a cross patonce sable) suggest that, like Admiral Horatio Nelson, he was descended from the Nelsons of Maudesley and Wrightington in Lancashire.

2. Mary Anne Everett Green, ed., *Calendar of State Papers, Domestic Series 1653–1654* (London 1879) 152. Robert Nelson to John Thurloe, February 18, 1655; Examination of Ellen Aske, February 17, 1655; letter to Nelson, n.d.; Thomas Waddington to Thurloe, December 28, 1657; all in Rawlinson Manuscripts, A, 23.153; 151.141; 155.56; 56.339, respectively, Bodleian Library, Oxford. There is, however, no record of Nelson's having acted as a sessional justice: J. C. Jeaffreson, ed., *Middlesex County Records* III (London, 1888), *passim*.

3. Morden and Lea's Prospect of London and Westminster, 1682; *Survey of London: Volume XX, Trafalgar Square and Neighbourhood (The Parish of St. Martin-in-the-Fields, Part III)* (London, 1940), 116.

4. Assessment for payment of the Scottish Army, 1646, Parish Poor Rates for 1653 and 1655, Records of the Parish of St. Martin-in-the-Fields, Westminster City Library, London. The sums assessed against Nelson place him amongst the wealthiest third of the householders living in this exceptionally prosperous area. Fleetwood and Lady Armine's two sons were also members of Gray's Inn.

5. Robert Nelson to William Ceelye, December 17, 1650, Additional Manuscripts, 46932, fols. 139–139v, British Library, London; Mary Anne Everett Green, ed., *Calendar of the Proceedings of the Committee for Compounding &c., 1643–1660: Part II, 1643–1646* (London, 1890), 899.

6. Parish Register of St. Martin-in-the-Fields, *sub.* December 21, 1651, Westminster City Library, London; Will of Temple Nelson, proved November 15, 1671, Probate 11/337, fol. 136, Public Record Office, London; *Allegations for Marriage Licences issued from the Faculty Office of the Archbishop of Canterbury, London, 1543–1869*, Harleian Society, XXIV (1886), 8; Robert Nelson to [Thomas Temple], May 1, 1670, Lloyd, Vassall, Borland Papers, no. 2, Houghton Library, Harvard University; Robert Nelson to Sir Richard Temple, June 19, [no year], STT 1505, Stowe-Temple Mss. No record survives of John Nelson's birth, traditionally ascribed to 1654, but the most reliable record, which tells of his death on November 15, 1734, at the age of "four score and one years" would set his birth in late 1652 or 1653: Timothy Cutler, *The Final Peace, Security, and Happiness of the Upright, A Sermon Deliver'd at Christ-Church in Boston, Novemb. 28, 1734. On Occasion of the Death of John Nelson Esq. and of Mrs. Elizabeth Nelson, His Consort* (Boston, 1735), 15.

7. Robert Nelson to [Thomas Temple], May 1, 1670, Lloyd, Vassall, Borland Papers, no. 2; "Record of my Great Grandmother, Lady Temple," Temple-Nelson Papers, no. 45; *Gazetteer and London Daily Advertiser*, August 17, 1754; Thomas Fuller, *The History of the Worthies of England*, ed. P. Austin Nuttall (London, 1840) I:210. Nelson's mother, for example, was the eighth daughter of a father who himself had had ten sisters and four brothers.

8. Will of Robert Nelson, proved August 4, 1698, Probate 11/447, fol. 190, Public Record Office, London. Martin H. Quitt has found a similar pattern of estrangment from one or both of their parents in a number of immigrants

to Virginia in these years: Quitt, "Immigrant Origins of the Virginia Gentry: A Study of Cultural Transmission and Innovation," *William and Mary Quarterly*, 3rd ser., XLV (1988): 632–634.

9. Statement of Thomas Temple's claim, [August 20, 1660], C.O.1/14, no. 36, and Order of the King in Council, August 26, 1661, C.O.5/903, p. 16. Temple's first will, made in 1671, acknowledged a debt to Robert Nelson "provided that he give up my Patent of Nova Scotia," evidently retained by Nelson as a surety: Temple Prime, *Some Account of the Temple Family: Appendix* (New York, 1899), 95.

10. Stephen Temple to [Thomas Temple], September 20, 1671, Temple-Nelson Papers, no. 13.

11. Thomas Temple to John Nelson, October 9, 1667, Temple-Nelson Papers, no. 8; for John Rhoades, Brown *et al., Dictionary of Canadian Biography* I:573.

12. Commission of Sir Thomas Temple to John Nelson, March 17, 1670, Temple-Nelson Papers, no. 11.

13. Secretary Edward Rawson of Massachusetts to Secretary of State Lord Arlington, May 20, 1669, *Calendar of State Papers, Colonial, 1669–74*, no. 68.

14. Testimony of John Nelson, [October 11, 1682], Mass. Archives, XXXIX, 755; Reid, *Acadia, Maine, and New Scotland*, 156–157; Memoire of Intendant Talon to the King, November 2, 1671, and Colbert to Talon, June 4, 1672, *Collection de Manuscrits contenant Lettres, Mémoires, et Autres Documents Historiques Relatifs à la Nouvelle-France* (Quebec, 1883–1885) I:213, 223 (hereafter cited as *Collection de MSS*); Report of Sieur du Patoulet, January 25, 1672, Archives des Colonies, Série C^{IIA}, vol. III, fol. 276, Archives Nationales, Paris; Buffinton, "Sir Thomas Temple," Pubs. Col. Soc. Mass., *Transactions* XXVII (1932): 315, 319; Prime, *Some Account of the Temple Family: Appendix*, 99. Years later, the Crown's failure to reimburse Temple was advanced as flimsy justification for the continued validity of his title to Nova Scotia.

15. Prime, *Some Account of the Temple Family: Appendix*, 96, 99.

16. *Suffolk Deeds* IX:262, and X:236; John Nelson to Nathaniel Elkins, October 17, 1678, Greenough Collection (photostat), Mass. Hist. Soc.; Petitions of William Tailer, July 16 and 19, 1677, Mass. Archives, LXI, 156, 159, respectively.

17. Discharge given by John Nelson, October 26, 1680, Mass. Archives, XVI, 195; Samuel Eliot Morison, ed., "Records of the Suffolk County Court, 1671–1680," Pubs. Col. Soc. Mass., *Collections* XXIX (1933): 476–477; Suffolk County Court Files, nos. 4631 and 4688, New State Archives Building, Boston; Suffolk County Court Records, 1680–1692, p. 63, New State Archives Building; Record Book of the Suffolk County Inferior Court of Common Pleas, 1698–1701, p. 35, New State Archives Building.

18. Henri Brunet to M. Delagny, February 4, 1675, in Louis-André Vigneras, "Letters of an Acadian Trader, 1674–1676," *New England Quarterly* XIII (1940): 106.

19. Rawlyk, *Nova Scotia's Massachusetts*, 37–39; Reid, *Acadia, Maine, and New Scotland*, 161–162; *Publications of the Bostonian Society* VI (1910): 33–60.

20. *New England Historical and Genealogical Register* XVI (1862): 144.

21. Brown *et al.*, *Dictionary of Canadian Biography* I:398–400; *ibid.* II:4–7; Pierre Daviault, *Le Baron de Saint-Castin: Chef Abénaquis* (Montreal, 1939); Report of Gov. Denonville, November 10, 1686, Instructions to Gov. Meneval, 1687, *Collection de MSS* I:388, 399.
22. Order of Massachusetts Council, January 29, 1677; Petitions of William Tailer, July 16 and 19, 1677; Stores desired by Marson and Saint-Castin, [1677]: all in Mass. Archives, LXI, 147, 156, 159, 157, respectively.
23. Goods brought in by Capt. Samuel Mosely, April 2, 1675, *loc.cit.* p. 77. For similar cargoes in the 1690s, see Jean Daigle, "Les Relations Commerciales de l'Acadie avec le Massachusetts: le Cas de Charles-Amadour de Saint-Étienne de la Tour, 1695–1697," *Revue de l'Université de Moncton* IX (1976): 56–57.
24. Gov. Grandfontaine to Gov. Richard Bellingham, January 12, 1672; Petition of William Waldron, [1675]; Deposition of George Manning, December 27, 1674; and Petition of John Poole, March 2, 1676; in Mass. Archives, II, 511; LXI, 62, 65, and 148, respectively. Morrison, "Records of the Suffolk County Court," Pubs. Col. Soc. Mass., *Collections* XXIX (1933): 135–139; and, generally, Jean Daigle, "Nos Amis les Ennemis: Relations Commerciales de l'Acadie avec le Massachusetts, 1670–1711" (Ph.D. diss., Univ. of Maine, 1975), chap. 3.
25. Tailer also acted as banker for French merchants trading to Boston: Vigneras, "Letters of an Acadian Trader," 105, 106. For the Atherton Associates, see Richard R. Johnson, *Adjustment to Empire: The New England Colonies, 1675–1715* (New Brunswick, N.J., 1981), 20.
26. Interrogation of Mathieu-François de Lino, January 17, 1693, Bibliothèque de l'Arsenal, Archives de la Bastille, vol. 10496, fol. 165; Hutchinson, *History of Massachusetts-Bay* I:321 n.
27. Gov. Perrot to Minister, August 29, 1686, Archives des Colonies, C^{11D}, vol. II, fol. 14; "Mémoire touchant le Canada and l'Acadie—Envoyé par M. de Meulles, [1686]," *Revue d'histoire de l'Amérique Française* II (1948–1949): 437. A 1686 sketched plan of Port Royal depicts two storehouses identified as belonging to Englishmen located alongside the governor's residence: John Clarence Webster, ed., *Relation of the Voyage to Port Royal in Acadia or New France by the Sieur de Dièreville* (Toronto, 1933), end map. One storehouse was undoubtedly Nelson's, as evidenced by both de Meulles's report and William Phips's identification of "Mr. Nelson's Warehouse" in 1690 (*A Journal of the Proceedings in the Late Expedition to Port-Royal* [Boston, 1690], 6–7).
28. *Collection de MSS* I:215–216; Census of M. de Meulles, 1686, *La Société Historique Acadienne*, 29ième cahier (1968), 341–342; Gisa Hynes, "Some Aspects of the Demography of Port Royal, 1650–1755," *Acadiensis* III, no. 1 (Autumn 1973), 3–17; Louis XIV to Gov. Frontenac, May 12, 1678, *Collection de MSS* I:266. A French account of 1686 estimated that as many as 800 English vessels of 10 to 30 tons apiece had come to fish off Acadia in the 1660s and reported that in the 1680s 80 boats were coming to Acadian waters several times a year from Salem alone: "Mémoire sur ce qu'on peut faire en Acadie," Archives des Colonies, C^{11D}, vol. II, fols. 32v, 33.
29. John Clarence Webster, *Acadia at the End of the Seventeenth Century: Letters, Journals and Memoirs of Joseph Robineau de Villebon, Comman-*

dant in Acadia, 1690–1700, and Other Contemporary Documents (Saint John, New Brunswick, 1934), 141. For French–Indian trade and an analysis of Abenaki and Micmac attitudes to traders, see Kenneth M. Morrison, *The Embattled Northeast: The Elusive Idea of Alliance in Abenaki–Euramerican Relations* (Berkeley, 1984), 28–34.

30. Intendant Talon to the King, November 10, 1670, *Collection de MSS* I:203; Frontenac to Massachusetts, November 3, 1681, Mass. Archives, II, 518.

31. Simon Bradstreet to Frontenac, [June 8, 1682], Prince Papers, no. 14, Mass. Hist. Soc.; John Nelson, "Observations on my Voyage to Canada made in July 1682," Stowe MSS, 163, fols. 172–173, British Library; and in Arthur H. Buffinton, "John Nelson's Voyage to Quebec in 1682: A Chapter in the Fisheries Controversy," in Pubs. Col. Soc. Mass., *Transactions* XXVI (1927): 434–437. The character of Nelson's "Observations" suggests that they were written out at a later date, as part of his schemes put forward in London during the 1690s.

32. "Extract of what was said to Intendant Du Chesneau in September 1682," Archives des Colonies, C¹¹ᴬ, vol. VI, fol. 116 (concerning information received from "le Sieur de Melson [*sic*] gentilhomme anglois"). This document credits Nelson with a huge trade in furs but seems to confuse his activities with those of the northern English colonies as a whole.

33. Gov. Frontenac to Massachusetts, August 2, 1682, Mass. Archives, II, 520–521. The Quebec fire broke out August 4, 1682—July 25 by the English (Old Style) reckoning: Archives de Colonies, C¹¹ᴬ, vol. VI, fol. 10.

34. Order of Gov. La Vallière, October 22, 1685, C.O. 1/55, no. 37v; Petition of William Vaughan and others, [December 5, 1684], C.O. 1/56, no. 105; Nathaniel B. Shurtleff, ed., *Records of the Governor and Company of the Massachusetts Bay in New England* (Boston, 1853–1854) V:373–374; Rawlyk, *Nova Scotia's Massachusetts*, 43–46.

CHAPTER III

1. Oliver H. Roberts, *History of the Military Company of the Massachusetts now called the Ancient and Honorable Artillery Company of Massachusetts, 1637–1888* (Boston, 1895) I:260; Annie Haven Thwing, *The Crooked and Narrow Streets of the Town of Boston, 1630–1822* (Boston, 1920), 83. Thwing's notes preserved at the Massachusetts Historical Society (as "Inhabitants and Estates of the Town of Boston, 1639–1800") provide details of the holdings of Nelson, Tailer, and others. For the streets of Boston in 1722, see the map reproduced on page 113 of this book.

2. M. Halsey Thomas, ed., *The Diary of Samuel Sewall, 1674–1729* (New York, 1973) I: 52, and II: 1013; "Diary of Noadiah Russell," *New England Historical and Genealogical Register* VII (1853): 56; *Suffolk Deeds* XII:392; Suffolk County Probate Records, new series, I: 373–381, and II: 391, Old Court House, Boston. Increase Mather first preached his *A Call to the Tempted. A Sermon on the Horrid Crime of Self-Murder* (Boston, 1724) on the occasion of Tailer's death.

3. Nelson was certainly married to Elizabeth Tailer by July 1684, as evidenced by Edward Randolph's letter (Mass. Hist. Soc., *Collections*, 4th ser., VIII

[1868]: 524–525), and Cutler, *Final Peace, Security, and Happiness of the Upright*, 13–14. The marriage is unlikely to have taken place at any much earlier date since Elizabeth was born in 1667.

4. *Reports of the Records Commissioners of the City of Boston* (Boston, 1876–1909), I:102. Some corroboration of this status is provided by an estimate of the wealth of subscribers to a petition of 1690, in which Nelson's estate was set at £6,000, fifth in a list of sixty: C.O.5/856, no. 157. For property dealings involving Nelson, see *Suffolk Deeds* XII: 110, 215, 356; Mass. Archives, XL, 444–445.

5. Depositions of Pierre Arconneau, Pierre Collare de la Rochelle, and Abraham Boudrot, August 29, 1683, Mass. Archives, LXI, 256–258; Suffolk County Court Records, 1680–1692, pp. 159, 163, 271; Indenture between John and Elizabeth Nelson and John Coney, Goldsmith, January 11, 1700, MSS Large, Mass. Hist. Soc.

6. Peter Bulkeley to Edward Bulkeley, January 17, 1677, Mass. Hist. Soc., *Proceedings*, 2nd ser., XIV (1900–1901): 214; John Higginson, *The Cause of God and his People in New-England* (Cambridge, Mass., 1664), 11. See also J. Franklin Jameson, ed., *Johnson's Wonder-working Providence* (New York, 1910), 35, 254; Perry Miller, "Declension in a Bible Commonwealth," American Antiquarian Society, *Proceedings*, new ser., LI (1941): 37–94; and Bailyn, *New England Merchants*.

7. Mass. Hist. Soc., *Collections*, 2nd ser., VII (1826): 105; Paul R. Lucas, "Colony or Commonwealth: Massachusetts Bay, 1661–1666," *William and Mary Quarterly*, 3rd ser., XXIV (1967): 88–107.

8. Pubs. Col. Soc. Mass., *Transactions* X (1907): 352–354.

9. Sewall, *Diary* I:32; "Journal of Dr. Benjamin Bullivant," Mass. Hist. Soc., *Proceedings* XVI (1878): 106.

10. Douglas E. Leach, "The Question of French Involvement in King Philip's War," Pubs. Col. Soc. Mass., *Transactions* XXXVIII (1947–1951): 414–421; Massachusetts Council to the Secretary of State (draft), April 5, 1676, James P. Baxter, ed., *Documentary History of the State of Maine* (Maine Hist. Soc., *Collections*, 2nd ser. [Portland, 1869–1916]), VI:111.

11. John Talcott to Gov. Edmund Andros, December 5, 1687, Mass. Hist. Soc., *Collections*, 3rd ser., III (1833): 168–169; also Gov. John Easton to Massachusetts, November 17, 1691, Mass. Archives, XXXVII, 212–213.

12. Orders in Council, September 19 and October 17, 1678, Mass. Archives, LXI, 179–180; Examination of Henry Smith, October 31, 1688, Baxter, *Documentary History of Maine* VI:447.

13. Hutchinson, *History of Massachusetts-Bay* I:321 n.

14. Cutler, *Final Peace, Security, and Happiness of the Upright*, 14; "The Petition of John Nelson Gentleman," November 30, 1698, Mass. Archives, LXX, 389. Nelson's use of his family's coat of arms can be seen in legal documents, as the indenture cited in note 5, this chapter. He began to be accorded the title of "Esquire" in the 1690s, even before his appointment as Massachusetts justice of the peace, an office customarily carrying such rank as a courtesy. In 1728, of 87 pewholders of Boston's Anglican church of King's Chapel, he was one of only eight recorded as "Esq.": Fulham Papers, Lambeth Palace Library, IV, fol. 266. For some suggestive remarks about social status in early America, see Norman H. Dawes, "Titles as

Symbols of Prestige in Seventeenth-Century New England," *William and Mary Quarterly*, 3d ser., VI (1949): 69–83.

15. Richard Wharton to William Blathwayt, December 6, 1684, Blathwayt Papers, VI, Colonial Williamsburg.

16. Michael G. Hall, *Edward Randolph and the American Colonies, 1676–1703* (Chapel Hill, 1960), 21–97; Viola Barnes, "Richard Wharton, A Seventeenth Century New England Colonial," Pubs. Col. Soc., Mass., *Transactions* XXVI (1924–1926): 238–270; *Suffolk Deeds* XII:392; and, generally, Johnson, *Adjustment to Empire*, 28–50.

17. Mass. Hist. Soc., *Proceedings*, 2nd ser., XIII (1899–1900): 248–249; Randolph to Samuel Shrimpton, July 18 and 24, 1685, Mass. Hist. Soc., *Collections*, 4th ser., VIII (1868): 524–525, 526.

18. W. J. Eccles, *Canada under Louis XIV, 1663–1701* (Toronto, 1964), 119–154.

19. Rawlyk, *Nova Scotia's Massachusetts*, 46–47.

20. Franklin B. Hough, ed., "Pemaquid Papers," Maine Hist. Soc., *Collections* V (1857): 80.

21. *Ibid.*, 89–91, Thomas Dongan to John Nelson, December 3, 1683, and March 6, 1684; Nelson to Richard Coote, Earl of Bellomont, September 30, 1699; all in Temple-Nelson Papers, nos. 14, 15, 44, respectively. Dongan himself, however, had served in the French army back in the 1660s.

22. As in the great collections of *Memorials of the English and French Commissaries* and *Mémoires des Commissaires du Roi et de Ceux de sa Majesté Britannique* cited in chap. 1, note 6.

23. Depositions of George Gore, William Card, and Joseph Berry, July 23–29, 1686, C.O.1/61, nos. 36i–iii; Suffolk County Court Records, 1680—1692, p. 243; Memorial of the French Ambassador and Envoy, [October 30, 1687], C.O.1/63, no. 54; *Memorials of the English and French Commissaries* I: 615–616; *Collection de MSS* I: 407–408. Nelson's associate is identified in a Suffolk County Court warrant of September 25, 1686, as "John Watkins of London and Malaga," probably the shipper of the cargo: Mass. Archives, LXI, 292.

24. Thomas C. Barrow, *Trade and Empire: The British Customs Service in Colonial America, 1660–1775* (Cambridge, Mass., 1967), 89, 148, 162. See also Ralph Greenlee Lounsbury, "Yankee Trade at Newfoundland," *New England Quarterly* III (1930): 607–626.

25. Depositions of George Gore, William Card, and Joseph Berry, July 23–29, 1686, C.O.1/61, nos. 36i–iii; John Palmer to Edward Randolph, July 24, 1686, in Robert N. Toppan and Alfred T. S. Goodrick, eds., *Edward Randolph: Including his Letters and Official Papers from the New England, Middle, and Southern Colonies in America, with Other Documents Relating Chiefly to the Vacating of the Royal Charter of the Colony of Massachusetts, 1676–1703* (Boston, 1898–1909) IV:96–97; Answer of John Palmer to French Ambassador, November 12, 1686, C.O.1/63, no. 61. For Palmer's career, see Paul M. Hamlin and Charles E. Baker, *Supreme Court of Judicature of the Province of New York, 1691–1704* (New York, 1959) I:425–426.

26. John Palmer to John West, October 6, 1686, Maine Hist. Soc., *Collections* VIII (1881): 189–191; Mass. Archives, LXII, 292; Suffolk Court Files, no.

4061; Suffolk County Court Records, 1680–1692, p. 317; Records of the Massachusetts Superior Court of Judicature, 1686–1700, p. 5.

27. President and Council of New England to the Lords of Trade and Plantations, [received October 21, 1686], C.O. 1/60, no. 80; Edward Randolph to William Blathwayt, July 28, 1686, Toppan and Goodrick, *Randolph Letters* IV:97–99.

28. Frances G. Davenport, *European Treaties Bearing on the History of the United States and its Dependencies* (Washington, D.C., 1917–1937) II:309–329; Max Savelle, *The Origins of American Diplomacy: The International History of Anglo-America, 1492–1763* (New York, 1967), 182–183, 186–190; Reid, *Acadia, Maine, and New Scotland*, 178–180; Garrett Mattingly, "No Peace Beyond What Line?" *Transactions of the Royal Historical Society*, 5th ser., XIII (1963): 145–162; Ian K. Steele, *The English Atlantic, 1675–1740: An Exploration of Communication and Community* (New York, 1986), 189–192.

29. Gov. Perrot to Gov. Thomas Dongan, August 29; *idem*, to President Dudley, August 20; *idem*, to Minister, August 29, 1686; all in *Collection de MSS* I: 366–368 (Archives des Colonies, C^{11D}, vol. II, fols. 11–14); Wait Winthrop to Fitz-John Winthrop, April 26 and 28, 1687, Mass. Hist. Soc., *Collections*, 5th ser., VIII (1882): 471–473; Saint-Castin to Gov. Denonville, July 2, 1687, *Collection de MSS* I:401.

30. Jean Daigle *et al.*, "L'Acadie au Temps du Sieur Perrot," La Société Historique Acadienne, *Dix-Neuviéme Cahier*, Vol. II, no. IX (1968), 316. Other French officials also planned to send their children to Boston at this time: Gov. Simon Bradstreet to M. de Meulles, January 14, 1684, Prince Papers.

31. The proceedings can be followed in *Calendar of State Papers, Colonial, 1685–1688*, nos. 1079, 1492, 1509, 1545, 1560, 1592, 1595, 1596, 1608, 1615; "Andros Records," American Antiquarian Society, *Proceedings*, new ser., XIII (1900): 496.

32. Viola Barnes, *The Dominion of New England: A Study of British Colonial Policy* (New Haven, 1923), *passim*; Johnson, *Adjustment to Empire*, 74–84; Henry W. Foote, *Annals of King's Chapel* (Boston, 1882–1896) I:89; *ibid.* II: 603, 605; Sewall, *Diary* I:128.

33. Sewall, *Diary* I:133.

34. Nathaniel B. Shurtleff, *A Topographical and Historical Description of Boston*, 3rd ed. (Boston, 1890), 532–534; *Suffolk Deeds* XIII:24–25. Nelson owned all but 4½ acres of the 216-acre island by 1690. For references to "Isle Nelson," see *Collection de MSS* II:259 and 269, and the 1693 map of Boston Harbor by Jean-Baptiste-Louis Franquelin, reproduced in A. L. Pinart, ed., *Recueil des Cartes, Plans, et Vues Relatifs aux États-Unis et au Canada, New York, Boston, Montréal, Québec, Louisbourg (1651–1731)* (Paris, 1893), plate 4; Boston Museum of Fine Arts, *New England Begins: The Seventeenth Century* (Boston, 1982) I:21; and page 44 in this book.

35. For Shrimpton, the richest man in Boston during the 1680s, see Bailyn, *New England Merchants*, 192; and Worthington C. Ford, "The Case of Samuel Shrimpton," Mass. Hist. Soc., *Proceedings*, 2nd ser., XIX (1905): 38–51. For charges against Shrimpton, see *Calendar of State Papers, Co-*

lonial, 1681–1685, no. 1862; *ibid., 1689–1892*, no. 2031. See also William Dyre to [William Blathwayt], September 17, 1684; *idem*, to Simon Bradstreet, March 5, 1685, Blathwayt Papers, IV, Colonial Williamsburg. Farther up the coast, in Salem, a group of settlers from the Channel Isle of Jersey strove for a similar social and commercial autonomy: David Thomas Konig, *Law and Society in Puritan Massachusetts, 1629–1692* (Chapel Hill, 1979), 70–74.

36. License for John Nelson to leave for Port Royal, June 8, 1687, Mass. Archives, VII, 24; M. de Gargas, "Mon séjour de l'Acadie, 1687–88," in William I. Morse, *Acadiensia Nova, 1598–1779* (London, 1935) I:176, 197–198; Letter of Mathieu de Goutin, September 2, 1689, Archives des Colonies, C¹¹ᴰ, vol. II, fols. 153–155; Sewall, *Diary* I:145.

37. Bruce T. McCully, "The New England–Acadia Fishery Dispute and the Nicholson Mission of August, 1687," *Essex Institute Historical Collections* XCVI (1960): 277–290.

38. Edward Randolph to John Povey, June 21, 1688, Toppan and Goodrick, *Randolph Letters* IV:224–228; Saint-Castin to Gov. Denonville, July 2, 1687; *idem*, to Gov. Meneval, September 15, 1687, *Collection de MSS* I:399–401, 403; Daviault, *Le Baron de Saint-Castin*, 69–71.

39. Memorial of John Nelson, July 2, 1697, Lansdowne MSS 849, fols. 59–60, British Library.

40. Morrison, *Embattled Northeast*, 113–124.

41. Edward Randolph to the Lords of Trade, May 29, 1689, Toppan and Goodrick, *Randolph Letters* IV:276–278.

42. Rawlyk, *Nova Scotia's Massachusetts*, 51–53; Instructions to Gov. Meneval, 1687, Memorial of Meneval, 1687, *Collection de MSS* I:396–399, 411; Governor Andros to the King, July 9, 1688, C.O.1/65, no. 20.

43. Lt.-Gov. Francis Nicholson to [John Povey?], August 31, 1688, Edmund B. O'Callaghan and Berthold Fernow, eds., *Documents Relative to the Colonial History of the State of New York* (Albany, 1853–1887) III: 553 (hereafter cited as *N.Y. Col. Docs.*); Reports of the English attack, August 10–15, 1688, *Collection de MSS* I:428–431.

44. Edward Randolph to John Povey, June 21, 1688, Toppan and Goodrick, *Randolph Letters* IV:225.

45. *Ibid.*, 227; Examination of Henry Smith, October 31, 1688, Baxter, *Documentary History of Maine* VI:447.

46. Johnson, *Adjustment to Empire*, 83–84.

47. Sir Purbeck Temple to John Nelson, March 17, 1689, Temple-Nelson Papers, no. 17.

CHAPTER IV

1. David S. Lovejoy, *The Glorious Revolution in America* (New York, 1972), 174–177.

2. Steele, *English Atlantic*, 94–110.

3. Letter of John Nelson, March 25, 1689, Mather Papers, VII, 81 (MS Am 1502), Boston Public Library; Steele, *English Atlantic*, 97, 101–102.

4. For the Damours and Bourgeois families, see Brown *et al.*, *Dictionary of Canadian Biography* I:245; *ibid.* II:94, 166–167.

5. Cotton Mather, *The Life of Sir William Phips*, ed. Mark Van Doren (New York, 1929), 52; Hutchinson, *History of Massachusetts-Bay* I:323; Johnson, *Adjustment to Empire*, 88–93; Robert Earle Moody and Richard Clive Simmons, eds., *The Glorious Revolution in Massachusetts: Selected Documents, 1689–1692* (*Publications of the Colonial Society of Massachusetts* LXIV [Boston, 1988]): 45–53.

6. Nathaniel Byfield, *An Account of the Late Revolution in New England* (London, 1689), reprinted in Charles M. Andrews, ed., *Narratives of the Insurrections, 1675–1690* (New York, 1915), 173; *ibid.*, Samuel Prince to Thomas Hinckley, April 22, 1689, p. 188; *ibid.*, "A Particular Account of the Late Revolution, 1689," 200, 202, 204; Mass. Archives, Council Records, VI, April 20, 1689.

7. M. de Chevry to M. de Lagny, January 28, 1697, *Collection de MSS* II:258–259. De Chevry's information came from a prisoner in Boston in the early 1690s, a son of Perrot, the former governor of Arcadia. Since young Perrot lodged in the Nelson household during part of his detention, he must have received a firsthand, though possibly inflated, account of his host's role in the uprising.

8. "A Particular Account of the Late Revolution, 1689," in Andrews, *Narratives of the Insurrections*, 198, 200, 203, 209; C.D., *New England's Faction Discovered, 1690*, reprinted in *Narratives of the Insurrections*, 263; Edward Randolph to the Lords of Trade, May 29, 1689, in Toppan and Goodrick, *Randolph Letters* IV:271; Mass. Archives, Council Records, VI, April 23, May 4, 1689. Foster remained in Boston to become a long-serving member of the Massachusetts Council and a close ally of the Mathers; Waterhouse returned to London and prominence in the timber and naval stores trade with New England.

9. The prominence of a similar small group of English-born settlers hitherto excluded from political power in leading the revolt in Maryland later in 1689 is noted by Lois Green Carr and David William Jordan, *Maryland's Revolution of Government, 1689–1692* (Ithaca, 1974), 54–55.

10. A more detailed account is given by Johnson, *Adjustment to Empire*, 95–107. Nelson attended just over half the meetings of the Council between April 20 and May 25.

11. Byfield, *An Account*, in Andrews, *op. cit.*, 174; "A Particular Account," in Andrews, *op. cit.*, 205–206. Andros sought to escape a second time, in August, and reached Rhode Island before being recaptured.

12. Andrews, *op. cit.*, 200, 206–208; List of those imprisoned with Sir Edmund Andros, [July 29, 1689], C.O.5/855, no. 24; "The Humble Address of the President and Councel for the Safety of the People," May 20, 1689, C.O.5/855, no. 7; Log of the frigate *Rose*, May 16, 1689, Admiralty 51/3955, Public Record Office; Foote, *Annals of King's Chapel* I:109.

13. Mass. Archives, Council Records, VI, May 25, 1689; a slightly different version is in Mass. Hist. Soc., *Collections*, 5th ser., VIII (1882): 491–492. Foster, however, was chosen as one of the colony's treasurers.

14. Report of the Committee for the Eastern Business, June 11, 1689, Mass. Archives, CVII, 100–101; Johnson, *Adjustment to Empire*, 113–124.

15. Petition of 12 merchants, [June 10, 1689], Mass. Archives, CVII, 92. For this incident and its intriguing aftermath, when some of the frigate's sailors turned pirate in an apparent attempt to get the frigate released, see John H. Edmonds, "Captain Thomas Pounds, Pilot, Pirate, Cartographer, and Captain in the Royal Navy," Pubs. Col. Soc. Mass., *Transactions* XX (1917–1919): 24–84.

16. Thomas Danforth to Increase Mather, July 30, 1689, *Hutchinson Papers* (Albany: Prince Society Publications, 1865) II:313.

17. Johnson, *Adjustment to Empire*, 120–121, 185–186; Moody and Simmons, *Glorious Revolution in Massachusetts*, 406–407, 415–418.

18. John Nelson and others to Secretary of State Henry Sydney, [April 9, 1691], C.O.5/856, no. 142.

19. Gov. Frontenac to Minister of Marine Pontchartrain, November 15, 1689, *Rapport de l'Archiviste de la Province de Québec pour 1927–1928* (Québec, 1928), 18.

20. Sir Purbeck Temple to John Nelson, January, 1690, Temple-Nelson Papers, no. 18; Petition of Robert Nelson, [1689], C.O.5/855, no. 51. No action was taken on the petition.

21. Sir Purbeck Temple to John Nelson, January 1690, Temple-Nelson Papers, no. 18.

22. Edward Randolph to the Lords of Trade, June 19, 1690, Answer of the Massachusetts agents, [June 26, 1690], Toppan and Goodrick, *Randolph Letters* V: 43, 51. Later evidence stemming from a court case suggests that Randolph's accusation was inaccurate: Nelson's brigantine, sailing from Boston to Barbados and then Virginia, proceeded to the legal port of Newcastle in England (rather than to Hamburg, as Randolph charged) before returning to Boston. Record Book of the Suffolk County Inferior Court of Common Pleas, 1698–1701, p. 6 (session of April 4, 1699).

23. Instructions to the Massachusetts Commissioners, August 21, 1689, Mass. Archives, CVII, 284.

24. Richard R. Johnson, "The Search for a Usable Indian: An Aspect of the Defense of Colonial New England," *Journal of American History* LXIV (1977): 635–637.

25. Petition of Bartholomew Gedney and others, [September, 1689], Mass. Archives, XXXV, 1; Commissioners of the United Colonies of New England to Massachusetts, December 6, 1689, *loc. cit.*, 106; Vote of the General Court, December 16, 1689, *loc. cit.*, 126. In the same month, with equal symbolism, the Massachusetts leadership voted to empower agents to negotiate with the Crown in England for a settlement of government.

26. As Mass. Archives, XXXV, 52; *loc. cit.*, C, 416, 452; *loc. cit.*, CVII, 271a, 288a.

27. Harry M. Ward, *The United Colonies of New England, 1643–1690* (New York, 1961), esp. 178–192; Arthur H. Buffinton, "The Puritan View of War," Pubs. Col. Soc. Mass., *Transactions* XXVIII (1930–1933): 82–84.

28. Proposals of John Nelson, January 4, 1690, Baxter, *Documentary History of Maine* V: 26–28 (from Mass. Archives, XXXV, 161–162).

29. Vote of the Representatives, January 4, 1690, Baxter, *Documentary History of Maine* V: 25 (Mass. Archives, XXXV, 160b); Mass. Archives, Council Records, VI, January 10, 1690.

30. Arthur H. Buffinton, "The Policy of the Northern English Colonies towards the French to the Peace of Utrecht," (Ph.D. diss., Harvard University, 1925), 236–240; Rawlyk, *Nova Scotia's Massachusetts*, 62.

31. Answer to the Council and Representatives, January 16, 1689 [/90], *Documentary History of Maine* V: 30–31 (Mass. Archives, XXXV, 172–173).

32. Mass. Archives, Court Records, VI, February 6, 1690.

33. Parkman, *Count Frontenac*, 208–228.

34. Sewall, *Diary* I:252; "Journal of Dr. Benjamin Bullivant," Mass. Hist. Soc., *Proceedings* XVI (1878): 106.

35. The King to Massachusetts, August 12, 1689, C.O.5/751, no. 3; Mass. Archives, Council Records, VI, December 3, 4, 1689, January 24, and March 14, 1690.

36. Cotton Mather, *The Present State of New-England* (Boston, 1690).

37. Mass. Archives, Court Records, VI, March 14 and 18, 1690; Gov. Samuel Bradstreet to Gov. Thomas Hinckley, March 11, 1690, Mass. Hist. Soc., *Collections*, 4th ser., V (1861): 230; Johnson, *Adjustment to Empire*, 193–195.

38. "Journal of Dr. Benjamin Bullivant," Mass. Hist. Soc., *Proceedings* XVI (1878): 106; Sewall, *Diary* I: 255; Mass. Archives, XXXV, 321, 345, 361, Council Records, VI, March 18, 20, and 22, 1690.

39. Viola F. Barnes, "The Rise of Sir William Phips," *New England Quarterly* I (1928): 274–280; Cyrus H. Karraker, "The Treasure Expedition of Captain William Phips to the Bahama Banks," *New England Quarterly* V (1932): 740–741.

40. Sewall, *Diary* I: 255; "Journal of Dr. Benjamin Bullivant," Mass. Hist. Soc., *Proceedings* XVI (1878): 105; Votes for the nomination and election of magistrates, [May, 1690], Mass. Archives, XXXVI, 54, C.O.5/855, no. 99.

41. Parkman, *Count Frontenac*, 236–240; Account of the taking of Port Royal, May 19–27, 1690, Gov. Meneval to the Minister, May 29, 1690, *Collection de MSS* II:6–8, 10–11; *Journal of the Proceedings in the late Expedition to Port-Royal*, 6–7. One reason the garrison surrendered so easily, it was later charged, was that they believed Nelson was among the expedition's leaders: Memoir of 1690, Archives des Colonies, C^{11D}, vol. II, fol. 149d.

42. Gov. Meneval to the Council of Massachusetts, December 4, 1690, Mass. Hist. Soc., *Collections* I (1825): 115–117; Johnson, *Adjustment to Empire*, 195–198. Nelson, it was said, contributed £87 to the cost of the expedition: *Collection de MSS* II:97.

43. Sewall, *Diary* I:271–274; Memorials of Gov. Meneval, April 6, 1691, and [1700], *Collection de MSS* II:42–43, 339–340; Certificate of Gov. Bradstreet, December 6, 1690, and Order of Sir William Phips, December 25, 1690, Mass. Archives, XXXVI, 233, 262.

44. Brown *et al.*, *Dictionary of Canadian Biography* I:576; Rawlyk, *Nova Scotia's Massachusetts*, 71–72.

45. Permission for Capt. John Alden, November 6, 1690, Baxter, *Documentary History of Maine* V: 159; Daigle, "Nos amis les ennemis," 125.

46. Daigle, "Nos amis les ennemis," 127; Brown *et al.*, *Dictionary of Canadian Biography* II:46, 449, 459. For Boudrot, whom both sides sought to use as

a spy, see Mass. Archives, XXXVII, 90, 94, 96; and Webster, *Acadia at the End of the Seventeenth Century*, 68. A list, ca. 1697, of Frenchmen "who have been to Boston" is given in *Collection de MSS* II:260.

47. Michael Perry to John Usher, May 3, 1693, Jeffries Papers, III, 76, Massachusetts Historical Society.

48. Mass. Archives, Council Records, VI, June 2, 1691; Proposals of the undertakers, [June 4, 1691], Mass. Archives, XXXVI, 108–109 (a number of documents relating to this episode are bound in with materials of the June 1690 Canada expedition).

49. Memorandum [June? 1691], *loc. cit.*, XXXVII, 35.

50. Those joining with the undertakers, n.d., *loc. cit.*, XXXVI, 110; Francis Foxcroft to Francis Nicholson, October 29, 1691, C.O.5/1037, no. 64; [David] Jeffreys to [John] Usher, November 11, 1691, C.O.5/856, no. 206. Samuel Sewall later reported that the failure of the expedition cost Boston merchants £18,000, but this seems excessive: Sewall, *Diary* I:283.

51. Commission and instructions for Col. Edward Tyng, July 20, 1691, Mass. Archives, XXXVII, 85, 86; Further proposals of the undertakers, n.d., *loc. cit.*, 110a.

52. Gov. Simon Bradstreet to M. Castine (draft), July 30, 1691, *loc. cit.*, 101–102; Saint-Castin to Frontenac, September 3, 1691, in Robert Le Blant, *Une Figure Légendaire de l'Histoire Acadienne: Le Baron de Saint-Castin* (Dax, n.d.), 132–133; M. de Monseignat to the Minister, September 10, 1691; and Gov. Frontenac to the Minister, October 20, 1691, *Collection de MSS* II:63, 66.

53. Sewall, *Diary* I:261; Account of guardianship of William Tailer, September 29, 1696, Suffolk County Probate Records, new ser., I, 373–381 (William's elder brother seems to have died young). See also Chapter II, n. 5.

54. Power of attorney in favor of James Lloyd, August 4, 1691, Temple-Nelson Papers, no. 19 (and *Suffolk Deeds* XIV: 262).

55. Daviault, *Le Baron de Saint-Castin*, 98–99; Proceedings of May 10, 1692, Amirauté de Guyenne au siège de La Rochelle, register B.222, fols. 63–64. This may have been only a part of the cargo gathered, since an English report spoke of trading to the value of £1,200: Francis Foxcroft to Francis Nicholson, October 26, 1691, C.O.5/1037, no. 64.

56. [David] Jeffreys to [John] Usher, November 19, 1691, C.O.5/856, no. 206. The King to Count Frontenac and Intendant Jean Bochart de Champigny, April 7, 1691; the King to Gov. Villebon, April 6, 1691; both in Archives des Colonies, Série B, XVI pt. 1, fols. 31, 46.

57. Details of the capture are given in Testimonies of Capt. Simon-Pierre Denys de Bonaventure [captain of the *Soleil d'Afrique*], Ensign Anthoine Gaigneau, and Mathieu De Goutin, [April, 1692], Archives départementales de la Charente-Maritime, Amirauté de La Rochelle, Série B, 5906, pièce no. 4; [Charles de Monseignat], "Narrative of the most remarkable Occurrences in Canada. 1690, 1691," *N.Y. Col. Docs.* IX:527; and Journal of Gov. Villebon, October 13, 1691 to October 25, 1692, Webster, *Acadia*, 32, 36. By French (New Style) dating, the capture took place on October 2.

CHAPTER V

1. [Monseignat], "Narrative," *N.Y. Col. Docs.* IX:527.
2. Reuben G. Thwaites, ed., *New Voyages to North-America by the Baron de Lahontan* (Chicago, 1901) I:265, 388–390; J.-Edmond Roy, *Le Baron de Lahontan* (Montreal, 1974), 50–51.
3. Interrogation of Mathieu-François de Lino, January 17, 1693, Archives de la Bastille, vol. 10496, fol. 165; Account of Samuell Danuell, John Harrod, and Edward Young, [1694?], C.O.388/3, p. 293.
4. "Projet d'une expedition contre Manathe et Boston," May 10, 1690, *Collection de MSS* II:5; and, generally, *N.Y Col. Docs.* IX:404–430, 505–506.
5. "Memoire sur l'entreprise de Baston," April 21, 1697, *Collection de MSS* II:268–273. A roughly contemporary memorandum by Le Moyne d'Iberville on the same topic envisioned what he imaginatively estimated to be the 1,500 Irish inhabitants of Boston rising in support of the French: Archives des Colonies, C^{11E}, vol. X, fols. 13–28.
6. Frontenac to Minister of Marine Pontchartrain, September 15, 1692, *N.Y. Col. Docs.* IX:533 (and *Rapport de l'Archiviste de la Province de Québec pour 1927–1928*, 117).
7. Gov. Villebon's Journal, Webster, *Acadia*, 32, 33, 37–38, 39–40; Instructions to John Alden, March 19, 1692, Baxter, *Documentary History of Maine* V:373–374.
8. Relation of Mark Emerson enclosed in letter from Samuel Ravenscroft to Francis Nicholson, November 5, 1691, C.O.5/1037, no. 67. The Alden son remaining in captivity was the eldest, John, and not, as is sometimes suggested, his younger brother William.
9. Johnson, *Adjustment to Empire*, 220, 227; Journal of the Lords of Trade, September 3, 7, 9, 1691, C.O. 391/7, pp. 44–49; Abner C. Goodell and Melville M. Bigelow, eds., *Acts and Resolves, Public and Private, of the Province of Massachusetts Bay* (Boston, 1869–1922) I:8–9 (hereinafter cited as *Mass. Acts and Resolves*). The only restrictions placed on Massachusetts control were the reservation of trees of a certain size for naval stores and a prohibition of the granting of land east of the Kennebec River without royal sanction.
10. Memoire of M. De Meneval, [1700], *Collection de MSS* II:339.
11. Robert Calef, *More Wonders of the Invisible World* (London, 1700), in George Lincoln Burr, ed., *Narratives of the Witchcraft Cases, 1648–1706* (New York, 1914), 353; Hutchinson, *History of Massachusetts-Bay* II:36–37.
12. J. Nelson to Massachusetts, August 26, 1692, Hutchinson, *History of Massachusetts-Bay* I:321 n; [Charles de Monseignat], "Narrative of the most remarkable Occurrences in Canada. 1692, 1693," *N. Y. Col. Docs.* IX:555.
13. Isaac Addington to [Gov. Phips], September 26, 1692, Mass. Archives, III, 473.
14. John Nelson, "State & Case of my affaires and Circumstances with the French Court,"[November 6, 1696], C.O.388/75, no. 5; Brown *et al.*, *Dictionary of Canadian Biography* II:604–605. Several subsequent French accounts state that the deserters were under orders to assassinate Saint-

Castin if they could not take him alive: *N. Y. Col. Docs.* IX:544; *Collection de MSS* II:100.

15. Nelson, "State and Case of my affaires and circumstances" [November 6, 1696], C.O.388/75, no. 5 (an undated draft, differing in some details, is in Temple-Nelson Papers, no. 31).

16. Letter of Cotton Mather, March 20, 1711, Mather Papers, American Antiquarian Society, Worcester, Mass. The letter (printed in full in the Appendix) is in draft form in Mather's handwriting, with many glosses and interlineations. Mather passed over French reports that other members of the garrison had been held against their will and had even been sold off to labor in Barbados. None of the numerous biographical studies of Mather deals with this affair.

17. For Phips's eastern speculations, see Baxter, *Documentary History of Maine* VIII:12–15; Phips to William Blathwayt, September 11, October 3, 1693, Blathwayt Papers, V, Colonial Williamsburg; and Johnson, *Adjustment to Empire*, 279.

18. Cotton Mather, in his 1711 account, maintained that one of the deserters betrayed the other, but the more contemporary French sources tell the story as I have it here. Saint-Aubin had had dealings with Nelson in the past, as when Nelson secured judgment against him in 1683 for the large sum of 250 pistoles (£250 New England money): Suffolk County Court Records, 1680–1692, 159.

19. Journal of Pierre Le Moyne D'Iberville, 1692, Archives de la Marine, Série B⁴, Campagnes, XIV, fols. 221–230; Statement on behalf of Sieurs Saint-Aubin and Petitpas, November 9, 1692, *Collection de MSS* II:92. The tradition popular in New England that the deserters were returned to Quebec and shot in Nelson's presence seems to derive from Thomas Hutchinson's reliance on the recollections of Nelson's son Pascal half a century later. Pascal's account, however, cites his father's vivid memory that *some* of the deserters were shot before his eyes; i.e., some other than the two who reached Boston and were then employed by Phips. Memorial of Paschal Nelson, [ca. 1750], Temple-Nelson Papers, no. 60.

20. "Le plus vif, le plus animé contre le Canada et le plus propre aux desseins des Anglois pour y faire des enterprises:" Pontchartrain to Gov. Frontenac, April 1692, Archives des Colonies, B, vol. XVI, pt. 2, fol. 35.

21. Frontenac to Minister of Marine Pontchartrain, September 15, 1692, *Rapport de l'Archiviste de la Province de Québec pour 1927–1928*, 117.

22. John Dottin to John Ive, January 31, 1693, C.O.5/1038, no. 2.

23. Louis XIVᵉ to Frontenac, February 14, 1693, Archives des Colonies, B, vol. XVI, pt. 2, fol. 46; Pontchartrain to Frontenac, [March 1693], *Rapport de l'Archiviste de la Province de Québec pour 1927–1928*, 135–136; Brown et al., *Dictionary of Canadian Biography* II:464–465; François Ravaisson, ed., *Archives de la Bastille: Documents Inédits* IX (Paris, 1877): 501–507.

24. Jacques Saint-Germain, *La Reynie et la Police au Grand Siècle* (Paris, 1962), *passim* ; Orest Ranum, *Paris in the Age of Absolutism* (Bloomington, 1968), 272–282.

25. Interrogations of Mathieu-François de Lino, January 17 and 20, 1693, Archives de la Bastille, vol. 10496, fols. 160–170 (a transcription is in Parkman Papers, III, 311–329, Massachusetts Historical Society); letter of Gabriel

Nicolas de La Reynie, January 18, 1693, Archives des Colonies, C^{11A}, vol. XII, 364; Frontenac to Minister of Marine Pontchartrain, October 25, 1693, *Rapport de l'Archiviste de la Province de Québec pour 1927–1928*, 163.

26. Nelson, "State and Case of my affaires and Circumstances,"[November 6, 1696], C.O.388/75, no. 5.

27. Frontenac's colleague in Canada, Intendant Jean Bochart de Champigny, did not scruple to make this point: Champigny to Minister of Marine Pontchartrain, November 4, 1693, Archives des Colonies, C^{11A}, vol. XII, fol. 279v.

28. Petition of [John] Nelson and [John] Alden, [August 16, 1694], and Testimony of Robert Heysham, Jeremiah Johnson, and David Waterhouse, [March 14, 1694], C.O.388/3, pp. 296, 289, respectively.

29. Minister of Marine Pontchartrain to Intendant Michel Bégon, February 7, 1693, and January 13, 1694, Archives des Colonies, B, vol. XVI, pt. 2, fol. 20; and vol. XVII, fol. 25, respectively; [Joseph W. Porter], "Captain John Alden, Jr., of Boston and Maine, 1659–1702," *Bangor Historical Magazine* VII (1891–1892): 214.

30. Louis XIVe to M. Desbauries, January 28, 1693, Temple-Nelson Papers, no. 20; Minister of Marine Pontchartrain to Intendant Bégon, January 28, 1693, Archives des Colonies, B, vol. XVI, pt. 2, fols. 15–16.

31. Pierre Dubourg-Noves, "Forteresses et Résidences des Comtes d'Angloulême dans leur Capitale," Société Archéologique et Historique de la Charente, *Bulletin Mensuel* (1981), 47–61.

32. Hutchinson, *History of Massachusetts-Bay* I:322 n. For recent—and still quite different—solutions to the mystery of the man in the (velvet, not iron) mask, see Rupert Furneaux, *The Man behind the Mask: The Real Story of the "Ancient Prisoner"* (London, 1954); Pierre-Jacques Arrèse, *Le Masque de Fer: l'énigme enfin résolu* (Paris, 1970); and Jean-Christian Petitfils, *L'Homme au Masque de Fer* (Paris, 1970).

33. Drake, *Captain Nelson*, 132–146. This dramatic license was slight, however, compared to the premature death Drake invented for evil royal official Edward Randolph, killed in a dramatic masthead pistol duel with the captain of the ship returning him from New England after the overthrow of the Dominion: *ibid.*, 60–61.

34. Nelson, "State & Case of my affaires and Circumstances" [November 6, 1696], C.O.388/75, no. 5.

35. Bonaventure to the Minister, December 24, 1706, Archives des Colonies, C^{11D}, vol. V, 245v–246.

36. Minister of Marine Pontchartrain to M. Desbauries, July 8, 1693, Ravaisson, *Archives de la Bastille* IX:508. See also Pontchartrain to Intendant Michel Bégon, January 13, 1694, Archives de Colonies, B, vol. XVII, fols. 24–25.

37. "Un esprit fort remuant": Frontenac and Intendant Champigny to Minister of Marine Pontchartrain, September 15, 1692, *Rapport de l'Archiviste de la Province de Québec pour 1927–1928*, 111.

38. John Paschal to John Nelson, June 14, 1694, Temple-Nelson Papers, no. 22. Nelson's mother's sister, Hester Temple, had married Edward Paschal. For John Paschal's 1694 appointment, and the charges of mismanagement that dogged his career, see *Calendar of State Papers, Domestic, 1694–95*, 278–279, 287; and Historical Manuscripts Commission, *The Manuscripts of*

the House of Lords, new ser. (London, 1900–1962) IV:393; *ibid*. V:437–440, 445–449. London's Lord Mayor that year was Sir William Ashurst, brother to the Massachusetts agent Sir Henry Ashurst. Hutchinson, *History of Massachusetts-Bay* I:322 n., suggests that Sir Purbeck Temple helped advertise Nelson's plight, but no contemporary evidence supports this.

39. See for example, the numerous petitions and orders calendared in W. L. Grant and James Munro, eds., *Acts of the Privy Council of England, Colonial Series* (London, 1908–1912) II:158–172, 219–226, 279–282; and the materials relating to convoys, 1692–1695, in C.O.388/2–4, *passim*. The comparable activities of a larger and more influential "interest" are well described by Alison G. Olson, "The Virginia Merchants of London: A Study in Eighteenth-Century Interest-Group Politics," *William and Mary Quarterly*, 3rd ser., XL (1983): 363–388.

40. Johnson, *Adjustment to Empire*, 175, 209–210.

41. Petition of the New England traders, September 12, 1692, Grant and Munro, *Acts of the Privy Council, Colonial*, no. 464.

42. Testimony of Robert Heysham, Jeremiah Johnson, and David Waterhouse, [March 14, 1694]; Affidavit of Waterhouse and Elisha Hutchinson, May 31, 1694; and "The case of Mr. John Nelson,"[August 9, 1694], C.O.388/3, pp. 289, 291, and 295, respectively.

43. Petition of John Nelson and John Alden, [August 16, 1694], C.O.388/3, p. 296.

44. For this correspondence, see *ibid.*, 281, 283–285, 297–298, 303, 315; Journal of the Board of Trade, October 15, 1694, C.O.391/7, pp. 359–369; and Archives de la Marine, B³, vol. LXXXI, fols. 103, 135, 159, 195, 208; *loc. cit.*, vol. LXXXII, fols. 191, 241–242, 251; *loc. cit.* vol. LXXXVI, fol. 408; *loc. cit.*, vol. LXXXIX, fols. 258, 269, 270.

45. "Newsletter to the Earl of Derwentwater," May 4, 1695, *Calendar of State Papers, Domestic, 1695*, 327.

46. Report of the commissioners for victualling the Navy to the Lords of the Treasury, November 19, 1696, Treasury 1/41, no. 28, Public Record Office; Bond of M. Duport, August 12, 1695, Temple-Nelson Papers, no. 23. The Duport brothers also serviced other English prisoners in France: *Calendar of State Papers, Colonial, 1696–1697*, nos. 560i, 561.

47. Brown *et al.*, *Dictionary of Canadian Biography* I:298; *ibid.*, II:182; Intendant de Lagny to the Commissioners for the exchange of prisoners, June 28 and 29, September 30, October 15, 1694, C.O.388/3, pp. 283–285, 297–298.

48. Memorial of John Nelson to the Board of Trade, [September 23, 1696], C.O.232/2, no. 10 (pp. 145–146).

49. John Nelson to [the Duke of Shrewsbury] (draft), January 24, 1696, Temple-Nelson Papers, no. 26; Nelson to Shrewsbury (draft), February 1696, *loc. cit.*, no. 32; James Vernon to Shrewsbury, November 26, December 5, 1696, G.P.R. James, ed., *Letters Illustrative of the Reign of William III from 1696 to 1708 addressed to the Duke of Shrewsbury by James Vernon Esq.* (London, 1841) I:83, 102–103. French forewarning of the attack on Brest from informants including John Churchill, Earl of Marlborough, is discussed by C. T. Atkinson, *Marlborough and the Rise of the British Army* (New York, 1921), 142–147.

50. Journal of M. du Junca, in Ravaisson, *Archives de la Bastille* IX:513. A little over three years later, the famed man in the mask would arrive at the Bastille to spend the last five years of his life in another of the fortress' eight towers.
51. Saint-Germain, *La Reynie et la Police*, 200–206; Minister of Marine Pontchartrain to Gov. Besmans of the Bastille, September 3 and 4, 1695, Archives de la Bastille, vol. 10501, pièces 118, 115.
52. Memorial of John Nelson to the Board of Trade, [September 23, 1696], C.O.323/2, no. 10 (pp. 145–146); Letter of the Minister to Gov. Philippe Rigaud de Vaudreuil, Marquis de Vaudreuil, August 10, 1710, *Collection de MSS* II:520.
53. Minister of Marine Pontchartrain to Intendant de Lagny, September 21, 1695, in Ravaisson, *Archives de la Bastille* IX:513; Memorial of John Nelson to the Board of Trade, [September 23, 1696], C.O.323/2, no. 10 (pp. 147–148); Nelson, "State & Case of my affaires and Circumstances," [November 6, 1696] C.O. 388/75, no. 5.
54. John Nelson to Gov. Besmans of the Bastille, December 10, 1695, Archives de la Bastille, vol. 10501, pièce 111; Journal of M. du Junca, in Ravaisson, *Archives de la Bastille* IX:514; Passports to John Nelson, November 30 and December 21, 1695, Temple-Nelson Papers, nos. 24, 25.

CHAPTER VI

1. K. G. Davies, *The Royal African Company* (New York, 1970), 202; and, generally, David Ogg, *England in the Reigns of James II and William III* (Oxford, 1955), 426–437.
2. For these negotiations, see the letters in Mass. Archives, II, 522–535, 542–543; *loc. cit.*, XXX, 377; *Collection de MSS* II:184–185, 191–193, 223. Nelson later claimed £20 for money disbursed by his family and friends back in New England in rounding up these captives: Petition of John Nelson, November 30, 1698, Mass. Archives, LXX, 389–391.
3. James Axtell, "The Scholastic Philosophy of the Wilderness," *William and Mary Quarterly*, 3rd ser., XXIX (1972): 361–362.
4. Minister of Marine Pontchartrain to Intendant Bégon, September 1696, Archives Maritimes, Port de Rochefort, Série E, Sous-Série 1E, Dépêches de la Cour aux intendants, 1672–1763, 688; M. de Lagny to John Nelson, February 11, 1697, in Ravaisson, *Archives de la Bastille* IX:517–518.
5. John Kick to John Nelson, January 23, 1696, Temple-Nelson Papers, no. 26.
6. John Nelson to the Duke of Shrewsbury (draft), January 24, 1696, Temple-Nelson Papers, no. 26.
7. John Nelson to the Duke of Shrewsbury (draft), February 1696, Temple-Nelson Papers, nos. 27, 32. A slightly less detailed version of this draft is printed in the Historical Manuscripts Commission's *Report on the Manuscripts of the Duke of Buccleuch and Queensbury Preserved at Montagu House, Whitehall* (London, 1899–1926), vol. II, pt. 2, pp. 723–729; a transcript of a third version is in the Nelson Papers, Gay Transcripts, Massachusetts Historical Society. For its submission to the Board of Trade, see note 16, this chapter.

8. Nelson to Shrewsbury (draft), February 1696, Temple-Nelson Papers, no. 32.

9. *Ibid.*; William Kellaway, *The New England Company, 1649–1776: Missionary Society to the American Indians* (London, 1961), *passim*; Hall, *Edward Randolph*, 116.

10. Nelson to Shrewsbury (draft), February 1696, Temple-Nelson Papers, nos. 27, 32.

11. John Nelson to [the Duke of Shrewsbury], n.d., Historical Manuscripts Commission, *Report on the Manuscripts of the Duke of Buccleuch and Queensbury*, vol. II. pt. 2, pp. 722–723. Nelson seems to have based his calculations on the revenues obtained by the group of "farmers" who monopolized Canadian fur-trade purchases in return for an annual lump-sum payment to the Crown: Francis H. Hammang, *The Marquis de Vaudreuil: New France at the Beginning of the Eighteenth Century* (Louvain, 1938), 91–92.

12. Robert C. Ritchie, *Captain Kidd and the War against the Pirates* (Cambridge, Mass., 1986), 52–54.

13. Edward Randolph to John Nelson, October 29, 1691, Temple-Nelson Papers, no. 28.

14. Ian K. Steele, *Politics of Colonial Policy: The Board of Trade in Colonial Administration, 1696–1720* (Oxford, 1968), 10–18.

15. Journal of the Board of Trade, September 12 and 14, 1696, C.O.391/9, p. 103.

16. Journal of the Board of Trade, September 16, 23, and 24, 1696, *loc. cit.*, 109–111, 136, 139–140.

17. Memorial of John Nelson to the Board of Trade, [September 23, 1696], C.O.323/2, no. 10 (printed in *N. Y. Col. Docs.* IV:206–211).

18. Johnson, *Adjustment to Empire*, 191–193.

19. John Nelson, "A Scheme or Methods for the Reduction of Canada,"[September 23, 1696], C.O.323/2, no. 12 (quotation from p. 155). A second version, with some concluding additions made in late 1697 or early 1698 is in the Historical Manuscripts Commission's *Report on the Manuscripts of the Duke of Buccleuch and Queensbury*, vol. II, pt. 2, pp. 729–733.

20. Journal of the Board of Trade, September 25, 1696, C.O.391/9, pp. 145–146.

21. Board of Trade to the Lords Justices, September 30, 1696, *N. Y. Col. Docs.* IV:227–230. For Locke's authorship, see his notes on Nelson's paper, [September 1696], Locke Manuscripts, c.30, fol. 40, Bodleian Library, Oxford University; and William Popple to Lord Townshend, July 22, 1720, Historical Manuscripts Commission, *The Manuscripts of the Marquess Townshend. Eleventh Report*, Appendix, Part IV (London, 1887), 296. Locke attended all the September meetings at which Nelson gave evidence.

22. Hall, *Edward Randolph*, 154–170.

23. Gertrude Ann Jacobsen, *William Blathwayt, a Late Seventeenth Century Administrator* (New Haven, 1932), chaps. 5, 6, 10.

24. Edward Randolph to John Nelson, October 29, 1696, Temple-Nelson Papers, no. 28.

25. John Nelson to William Blathwayt, June 21, 1697, BL 251, Blathwayt Man-

uscripts, Huntington Library; Nelson to Blathwayt, October 29, 1698, C.O.5/860, no. 39.

26. E. E. Rich, *The History of the Hudson's Bay Company, 1670–1870* (London, 1958–1959) I:337–341; Journal of the Board of Trade, November 6 and 20, 1696, C.O.391/9, pp. 216, 239; Nelson, "State and Case of my affaires and Circumstances," [November 6, 1696], C.O.388/75, no. 5; Petition of John Nelson to the King (draft), December 1, 1696, Temple-Nelson Papers, no. 30.

27. Petition of John Nelson to the Lords of the Treasury, [September 8, 1696], Report of the commissioners for victualling the Navy to the Lords of the Treasury, November 19, 1696, Treasury 1/41, no. 28.

28. Address of Massachusetts to the King, September 24, 1696, Baxter, *Documentary History of Maine* V:447–451 (C.O.5/859, no. 44i); and, generally, *Mass. Acts and Resolves* VII:122–123, 127–129, 513–516, 521.

29. Journal of the Board of Trade, November 20, 1696, C.O.391/6, pp. 239–240; Notes taken by the Earl of Bridgewater, [November 20, 1696], EL 9630, Ellesmere MSS, Huntington Library; "A brief information whereon to ground an Enterprise for intercepting the Canada fleet," October 16, 1696, Locke MSS, c.30, fol. 42; Board of Trade to the King, November 25, 1696, C.O.5/907, p. 51.

30. Johnson, *Adjustment to Empire*, 258–259; Lawrence H. Leder, *Robert Livingston and the Politics of Colonial New York, 1654–1728* (Chapel Hill, 1961), 109–110.

31. Jacobsen, *William Blathwayt*, 310–311, 316; Steele, *Politics of Colonial Policy*, 62–63. For the rivalry on the Board between Locke and Blathwayt, see Steele, *op. cit.*, 24–25.

32. Notes taken by the Earl of Bridgewater, February 1, 1697, EL 9652, Ellesmere MSS; Memorial of the inhabitants, traders and proprietors, [February 1, 1697], C.O.5/859, no. 62; John Nelson and John Alden to the Queen, [August 16, 1695], C.O.388/3, p. 296. A second memorial seeking the same kind of confederation was submitted by one of Kidd's backers: Memorial of Edmund Harrison, [February 1, 1697], C.O.5/859, no. 60.

33. John Nelson and others to the King, January 25, 1690, C.O.5/855, no. 56. Nelson and the Anglican lawyer (and former attorney general of New York and Massachusetts) Thomas Newton were the only men to sign both the 1690 and 1697 memorials.

34. Journal of the Board of Trade, February 8, 1697, C.O.391/9, p. 393; Notes taken by the Earl of Bridgewater, February 8, 1697, EL 9655, Ellesmere MSS; Memorial of the New England Traders, [April 5, 1697], C.O.5/859, no. 212 (11 of its 59 signers had subscribed the February 1 memorial).

35. Johnson, *Adjustment to Empire*, 260–262.

36. Notes taken by the Earl of Bridgewater, March 15, 1697, EL 9681, Ellesmere MSS; Journal of the Board of Trade, March 17 and 26, 1697, C.O.391/10, pp. 32–33, 48–49; Board of Trade to Sir William Trumbull, March 19, 1697, C.O.324/6, p. 129.

37. William Popple to John Nelson, March 24, 1697, C.O.5/907, p. 145, and Temple-Nelson Papers, no. 34.

38. John Nelson to the Board of Trade, April 12, 1697; and Nelson to the Lords Justices, [April 13, 1697], C.O.5/859, nos. 88 and 87. Nelson's drafts of

both documents are in Temple-Nelson Papers, nos. 35, 42; and copies contained in Lansdowne MSS, 849, fols. 55–58, are printed in Baxter, *Documentary History of Maine* X:16–20. The memorials were forwarded to Secretary Trumbull: C.O.391/7, p. 77.

39. Petition of John Nelson to the King (draft), December 1, 1696, Temple-Nelson Papers, no. 30; Order in Council, March 18, 1697, Registers of the Privy Council (P.C.), Class 2, vol. 76, p. 596, Public Record Office; M. Hébert to M. de la Forest, December 31, 1696, *Calendar of State Papers, Colonial, 1696–1697*, no. 568; Memorial concerning the surrender of Fort Bourbon, [April 25, 1698], *loc.cit., 1697–1698*, no. 398; M. de Lagny to John Nelson, February 11, 1697, in Ravaisson, *Archives de la Bastille* IX:517–518; Sir William Trumbull to the Commissioners for the Exchange of Prisoners, March 23, 1697, *Calendar of State Papers, Domestic, 1697*, 69; and, generally, William Thomas Morgan, "A Crisis in the History of the Hudson's Bay Company, 1694–1697," *North Dakota Historical Quarterly* V, no. 4 (1931), 209–213.

40. Orders in Council, May 27 and June 3, 1697, P.C. 2/77, pp. 19, 25. While the date of Nelson's departure from England remains unknown, he was well embarked upon his plan by June 8: Sir William Trumbull to Ambassador Lord Villiers, June 18, 1697, State Papers (S.P.), Class 104, vol. 69, fol. 82d, Public Record Office.

41. James Lloyd to Samuel Breck, August 20, 1817, Temple-Nelson Papers, no. 71, printed in Mass. Hist. Soc., *Proceedings* VII (1863–1864): 371.

42. John Nelson to William Blathwayt, June 21, 1697, Rotterdam, BL 251, Blathwayt Papers, Huntington Library; Duke of Shrewsbury to William Blathwayt, August 13, 1697, Historical Manuscripts Commission, *Report on the Manuscripts of the Duke of Buccleuch and Queensbury*, vol. II, pt. 2, p. 531. As the brother of one of William's former mistresses, Villiers also had the ear of the king—he would soon become Earl of Jersey and Secretary of State.

43. John Nelson to William Blathwayt, June 21, 1697, Rotterdam, BL 251, Blathwayt Papers, Huntington Library; Brown *et al., Dictionary of Canadian Biography* II:112.

44. John Nelson to William Blathwayt, June 21, 1697, Rotterdam, BL 251, Blathwayt Papers, Huntington Library; James Vernon to the Duke of Shrewsbury, July 3, 1697, Shrewsbury Papers, Broughton House, Northamptonshire (microfilm) (misdated in James, *Letters Illustrative* I:309).

45. William Blathwayt to Matthew Prior, August 19 [N.S.], 1697, and James Vernon to Prior, May 4 and 18, 1697, in Historical Manuscripts Commission, *Calendar of the Manuscripts of the Marquess of Bath Preserved at Longleat, Wiltshire* (London, 1904–1908) III:148, 116, 120, respectively. Prior's journal of the negotiations paints an indelible picture, spiced by his deadpan wit, of their formality and complexity: *ibid.*, 508–548.

46. Sir William Trumbull to Ambassador Lord Villiers, June 18, 1697, S.P.104/69, fol. 82d; Minutes of the proceedings of the Lords Justices, July 1, 1697, S.P.44/275, pp. 103–104; Order in Council, July 1, 1697, P.C.2/77, p 34; warrant for the arrest of John Nelson (copy), July 1, 1697, Temple-Nelson Papers, no. 37.

47. James Vernon to Sir Joseph Williamson, July 2, 1697, *Calendar of State*

Papers, Domestic, 1697, 226–227 (S.P.32/7, no. 90); and, in a similar vein, Vernon to the Duke of Shrewsbury, July 1, 1697, in James, *Letters Illustrative* I:304–305. Vernon told of earlier meetings with Nelson in James, *op. cit.* I:83, 102.

48. Minutes of the proceedings of the Lords Justices, July 1, 1697, S.P.44/275, p. 103; James Vernon to Sir Joseph Williamson, July 2, 1697, *Calendar of State Papers, Domestic, 1697*, 226. La Forest was released the following month but died in London before he could return to France.

49. Sir William Trumbull to Lords Ambassador Pembroke and Villiers, June 4, 1697, Historical Manuscripts Commission, *Calendar of the Manuscripts of the Marquess of Bath* III:126; William Popple to John Nelson, June 22, 1697, Temple-Nelson Papers, no. 36; Nelson to the Board of Trade, July 2, 1697, C.O.388/6 (unfolioed).

50. Minutes of the proceedings of the Lords Justices, July 27, 1697, S.P.44/275, p. 149; Sir Richard Temple to John Nelson, Temple-Nelson Papers, no. 38.

51. James Vernon to Sir Joseph Williamson, August 13, 1697, S.P.32/7, no. 154; Duke of Shrewsbury to William Blathwayt, August 13, 1697, Historical Manuscripts Commission, *Report on the Manuscripts of the Duke of Buccleuch and Queensbury*, vol. II, pt. 2, p. 531.

52. Chap. 2, note 8.

53. Journal of the Board of Trade, October 18, 1697, C.O. 391/10, p.314; C.O.391/10, p. 314; William Popple to John Nelson "at Mr. Waterhouse his house in Georges Lane near the monument," October 19, 1697, Temple-Nelson Papers, no. 39; Memorial of John Nelson, November 2, 1697, C.O.5/859, no. 129 (printed, from the copy in Lansdowne MSS 849, fols. 61–64, in Baxter, *Documentary History of Maine* X:21–25).

54. Memorial of John Nelson, November 2, 1697, C.O.5/859, no. 129.

55. James Vernon to Sir Joseph Williamson, July 2, 1697, S.P.32/7, no. 90.

56. Journal of the Board of Trade, November 2, 1697, C.O.391/10, p. 334.

57. License for John Nelson to return to England, January 31, 1698, Temple-Nelson Papers, no. 41 (and *Calendar of State Papers, Domestic, 1698*, 61); John Nelson to John Locke, February 23, 1698, Locke MSS, c. 16, fol. 131.

58. John Nelson to the Board of Trade, December 2, 1697, C.O.323/2, no. 79 (a copy from Lansdowne MSS 849, fols. 67–68, is printed in *Documentary History of Maine* X:13–16). Nelson may also have sent further information to Blathwayt about French plans: Extract from a letter from Paris, [December 29, 1697], *Calendar of State Papers, Colonial, 1697–1698*, no. 130.

59. Nicholas Toinard to John Locke, December 6, 1697, January 16, 1698, Locke MSS, c. 21, fols. 187, 190; John Nelson to Locke, February 23, 1698, *loc. cit.*, c. 16, fols. 131–131v.

CHAPTER VII

1. Moses F. Sweetser, *King's Handbook of Boston Harbor*, 2nd ed. (Boston, 1883), 164; Edward Rowe Snow, *The Islands of Boston Harbor: Their History and Romance, 1626–1935* (Andover, 1935), 292.

2. Vote of the House of Representatives, February 17, 1694, Mass. Archives, C, 467; Testimony of Samuel Marshall and Thomas Barker, September 27, 1695, Suffolk County Court Files 162374 and 162375; Petition of Mary

Dafforne, March 31, 1697, Mass. Archives, XL, 444–445. The fever-ridden English troops had been quartered on Nelson's Long Island by order of Sir William Phips: *Mass. Acts and Resolves* VII:384.

3. Suffolk County Probate Records, new series, vol. I, 373–381; *Lloyd Family Papers* I:138.

4. Sewall, *Diary* I:392.

5. Gov. Villebon to Minister of Marine Pontchartrain, October 3, 1698; and Memoire of Villebon, June 27, 1699; in Archives des Colonies, C^{11D} vol. III, 105 and 166; Webster, *Acadia*, 117. These accounts date Nelson's arrival at the St. John River as either September 22 or 24, New Style—mid-September by the English reckoning. It had been in September also, twenty-eight years before, that Nelson surrendered his command at St. John River to the French.

6. Gov. Villebon and Mathieu De Goutin to [John Nelson], May 5, 1699, Mass. Archives, II, 1690.

7. William Stoughton to Charles Mellanson, June 6, 1696, Mass. Archives, LXII, 98; Pass issued by Gov. Phips to Charles De La Tour, July 11, 1694, Chamberlain Manuscripts, Ch.E10.83, Boston Public Library; Attestation of Abraham Boudrot, October 16, 1693, Collection Clairambault, vol. 380, fol. 302, Bibliothèque Nationale, Paris; *Collection de MSS* II:305, 307, 336; and, generally, Jean Daigle, "Les Relations Commerciales de l'Acadie avec le Massachusetts," *Revue de l'Université de Moncton* IX (1976): 53–61, and "Nos Amis les Ennemis: Les Marchands Acadiens et le Massachusetts à la Fin du 17e Siècle," *Les Cahiers de la Société Historique Acadienne* VII, no. 4 (1976), 161–170.

8. Memoir for the instruction of Gov. Villebon, February 14, 1693, Archives des Colonies, ser. B, vol. XVI, pt. 2, pp. 171–172; Complaints against M. de Villebon, [1698], *Collection de MSS* II:307–308; Memoir of M. Tibierge, June 21, 1699, Archives des Colonies, C^{11D}, vol. III, fols. 218–218d.

9. John Nelson to William Blathwayt, October 29, 1698; Gov. Villebon to Lt. Gov. Stoughton, September 5, 1698; in C.O.5/860, nos. 39, 37i; Letter of the Minister to Gov. Villebon, March 26, 1698, *Collection de MSS* II: 295–296.

10. John Nelson to the Board of Trade, November 4, 1698; Nelson to William Blathwayt, October 29, 1698; Lt. Gov. Stoughton to the Board of Trade, October 24, 1698; all C.O.5/860, nos. 40, 39, 37, respectively; John Pascal to John Nelson, June 15, 1699, Temple-Nelson Papers, no. 43; Address of the Massachusetts General Court to the King, November 19, 1698, *Mass. Acts and Resolves* VII:194. Nelson also wrote to the Earl of Bridgewater, John Povey, and Privy Council clerk (and Blathwayt's son-in-law) Edward Southwell: John Nelson to Gov. Bellomont, September 30, 1699, Temple-Nelson Papers, no. 44.

11. Votes of the Massachusetts Council and House of Representatives, November 22 and December 1, 1698, *Mass. Acts and Resolves* VII:196, 201; "The Petition of John Nelson Gentleman," November 30, 1698, *loc.cit.*, 607, and Mass. Archives, LXX, 389.

12. Board of Trade to Secretary Vernon, February 17, 1699, C.O.324/7, pp. 12–30.

13. Alternatives proposed by the French Ambassador, [April 29, 1700], C.O.5/ 861, no. 34i.
14. Memoirs of Gov. Villebon, October 27, 1699, and [1699?], both in Webster, *Acadia*, 139, 140.
15. Extract of letters from Acadia, June 27, 1699; and Order of Gov. Villebon, April 27, 1699; both Archives des Colonies, C^{11D}, vol. III, fols. 182, 215; Gov. Villebon and Mathieu De Goutin to John Nelson, May 6, 1699, Mass. Archives, II, 591.
16. Journal of John Marshall, Mass. Hist. Soc., *Proceedings* XXI (1884): 153; Minutes of Massachusetts Council, June 6, 1699, Mass. Archives, LXXXI, 192.
17. Grant of the Hull selectmen, December 18, 1699, Bowdoin-Temple Papers, Massachusetts Historical Society. For Davis, see Brown *et al., Dictionary of Canadian Biography* II:172; and John T. Hull, *The Siege and Capture of Fort Loyall, Destruction of Falmouth, May 20, 1690 (O.S.)* (Portland, 1885), *passim.*
18. John Nelson to Gov. Bellomont, September 30, 1699, Temple-Nelson Papers, no. 44. For Nelson's role, see Gov. Bellomont to Board of Trade, July 15, 1700, C.O.5/861, no. 53.
19. John Nelson and Sylvanus Davis to Gov. Bellomont, November 24, 1699, C.O.5/861, no. 4xxii; *Mass. Acts and Resolves* I:384–385; Ronald O. MacFarlane, "The Massachusetts Bay Truck-Houses in Diplomacy with the Indians," *New England Quarterly* XI (1938): 43–65. Nelson had urged the establishment of a trading house among the Penobscot Indians back in 1692: Hutchinson, *History of Massachusetts-Bay* I:321 n.
20. Negotiations of John Phillips, Penn Townsend, Nathaniel Byfield, and John Nelson, June 3, 1701, *Mass. Acts and Resolves* VII:736–740; Morrison, *Embattled Northeast*, 146–153. Nelson preserved a copy of the treaty: Temple-Nelson Papers, no. 46.
21. Johnson, *Adjustment to Empire*, 329–341.
22. Thwing, "Inhabitants and Estates of the Town of Boston," citing Suffolk Deeds MSS, XIX, 248; *loc.cit.* XX,197; *loc.cit.* XXI, 147; Indenture between John and Elizabeth Nelson and John Coney, Goldsmith, January 11, 1700, MSS Large, Mass. Hist. Soc. The Nelsons did occasionally spend weeks at a time back in downtown Boston: they may have stayed at the Beacon Hill house that they had sold to Elizabeth's brother, Col. William Tailer.
23. Suffolk County Court of the General Sessions of the Peace, Record Books, 1702–1712, 1712–1719, 1719–1725, 1725–1732, New State Archives Building, Boston. These volumes include Nelson's name in the Suffolk County Commissions of the Peace dated July 1702, August 1706, February 1709, February 1715, January 1716, December 1728, and December 1732. Though omitted in one of June 1717, he was reappointed in a commission of November 1717 not transcribed in the court's records but noted in Mass. Archives, Executive Records of the Council, VI, 537. Possibly, as John Murrin has suggested to me, Nelson may have served as a local magistrate on Long Island without joining the bench of justices at quarter sessions. A son-in-law, Thomas Steel, did serve on the court in the 1720s.

24. M. de Bonaventure to Minister of Marine Pontchartrain, December 24, 1706, Archives des Colonies, C^{11D}, vol. V, fols. 245v–246.

25. M. de Bonaventure to the Minister, December 24, 1706, *Collection de MSS* II:463; Yves Zoltvany, *Philippe de Rigaud de Vaudreuil, Governor of New France, 1703–1725* (Toronto, 1974), 59–63; Minister of Marine Pontchartrain to Gov. Vaudreuil, June 9, 1706, *N.Y. Col. Docs.* IX:779; Gerald M. Kelly, "Louis Allain in Acadia and New England," La Société Historique Acadienne, *39ième Cahier* IV, no. 9 (1973), 370–372. For the Courtemanche mission, see Arthur H. Buffinton, "Governor Dudley and the Proposed Treaty of Neutrality, 1705," Pubs. Col. Soc. Mass., *Transactions* XXVI (1925): 211–229; and the many documents printed in *Mass. Acts and Resolves* VIII:497 *et seq.*

26. G. M. Waller, *Samuel Vetch, Colonial Enterpriser* (Chapel Hill, 1960), 79–93; Hutchinson, *History of Massachusetts-Bay* II:115.

27. Deposition of John Nelson, November 6, 1700, Miscellaneous Bound MSS, 1699–1705, Mass. Hist. Soc.; Petition of the Merchants, Traders, and Sailors, June 27, 1705, *Mass. Acts and Resolves* VIII:511–512; Deposition of John Nelson and John Alden, [1706], C.O.5/864, no.178iii.

28. John Winthrop to FitzJohn Winthrop, [June 1706], Mass. Hist. Soc., *Collections*, 6th ser., III (1889): 335; Wait Winthrop to FitzJohn Winthrop, June 24, 1706, *loc.cit.*, 6th ser., V (1892): 142.

29. Waller, *Samuel Vetch*, 3–93; Gov. Dudley to Gov. Vaudreuil, July 5, 1705, *Collection de MSS* II:439.

30. John Chamberlayne to [Charles Montague, Lord Halifax], February 27, 1706, Egerton MSS 929, fols. 90–94; Waller, *Samuel Vetch*, 102–104; and, generally, James D. Alsop, "Samuel Vetch's 'Canada Surveyed': The Formation of a Colonial Strategy, 1706–1710," *Acadiensis* XII, no. 1 (1982), 39–58. Suggestions for a Scots colony on New England's frontier antedated Vetch's coming: thus Gov. Dudley to Board of Trade, September 15, 1703, *Calendar of State Papers, Colonial, 1702–3*, no. 1094; and John Winthrop, Jr., to Alexander, Lord Forbes, December 23, 1644, in Allyn B. Forbes, ed., *Winthrop Papers, 1498–1649* (Boston, 1929–1947) IV:501.

31. [Samuel Vetch], "Canada Survey'd," July 27, 1708, *Calendar of State Papers, Colonial, 1708–1709*, no. 60.

32. Worthington C. Ford, ed., *The Diary of Cotton Mather* (New York, 1957) I:570; Sewall, *Diary* I:544; Samuel Sewall to Nathaniel Higginson, October 21, 1706, Mass. Hist. Soc., *Collections*, 6th ser., I (1886): 340.

33. See chap. 6, note 7; and Richmond P. Bond, *Queen Anne's American Kings* (Oxford, 1952).

34. John Winthrop to Wait Winthrop, [May 1709], Mass. Hist. Soc., *Collections*, 6th ser., V (1892): 187; *Year-Book of the Society of Colonial Wars in the Commonwealth of Massachusetts*, no. 3 (1897), 99; *Mass. Acts and Resolves* IX:191–192. Nelson's name appears on only one of the numerous petitions drawn up by merchants and other New Englanders during 1709 pleading for the conquest of Canada and Port Royal: compare C.O.5/9, no. 91, with C.O.5/9, nos. 36 and 82, and HM 1372, Miscellaneous MSS, Huntington Library.

35. Gerald S. Graham, *The Walker Expedition to Quebec, Publications of the Champlain Society* XXXII (Toronto, 1953): 106–107, 115.

36. Sewall, *Diary* II:941, 952, 974.
37. Nelson's entanglement in the disposition of Wharton's estate can be followed in Mass. Archives, XXXVII, 162–164; Warrant for the arrest of John Nelson, April 13, 1699, C.O.5/1259, no. 40xxix; Suffolk County Court Files, nos. 10676, and 10747; *Mass. Acts and Resolves* IX:424–425, 452; Record Books for Suffolk County Inferior Court of Common Pleas, 1714–1715, p. 100; 1715–1718, p. 26; and John Nelson to Henry Lloyd, January 31, 1710, *Lloyd Family Papers* I:187. Nelson also served as executor for James Lloyd between 1693 and 1707: *Lloyd Family Papers*, 117–154. Cotton Mather's ordeal is recounted in Kenneth Silverman, *The Life and Times of Cotton Mather* (New York, 1984), 312–319, 360–361.
38. *Mass. Acts and Resolves* IX:424. Blagrove, Byfield, and Saffin figure prominently and pungently in Sewall's diary and throughout the period's legal records. For Byfield, see also Johnson, *Adjustment to Empire*, 357–360, and Barbara A. Black, "Nathaniel Byfield, 1653–1733," in *Law in Colonial Massachusetts, 1630–1800* (Boston, 1984), 57–105.
39. M. Tibierge to [John Nelson], August 22, 1702; and Gov. Brouillan to [Pierre Maisonnat], August 23, 1702; both in Mass. Archives, II, 603a and 605a, "Mémoire pour 1705," Gov. Vaudreuil to Gov. Samuel Shute, June 7, 1722, *Collection de MSS* I:613; *ibid*. III:83; Le Blant, *Figure Légendaire*, 178.
40. Gov. Vaudreuil to [John] Nelson, October 7, 1712, February 12, 1713, Temple-Nelson Papers, no. 47.
41. Brown *et al.*, *Dictionary of Canadian Biography* II:301. See also chap. 2, note 21.
42. Gov Vaudreuil to [John] Nelson, August 4 and October 16, 1724; and [Nelson] to [Vaudreuil], January 12, 1725; all in Temple-Nelson Papers, nos. 51, 52, 53. References in these letters suggesting that they were part of a continuing, but now lost, correspondence are supported by other evidence, such as Memorial of Paschal Nelson, [ca. 1750], *loc.cit.*, no. 60; Gov. Dudley to Secretary of State Viscount Bolingbroke, April 26, 1714, C.O.5/752, no. 4; and (referring to Nelson's contacts with Canada in 1723) President of the Navy Board to Gov. Charles de Beauharnois de La Boische, May 12, 1728, in Archives des Colonies, Série B, vol. LII, fol. 522d.
43. [John Nelson] to [René Robinau de Portneuf?], [1725], Temple-Nelson Papers, no. 53.
44. Inventory of estate of Temple Nelson, August 4, 1739, Suffolk County Probate Records, new ser., XX, 503–507.
45. *Ibid*.
46. John Nelson to Henry Lloyd, June 28, 1715, *Lloyd Family Papers* I:206; Record Book of the Suffolk County Court of General Sessions of the Peace, 1712–1719, p. 14, New State Archives Building, Boston; Suffolk County Court Files, nos. 8887, 17266; Recognizance Bond of John Nelson, April 21, 1721, Norcross Papers, Box 1, Mass. Hist. Soc.
47. *Lloyd Family Papers* I:110, 115, 121, 144, 147, 161.
48. Margaret Nelson to Henry Lloyd, August 31, [1719], *Lloyd Family Papers* I:234. Around 1740, one-fifth of Boston families owned slaves, and black slaves composed at least 8½ percent of the town's population of some 16,000 people: Gary B. Nash, *The Urban Crucible: Social Change, Political Con-*

sciousness, and the Origins of the American Revolution (Cambridge, Mass., 1979), 107.

49. John Nelson to Henry Lloyd, April 13, 1712; Feb. 12, 1714; and June 28, 1715; all *Lloyd Family Papers* I:194, 204, 206 respectively; and, generally, *Lloyd Family Papers*, I:183–295, for family affairs. No letters survive from the pen of John's wife, Elizabeth.

50. Sewall, *Diary* II:1123.

51. For suits in which Nelson was the defendant for monies owed, see Sewall, *Diary* II:801; Suffolk County Court Files, nos. 16466, 18048, 18148, 21265, 20781.

52. Memorial of Paschal Nelson, [1750?], Temple-Nelson Papers, no. 60.

53. Will of John Nelson, January 29, 1730, Miscellaneous Bound MSS, 1728–1733, Mass. Hist. Soc.; and Suffolk County Probate Records, XXX, 448–450; Shurtleff, *Topographical and Historical Description of Boston*, 533–534, 629; Suffolk County Court Files, no. 14088; *Lloyd Family Papers* I: 204, 353.

54. John Nelson to Rebecca Lloyd, May 9, 1720; and Robert Temple to Henry Lloyd, June 29, 1742, *Lloyd Family Papers* I:236, 353.

55. Bailyn, *New England Merchants*, 195–197.

56. John Winthrop to Wait Winthrop, June, 1711, Mass. Hist. Soc. *Collections*, 6th ser., V (1892): 232; Jeremiah Dummer to [Gov. Joseph Dudley], June 5, 1711, Miscellaneous Bound MSS, 1701–1713, Mass. Hist. Society.

57. Foote, *Annals of King's Chapel* II:176–178, 586, 603, 605; Testimony of members of the Church of England, February 4, 1706; and John Nelson to Mr. Popple, February 11, 1706; in C.O.5/864, nos. 63 and 72.

58. Chap. 5, note 16.

59. Johnson, *Adjustment to Empire*, 346–353.

60. William Tailer to John Nelson, April 3, 1717, Temple-Nelson Papers, no. 48; Nelson to Henry Lloyd, May 24 and October 14, 1717, *Lloyd Family Papers* I:218, 224. Further details of Tailer's lobbying in England are contained in Tailer's letterbook, Belknap Papers, 1664–1744, no. 77, Mass. Hist. Society. Charles Dalton, ed., *English Army Lists and Commission Registers, 1661–1714* VI (London, 1904): 285, records his commission.

61. William Tailer to John Nelson, April 3, 1717; and Richard Temple, Viscount Cobham, to Tailer, August 18, 1719; in Temple-Nelson Papers, nos. 48 and 49; *Journal of the Commissioners for Trade and Plantations from November 1718 to December 1722* (London, 1925), 90–94; J. B. Brebner, "Subsidized Intermarriage with the Indians: An Incident in British Colonial Policy," *Canadian Historical Review* VI (1925): 33–36.

62. Francis Nicholson to "Mr. Thomas Nelson," March 31, 1720, Temple-Nelson Papers, no. 50. For petitions for land in Nova Scotia, including one submitted by Cobham, see Grant and Munro, *Acts of the Privy Council, Colonial* II:745–747, 764–765.

63. Brown *et al*, *Dictionary of Canadian Biography* II:590–591; William G. Godfrey, *Pursuit of Profit and Preferment in Colonial North America: John Bradstreet's Quest* (Waterloo, Ontario, 1982), 3–4.

64. Viscount Cobham to John Nelson, October 14, 1727; and Robert Temple to [Paschal Nelson], December 26, 1753; in Temple-Nelson Papers, nos. 56 and 64; Col. David Dunbar to Mr. Popple, June 4, 1731, *Calendar of State*

Papers, Colonial, 1731, no. 217. Part of Waldo and Nelson's agreement, dated April 29, 1729, is in Miscellaneous MSS, Mass. Hist. Society. For Waldo's use of this title (and of another purchased from the heirs of Sir William Phips), see Douglas Brymner, ed., *Report on Canadian Archives for 1886* (Ottawa, 1887), cliv–clvi.

65. John Nelson to Henry Lloyd, May 24, 1717, *Lloyd Family Papers* I:218. Perhaps in preparation for this venture, Nelson had sought and received permission to erect a warehouse in south Boston: *Reports of the Records Commissioners of the City of Boston* XXIX:216.

66. John B. Blake, *Public Health in the Town of Boston, 1630–1820* (Cambridge, Mass., 1959), 52–73, 248.

67. Zabdiel Boylston, *An Historical Account of the Small-Pox Inoculation in New England*, 2nd ed. (Boston, 1730), 38.

68. Memorial of Paschal Nelson, [ca. 1750], undated draft by Paschal Nelson, Temple-Nelson Papers, nos. 60, 61; *Lloyd Family Papers* I:242, 245–246, 262, 283–292; Deposition of Christopher Rhymes, November 13, 1723, *Calendar of State Papers, Colonial, 1724–25*, no. 85iii(a).

69. John Nelson to Gov. Vaudreuil, January 12, 1725, Temple-Nelson Papers, no. 53. In this letter, Nelson hoped to trade between Cape Breton and "Martineo & other Islands," what Vaudreuil in his reply (Temple-Nelson Papers, no. 55) called "Martinique" island. Both were referring to Matinicus and its neighboring islands in Penobscot Bay, then frequented by English fisherman. Thus *Collection de MSS* I:364, 410, 412.

70. Temple Nelson's only son, John, born in 1730, settled in Portsmouth, New Hampshire, where he speculated in frontier lands and traded with the West Indies. Later, he secured the post of collector of customs in the Caribbean island of Nevis. The last John Nelson in direct descent from his grandfather, he died in 1784, without known heirs, in the neighboring island of Grenada.

71. Clifford L. Shipton, *Sibley's Harvard Graduates: Biographical Sketches of Those Who Attended Harvard College. Volume VI: 1713–1721* (Cambridge, Mass., 1942), 503–504—an account, however, that must be checked against other sources.

72. *Ibid.*, 504–507; Viscount Cobham to Sir William Yonge, May 3, 1744, undated drafts [ca. 1752–1756] of petitions and memorials of Paschal Nelson, Temple-Nelson Papers, nos. 59, 65–69; *Journal of the Commissioners for Trade and Plantations from January 1749–1750 to December 1753* (London, 1932), 57–59; George Grenville to Paschal Nelson, July 18, 1756, Mass. Hist. Soc., *Collections*, 6th ser., IX (1897): 3.

73. Charles Knowles Bolton, *Scotch Irish Pioneers* (Boston, 1910), 130–146, 218–219; Roy Hidemichi Akagi, *The Town Proprietors of the New England Colonies* (Philadelphia, 1924), 259–261; Maine Hist. Soc., *Collections*, 2nd ser., IV (1893): 242–244.

74. Robert Temple to Henry Lloyd, June 29, 1742; and Samuel Fitch to Henry Lloyd, January 18, 1755; in *Lloyd Family Papers* I:353; II: 524–527, respectively; Gordon E. Kershaw, *"Gentlemen of Large Property and Judicious Men": The Kennebeck Proprietors, 1749–1775* (Somersworth, N.H., 1975): 79–81.

75. Mass. Hist. Society, *Collections*, 6th ser., IX (1897): xvi–xvii.

76. John Nelson to Henry Lloyd, February 21, 1726; and April 1, 1728; in *Lloyd*

Family Papers I:264, 295, respectively; Sewall, *Diary* II:1035. Tailer, however, died in 1732, leaving an estate valued at over £9,000.

77. David Dunbar to Mr. Popple, November 17, 1730, *Calendar of State Papers, Colonial, 1730*, no. 533.

78. *The Notebook of John Smibert* (Boston, 1969), 90; and page 31 of this book.

79. John Nelson to Henry Lloyd, September 2, 1728, *Lloyd Family Papers* I:300; *Boston Weekly News-Letter*, November 14–21, 1734. Timothy Cutler's funeral sermon, *The Final Peace*, dates Nelson's death as November 15.

CHAPTER VIII

1. John Nelson to Gov. Vaudreuil, January 12, 1725, Temple-Nelson Papers, no. 53.

2. P. M. G. Dickson and J. G. Sperling, "War Finance, 1689–1714," in J. S. Bromley, ed., *The New Cambridge Modern History* VI (Cambridge, 1970): 284–315; and, more generally, Samuel E. Finer, "State- and Nation-Building in Europe: The Role of the Military," in Charles Tilly, ed., *The Formations of National States in Western Europe* (Princeton, N.J., 1975), 84–163. For a penetrating analysis of the constitutional ambivalences that emerged, see Jack P. Greene, *Peripheries and Center: Constitutional Development in the Extended Polities of the British Empire and the United States, 1607–1788* (Athens, Ga., 1986).

3. *Journal of the Commissioners for Trade and Plantations from November 1718 to December 1722* (London, 1925), 92; Representation of September 8, 1721, *N. Y. Col. Docs*, V: 591–630.

4. [Sir Robert Southwell?] to Daniel Finch, Earl of Nottingham, March 23, 1689, Blathwayt Papers, BL 418, Huntington Library.

5. D. W. Meinig, *The Shaping of America: A Geographical Perspective on 500 Years of History. Volume 1: Atlantic America, 1492–1800* (New Haven, 1986), 100.

6. Thomas Dongan to John Nelson, March 6, 1684, Temple-Nelson Papers, no. 15; Representation of Richard Smithsend to the King, [December 3, 1691], C.O.5/856, no. 209; Memoir of M. de Meneval, April 6, 1691, *Collection de MSS* II:43.

7. Cotton Mather, *The Serviceable Man* (Boston, 1690), 61; Johnson, *Adjustment to Empire*, 133–134; and, generally, Philip S. Haffenden, *New England in the English Nation, 1689–1713* (Oxford, 1974), 38–71.

8. Cotton Mather, *Things for a Distress'd People to Think Upon* (Boston, 1696), 64, 74; *idem, Present State of New-England*, 28.

9. Mather, *The Serviceable Man*, 31, 53.

10. Edward Randolph to the King, September 20, 1676, Toppan and Goodrick, *Randolph Letters* II:217; and, for the new ceremonials of loyalty to the Crown, Richard L. Bushman, *King and People in Provincial Massachusetts* (Chapel Hill, 1985), 14–25.

11. Sewall, *Diary*, II:1012.

12. Relation of Grace Higiman, May 31, 1695, Mass. Archives, VIII, 36.

13. Cutler, *The Final Peace, Security, and Happiness of the Upright*, 14.

BIBLIOGRAPHY

PRIMARY SOURCES

Manuscripts

France [from transcripts and microfilm copies held in the Public Archives of
   Canada in Ottawa]

Archives départmentales de la Charente-Maritime, La Rochelle
   Admirauté de La Rochelle, Série B
Archives Maritimes, Port de Rochefort, Rochefort
   Série E, Sous-Série 1E
Archives Nationales, Paris
   Archives de la Marine, Série B
   Archives des Colonies, Séries B, C^{11A}, C^{11D}, C^{11E}
Bibliothèque de l'Arsenal, Paris
   Archives de la Bastille
Bibliothèque Nationale, Paris
   Collection Clairambault

Great Britain

Bodleian Library, Oxford University, Oxford
   Locke Manuscripts
   Rawlinson Manuscripts
British Library, London

Egerton Manuscripts
Lansdowne Manuscripts
Stowe Manuscripts
Broughton House, Northamptonshire, England
  Shrewsbury Papers, microfilm copy in the Library of the University of Washington, Seattle
Lambeth Palace Library, London
  Fulham Manuscripts, microfilm copy in the Library of Congress, Washington, D.C.
Public Record Office, London
  Colonial Office Papers, classes 1, 5, 323, 324, 388, 391
  Probate, class 11
  Registers of the Privy Council, class 2
  State Papers, classes 32, 44, 104
  Treasury Papers, class 1
Westminster City Library, London
  Parish Register of St. Martin-in-the-Fields
  Records of the Parish of St. Martin-in-the-Fields

United States

American Antiquarian Society, Worcester, Massachusetts
  Mather Papers
Boston Public Library, Boston, Massachusetts
  Mather Papers
  Chamberlain Manuscripts
Colonial Williamsburg, Williamsburg, Virginia
  Blathwayt Papers
Houghton Library, Harvard University, Massachusetts
  Lloyd, Vassall, Borland Papers
  Temple-Nelson Papers
Huntington Library, San Marino, California
  Blathwayt Manuscripts
  Ellesmere Manuscripts
  Miscellaneous Manuscripts
  Stowe-Temple Papers
Massachusetts Archives, New State Archives Building, Columbia Point, Boston
  Massachusetts Archives, Volumes II, III, VII, VIII, XXX, XXXV, XXXVI, XXXVII, XL, LXI, LXII, LXX, LXXI; Court Records, VI; Executive Records of Council, VI.
  Records of the Massachusetts Superior Court of Judicature, 1686–1700
  Suffolk County Court Files
  Suffolk County Court, Records, 1680–1692
  Suffolk County Court of General Sessions of the Peace, Record Books, 1702–1712, 1712–1719, 1719–1725, 1725–1732
  Suffolk County Inferior Court of Common Pleas, Record Books, 1698–1701, 1714–1715, 1715–1718
Massachusetts Historical Society, Boston
  Belknap Papers
  Bowdoin-Temple Papers

Greenough Collection
Jeffries Papers
Manuscripts Large
Miscellaneous Bound Manuscripts
Miscellaneous Manuscripts
Norcross Papers
Nelson Papers, Gay Transcripts
Parkman Papers
Prince Papers
William Tailer Letterbook, Belknap Papers
Annie Haven Thwing, "Inhabitants and Estates of the Town of Boston, 1639–1800"
Old Court House, Boston
Suffolk County Probate Records

Published Works

Andrews, Charles M., ed. *Narratives of the Insurrections, 1675–1690*. New York, 1915.
"Andros Records." American Antiquarian Society, *Proceedings*, new series, XIII (1900): 237–268, 463–499.
Boston. *Reports of the Records Commissioners of the City of Boston*. 39 vols. Boston, 1876–1909.
————. *Boston Weekly News-Letter*.
Boston Museum of Fine Arts. *New England Begins: The Seventeenth Century*. 3 vols. Boston, 1982.
Boylston, Zabdiel. *An Historical Account of the Small-Pox Inoculation in New England*. 2nd ed. Boston, 1730.
Brymner, Douglas, ed. *Report on Canadian Archives for 1886*. Ottawa, 1887.
Bullivant, Benjamin. "Journal of Dr. Benjamin Bullivant." Massachusetts Historical Society, *Proceedings*, XVI (1878): 101–108.
Burr, George Lincoln, ed. *Narratives of the Witchcraft Cases, 1648–1706*. New York, 1914.
Champlain, Samuel de. *The Works of Samuel de Champlain*. Edited by Henry P. Biggar. 6 vols. Toronto, 1922–1936.
Collection de Manuscrits contenant Lettres, Mémoires, et Autres Documents Historiques Relatifs à la Nouvelle-France. 4 vols. Quebec, 1883–1885.
Cutler, Timothy. *The Final Peace, Security, and Happiness of the Upright, A Sermon Deliver'd at Christ-Church in Boston, Novemb. 28, 1734. On Occasion of the Death of John Nelson Esq. and of Mrs. Elizabeth Nelson, His Consort*. Boston, 1735.
Dalton, Charles, ed. *English Army Lists and Commission Registers, 1661–1714*. Vol. VI. London, 1904.
Davenport, Frances G. *European Treaties bearing on the History of the United States and its Dependencies*. 4 vols. Washington, D.C., 1917–1937.
Fletcher, Reginald J. *The Pension Book of Gray's Inn, 1569–1669*. 2 vols. London, 1901.
Forbes, Allyn B., ed. *Winthrop Papers, 1498–1649*. 5 vols. Boston, 1929–1947.
Foster, Joseph. *Register of Admissions to Gray's Inn, 1521–1889*. London, 1889.

Fuller, Thomas. *The History of the Worthies of England.* Edited by P. Austin Nuttall. 3 vols. London, 1840.

Graham, Gerald S. *The Walker Expedition to Quebec. Publications of the Champlain Society.* Vol. XXXII. Toronto, 1953.

Great Britain. *Acts of the Privy Council of England, Colonial Series.* Edited by W. L. Grant and James Munro. 6 vols. London, 1908–1912.

———. *Calendar of the Proceedings of the Committee for Compounding &c., 1643–1660.* Edited by Mary Anne Everett Green. 5 vols. London, 1889–1892.

———. *Calendar of State Papers, Colonial Series, America and West Indies.* Edited by W. Noel Sainsbury *et al.* 44 vols. London, 1860–1969.

———. *Calendar of State Papers, Domestic Series, 1649–1660.* Edited by Mary Anne Everett Green. 13 vols. London, 1875–1886.

———. *Calendar of State ·Papers, Domestic Series, of the Reign of William and Mary.* Edited by William J. Hardy. 11 vols. London, 1895–1937.

———. Historical Manuscripts Commission. *Calendar of the Manuscripts of the Marquess of Bath Preserved at Longleat, Wiltshire.* 3 vols. London, 1904–1908.

———. Historical Manuscripts Commission. *Report on the Manuscripts of the Duke of Buccleuch and Queensbury Preserved at Montagu House, Whitehall.* 3 vols. London, 1899–1926.

———. Historical Manuscripts Commission. *The Manuscripts of the House of Lords.* New series, 11 vols. London, 1900–1962.

———. Historical Manuscripts Commission. *The Manuscripts of the Marquess Townshend. Eleventh Report*, Appendix, Part IV. London, 1887.

———. *Journal of the Commissioners for Trade and Plantations.* 14 vols. London, 1920–1938.

Higginson, John. *The Cause of God and his People in New-England.* Cambridge, Mass., 1664.

Hough, Franklin B., ed. "Pemaquid Papers." Maine Historical Society, *Collections* V (1857).

Howell, Thomas Bayly, ed. *Cobbett's Complete Collection of State Trials.* 33 vols. London, 1809–1833.

Jeaffreson, J. C., ed., *Middlesex County Records.* 4 vols. London, 1886–1892.

Johnson, Edward. *Johnson's Wonder-working Providence.* Edited by J. Franklin Jameson. New York, 1910.

Journal of the Proceedings in the Late Expedition to Port-Royal, A. Boston, 1690.

Lloyd Family Papers. *Papers of the Lloyd Family of the Manor of Queens Village, Lloyd's Neck, Long Island, New York 1654–1826. Collections of the New-York Historical Society,* vols. LIX–LX. New York, 1927.

Maine. *Documentary History of the State of Maine.* Edited by James P. Baxter. Maine Historical Society, *Collections*, 2nd series, I–XXIV. Portland, Me., 1869–1916.

Massachusetts. *Acts and Resolves, Public and Private, of the Province of Massachusetts Bay.* Edited by Abner C. Goodell and Melville M. Bigelow. 21 vols. Boston, 1869–1922.

———. *Records of the Governor and Company of the Massachusetts Bay in New England.* Edited by Nathaniel B. Shurtleff. 5 vols. Boston, 1853–1854.

Mather, Cotton. *The Diary of Cotton Mather*. Edited by Worthington C. Ford. 2 vols. New York, 1957.

———. *The Life of Sir William Phips*. Edited by Mark Van Doren. New York, 1929.

———. *Parentator. Memoirs of Remarkables in the Life and the Death of the Ever-Memorable Dr. Increase Mather*. Boston, 1724.

———. *The Present State of New-England*. Boston, 1690.

———. *The Serviceable Man*. Boston, 1690.

———. *Things for a Distress'd People to Think Upon*. Boston, 1696.

Mather, Increase. *A Call to the Tempted. A Sermon on the Horrid Crime of Self-Murder*. Boston, 1724.

Mémoires des Commissaires du Roi et de Ceux de sa Majesté Britannique sur les Possessions et les Droits Respectifs des Deux Coronnes en Amerique; avec les Acts Publics et Pièces Justificatives. 4 vols. Paris, 1755.

Memorials of the English and French Commissaries Concerning the Limits of Nova Scotia or Acadia. 2 vols. London, 1754.

Moody, Robert Earle, and Richard Clive Simmons, eds. *The Glorious Revolution in Massachusetts: Selected Documents, 1689–1692*. Publications of the Colonial Society of Massachusetts, vol. LXIV. Boston, 1988.

Morison, Samuel Eliot, ed. "Records of the Suffolk County Court, 1671–1680." Publications of the Colonial Society of Massachusetts, *Collections*, vols. XXIX–XXX. Boston, 1933.

Morse, William I. *Acadiensia Nova, 1598–1779*. 2 vols. London, 1935.

New York. *Documents Relative to the Colonial History of the State of New York*. Edited by Edmund B. O'Callaghan and Berthold Fernow. 15 vols. Albany, N.Y., 1853–1887.

Randolph, Edward. *Edward Randolph: Including his Letters and Official Papers from the New England, Middle, and Southern Colonies in America, with Other Documents Relating Chiefly to the Vacating of the Royal Charter of the Colony of Massachusetts, 1676–1703*. Edited by Robert N. Toppan and Alfred T. S. Goodrick. Prince Society Publications, vols. XXIV–XXVIII, XXX–XXXI. Boston, 1898–1909.

Rapport de l'Archiviste de la Province de Québec pour 1927–1928. Quebec, 1928.

Ravaisson, François, ed. *Archives de la Bastille: Documents Inédits*. 19 vols. Paris, 1866–1904.

Recueil des Cartes, Plans, et Vues Relatifs aux États-Unis et au Canada, New York, Boston, Montréal, Québec, Louisbourg (1651–1731). Edited by A. L. Pinart. Paris, 1893.

Sewall, Samuel. *The Diary of Samuel Sewall, 1674–1729*. Edited by M. Halsey Thomas. 2 vols. New York, 1973.

Smibert, John. *The Notebook of John Smibert*. Boston, 1969.

Suffolk Deeds. 14 vols. Boston, 1880–1906.

Thurloe, John. *A Collection of the State Papers of John Thurloe Esq*. Edited by Thomas Birch. 7 vols. London, 1742.

Thwaites, Reuben G., ed. *New Voyages to North-America by the Baron de Lahontan*. 2 vols. Chicago, 1901.

Vernon, James. *Letters Illustrative of the Reign of William III from 1696 to 1708 addressed to the Duke of Shrewsbury by James Vernon Esq*. Edited by G. P. R. James. 3 vols. London, 1841.

Webster, John Clarence, ed., *Relation of the Voyage to Port Royal in Acadia or New France by the Sieur de Dièreville*. Toronto, 1933.

Winthrop, John. *Winthrop's Journal "History of New England," 1603–1649*. Edited by James K. Hosmer. 2 vols. New York, 1908.

SECONDARY SOURCES

Akagi, Roy Hidemichi. *The Town Proprietors of the New England Colonies*. Philadelphia, 1924.

Alsop, James D. "Samuel Vetch's 'Canada Surveyed': The Formation of a Colonial Strategy, 1706–1710." *Acadiensis* XII, no. 1 (1982): 39–58.

Andrews, Charles M. *British Committees, Commissions, and Councils of Trade and Plantations, 1622–1675*. Baltimore, 1908.

Arsenault, Bona. *History of the Acadians*. Ottawa, 1978.

Axtell, James. "The Scholastic Philosophy of the Wilderness." *William and Mary Quarterly*, 3rd series, XXIX (1972): 335–366.

Bailyn, Bernard. *The New England Merchants in the Seventeenth Century*. Cambridge, Mass., 1955.

Barnes, Viola. *The Dominion of New England: A Study of British Colonial Policy*. New Haven, 1923.

———. "Richard Wharton, A Seventeenth Century New England Colonial." Publications of the Colonial Society of Massachusetts, *Transactions* XXVI (1924–1926): 238–270.

———. Viola F. Barnes, "The Rise of Sir William Phips." *New England Quarterly* I (1928) : 271–294.

Barrow, Thomas C. *Trade and Empire: The British Customs Service in Colonial America, 1660–1775*. Cambridge, Mass., 1967.

Bolton, Charles Knowles. *Scotch Irish Pioneers*. Boston, 1910.

Blake, John B. *Public Health in the Town of Boston, 1630–1820*. Cambridge, Mass., 1959.

Bond, Richmond P. *Queen Anne's American Kings*. Oxford, 1952.

Brebner, John Bartlet. *New England's Outpost: Acadia before the Conquest of Canada*. New York, 1927.

———. "Subsidized Intermarriage with the Indians: An Incident in British Colonial Policy." *Canadian Historical Review* VI (1925): 33–36.

Brewer, John. *The Sinews of Power: War, Money, and the English State, 1688–1783*. New York, 1989.

Brown, George W., *et al.*, eds., *Dictionary of Canadian Biography*. 11 vols. Toronto, 1965–1982.

Buffington, Arthur H. "Governor Dudley and the Proposed Treaty of Neutrality, 1705." Publications of the Colonial Society of Massachusetts, *Transactions* XXVI (1925): 211–229.

———. "John Nelson's Voyage to Quebec in 1682: A Chapter in the Fisheries Controversy." Publications of the Colonial Society of Massachusetts, *Transactions* XXVI (1927): 427–437.

———. "Sir Thomas Temple in Boston, a Case of Benevolent Assimilation."

Publications of the Colonial Society of Massachusetts, *Transactions* XXVII (1932): 308–319.

——. "The Policy of the Northern English Colonies towards the French to the Peace of Utrecht." Ph.D. diss., Harvard University, 1925.

Bushman, Richard L. *King and People in Provincial Massachusetts*. Chapel Hill, 1985.

Carr, Lois Green, and David William Jordan. *Maryland's Revolution of Government, 1689–1692*. Ithaca, N.Y., 1974.

Clark, Andrew Hill. *Acadia: The Geography of Early Nova Scotia to 1760*. Madison, 1968.

Comeau, Roger. "Pêche et Traite en Acadie jusqu'en 1713." Ph.D. diss., Université d'Ottawa, 1949.

Daigle, Jean. "Les Relations Commerciales de l'Acadie avec le Massachusetts: le Cas de Charles-Amadour de Saint-Étienne de la Tour, 1695–1697." *Revue de l'Université de Moncton* IX (1976): 53–61.

——. "Nos Amis les Ennemis: Les Marchands Acadiens et le Massachusetts à la Fin du 17e Siècle." *Les Cahiers de la Société Historique Acadienne* VII no. 4 (1976): 161–170.

——. "Nos Amis les Ennemis: Relations Commerciales de l'Acadie avec le Massachusetts, 1670–1711." Ph.D. diss., University of Maine, 1975.

——*et al.* "L'Acadie au Temps du Sieur Perrot." La Société Historique Acadienne, *Dix-Neuviéme Cahier* II, no. IX (1968): 313–346.

Daviault, Pierre. *Le Baron de Saint-Castin: Chef Abénaquis*. Montreal, 1939.

Davies, K. G. *The Royal African Company*. New York, 1970.

Dawes, Norman H. "Titles as Symbols of Prestige in Seventeenth-Century New England." *William and Mary Quarterly*, 3rd series, VI (1949): 69–83.

Dickson, P. M. G., and J. G. Sperling. "War Finance, 1689–1714." In *The New Cambridge Modern History*, vol. VI. Edited by J. S. Bromley. Cambridge, 1970.

Drake, Samuel A. *Captain Nelson: A Romance of Colonial Days*. New York, 1879.

Dubourg-Noves, Pierre. "Forteresses et Résidences des Comtes d'Angloulême dans leur Capitale." Société Archéologique et Historique de la Charente, *Bulletin Mensuel* (1981): 47–61.

Dunn, Richard S. *Puritans and Yankees: The Winthrop Dynasty of New England, 1630–1717*. Princeton, 1962.

Eccles, W. J. *Canada under Louis XIV, 1663–1701*. Toronto, 1964.

——. *Frontenac: The Courtier Governor*. Toronto, 1959.

Foote, Henry W. *Annals of King's Chapel*. 2 vols. Boston, 1882–1896.

Godfrey, William G. *Pursuit of Profit and Preferment in Colonial North America: John Bradstreet's Quest*. Waterloo, Ontario, 1982.

Greene, Jack P. *Peripheries and Center: Constitutional Development in the Extended Polities of the British Empire and the United States, 1607–1788*. Athens, Ga., 1986.

Haffenden, Philip S. *New England in the English Nation, 1689–1713*. Oxford, 1974.

Hall, Michael G. *Edward Randolph and the American Colonies, 1676–1703*. Chapel Hill, 1960.

Hammang, Francis. *The Marquis de Vaudreuil: New France at the Beginning of the Eighteenth Century*. Louvain, 1938.

Harris, R. Cole, ed. *Historical Atlas of Canada. Volume I: From the Beginnings to 1800*. Toronto, 1987.

Hutchinson, Thomas. *History of the Colony and Province of Massachusetts-Bay*. Edited by Lawrence Shaw Mayo. 3 vols. Cambridge, Mass., 1936.

Innis, Harold A. *The Cod Fisheries: The History of an International Economy*. Revised edition: Toronto, 1954.

Jacobsen, Gertrude Ann. *William Blathwayt, a Late Seventeenth Century Administrator*. New Haven, 1932.

Johnson, Richard R. *Adjustment to Empire: The New England Colonies, 1675–1715*. New Brunswick, N.J., 1981.

———. "The Search for a Usable Indian: An Aspect of the Defense of Colonial New England." *Journal of American History* LXIV (1977): 623–651.

———. "Charles McLean Andrews and the Invention of American Colonial History." *William and Mary Quarterly*, 3rd series, XLIII (1986): 519–541.

Kellaway, William. *The New England Company, 1649–1776: Missionary Society to the American Indians*. London, 1961.

Kelly, Gerald M. "Louis Allain in Acadia and New England." La Société Historique Acadienne, *39ième Cahier* IV, no. 9 (1973): 362–380.

Kershaw, Gordon E. *"Gentlemen of Large Property and Judicious Men": The Kennebeck Proprietors, 1749–1775*. Somersworth, N.H., 1975.

Konig, David Thomas. *Law and Society in Puritan Massachusetts, 1629–1692*. Chapel Hill, 1979.

Leder, Lawrence H. *Robert Livingston and the Politics of Colonial New York, 1654–1728*. Chapel Hill, 1961.

Le Blant, Robert. *Une Figure Légendaire de l'Histoire Acadienne: Le Baron de Saint-Castin*. Dax, no date.

Lounsbury, Ralph Greenlee. "Yankee Trade at Newfoundland." *New England Quarterly* III (1930): 607–626.

Lovejoy, David S. *The Glorious Revolution in America*. New York, 1972.

McCully, Bruce T. "The New England–Acadia Fishery Dispute and the Nicholson Mission of August, 1687." *Essex Institute Historical Collections* XCVI (1960): 277–290.

MacDonald, M. A. *Fortune and La Tour: The Civil War in Acadia*. Toronto, 1983.

MacFarlane, Ronald O. "The Massachusetts Bay Truck-Houses in Diplomacy with the Indians." *New England Quarterly* XI (1938): 48–65.

Mattingly, Garrett. "No Peace Beyond What Line?" *Transactions of the Royal Historical Society*, 5th series, XIII (1963): 145–162.

Meinig, D. W. *The Shaping of America: A Geographical Perspective on 500 Years of History. Volume I: Atlantic America, 1492–1800*. New Haven, 1986.

Morgan, William Thomas. "A Crisis in the History of the Hudson's Bay Company, 1694–1697." *North Dakota Historical Quarterly* V, no. 4 (1931): 197–218.

Morrison, Kenneth M. *The Embattled Northeast: The Elusive Idea of Alliance in Abenaki–Euramerican Relations*. Berkeley, 1984.

Nash, Gary B. *The Urban Crucible: Social Change, Political Consciousness, and the Origins of the American Revolution.* Cambridge, Mass., 1979.

Newton, Arthur P. *The Colonizing Activities of the English Puritans: The Last Phase of the Elizabethan Struggle with Spain.* New Haven, 1914.

Ogg, David. *England in the Reigns of James II and William III.* Oxford, 1955.

Olson, Alison G. "The Virginia Merchants of London: A Study in Eighteenth-Century Interest-Group Politics." *William and Mary Quarterly*, 3rd series, XL (1983): 363–388.

Parkman, Francis. *Count Frontenac and New France under Louis XIV.* Boston, 1880.

Prime, Temple. *Descent of John Nelson and his Children.* 2nd ed. New York, 1894.

———. *Some Account of the Temple Family.* New York, 1887.

———. *Some Account of the Temple Family: Appendix.* New York, 1899.

Quitt, Martin H. "Immigrant Origins of the Virginia Gentry: A Study of Cultural Transmission and Innovation." *William and Mary Quarterly*, 3rd series, XLV (1988): 629–655.

Rameau de Saint-Père, Edmé. *Une Colonie Féodale en Amerique (L'Acadie, 1604–1710).* Paris, 1877.

Ranum, Orest. *Paris in the Age of Absolutism.* Bloomington, Ind., 1968.

Rawlyk, George A. *Nova Scotia's Massachusetts: A Study of Massachusetts–Nova Scotia Relations, 1630–1784.* Montreal, 1973.

Reid, John G. *Acadia, Maine, and New Scotland: Marginal Colonies in the Seventeenth Century.* Toronto, 1981.

Rich, E. E. *The History of the Hudson's Bay Company 1670–1870.* 2 vols. London, 1958–1959.

Ritchie, Robert C. *Captain Kidd and the War against the Pirates.* Cambridge, Mass., 1986.

Roberts, Oliver H. *History of the Military Company of the Massachusetts now called the Ancient and Honorable Artillery Company of Massachusetts, 1637–1888.* 4 vols. Boston, 1895–1901.

Roy, J.-Edmond. *Le Baron de Lahontan.* Montreal, 1974.

Saint-Germain, Jacques. *La Reynie et la Police au Grand Siècle.* Paris, 1962.

Savelle, Max. *The Origins of American Diplomacy: The International History of Anglo-America, 1492–1763.* New York, 1967.

Shipton, Clifford L. *Sibley's Harvard Graduates: Biographical Sketches of Those Who Attended Harvard College. Volume VI: 1713–1721.* Cambridge, Mass., 1942.

Shurtleff, Nathaniel B. *A Topographical and Historical Description of Boston.* 3rd ed. Boston, 1890.

Silverman, Kenneth. *The Life and Times of Cotton Mather.* New York, 1984.

Snow, Edward Rowe. *The Islands of Boston Harbor: Their History and Romance, 1626–1935.* Andover, Mass., 1935.

Steele, Ian K. *The English Atlantic, 1675–1740: An Exploration of Communication and Community.* New York, 1986.

———. *Politics of Colonial Policy: The Board of Trade in Colonial Administration, 1696–1720.* Oxford, 1968.

Survey of London: Volume XX, Trafalgar Square and Neighbourhood (The Parish of St. Martin-in-the-Fields, Part III). London, 1940.

Sweetser, Moses F. *King's Handbook of Boston Harbor*. 2nd ed. Boston, 1883.

Thwing, Annie Haven. *The Crooked and Narrow Streets of the Town of Boston, 1630–1822*. Boston, 1920.

Waller, G. M. *Samuel Vetch, Colonial Enterpriser*. Chapel Hill, 1960.

Ward, Harry M. *The United Colonies of New England, 1643–1690*. New York, 1961.

Webster, John Clarence. *Acadia at the End of the Seventeenth Century: Letters, Journals and Memoirs of Joseph Robineau de Villebon, Commandant in Acadia, 1690–1700, and Other Contemporary Documents*. Saint John, New Brunswick, 1934.

Vigneras, Louis-André, "Letters of an Acadian Trader, 1674–1676." *New England Quarterly* XIII (1940): 98–110.

Zoltvany, Yves. *Philippe de Rigaud de Vaudreuil, Governor of New France, 1703–1725*. Toronto, 1974.

INDEX

187